In the sixteenth century the modern meaning of courtship –
'wooing someone' – developed from an older sense – 'being at
court'. *The rhetoric of courtship* takes this semantic shift as the
starting-point for an incisive account of the practice and
meanings of courtship at the court of Elizabeth I, a place where
'being at court' pre-eminently came to mean the same as
'wooing' the Queen. Exploring the wider context of social
anthropology, philology, and cultural and literary history,
Catherine Bates presents courtship as a judicious, sensitive, and
rhetorically aware understanding of public and private relations. Gascoigne, Lyly, Sidney, Leicester, Essex, and Spenser
are shown to reflect in the fictional courtships of their poetry
and prose the vulnerabilities of court life that were created by
the system of patronage. These writers exploited the structural
and semantic ambivalence of courtship in order to rehearse
alternative experiences of failure and success, producing richly
polyvalent and complex texts in which often conflicting strategies and devices are seen to compete and overlap with each
other. *The rhetoric of courtship* thus makes an important contribution to Renaissance cultural history, exploring the multiple
meanings of 'courtship' in the sixteenth century, and using the
court of Elizabeth I as a test case for representations of the
courtier's role and power in the literature of the period.

THE RHETORIC OF COURTSHIP IN ELIZABETHAN LANGUAGE AND LITERATURE

THE RHETORIC OF COURTSHIP IN ELIZABETHAN LANGUAGE AND LITERATURE

CATHERINE BATES

Lecturer in English, Peterhouse, Cambridge

CAMBRIDGE
UNIVERSITY PRESS

Published by the Press Syndicate of the University of Cambridge
The Pitt Building, Trumpington Street, Cambridge CB2 1RP
40 West 20th Street, New York, NY 10011-4211, USA
10 Stamford Road, Oakleigh, Melbourne 3166, Australia

First published 1992
Reprinted 1995

Printed in Great Britain by Watkiss Studios Ltd., Biggleswade, Beds.

A cataloguing in publication record for this book is available from the British Library

Library of Congress cataloguing in publication data

Bates, Catherine, 1964–
The rhetoric of courtship in
Elizabethan language and literature / Catherine Bates.
p. cm.
Includes bibliographical references.
ISBN 0 521 41480 6
1. English literature – Early modern, 1500–1700 – History and
criticism. 2. Great Britain – Court and courtiers – History – 16th
century. 3. Authors and patrons – England – History – 16th century.
4. Courts and courtiers in literature. 5. Courtly love in
literature. 6. Courtship in literature. 7. Courtesy in literature.
8. Rhetoric – 1500–1800. I. Title.
PR428.C64B38 1992
820.9′353 – dc20 91-31573 CIP

ISBN 0 521 41480 6 hardback

UP

For
M.D.X.

Contents

Illustrations

Acknowledgements

In the course of writing this study I have incurred many debts, none of which can be calculated or adequately repaid. In particular, I would like to thank the following – L. G. Black, Cedric Brown, John Carey, Heather Dubrow, Dennis Kay, Arthur Kinney, Roger Lonsdale, Arthur Marotti, David Norbrook, Annabel Patterson, Christopher Ricks, A. V. C. Schmidt, Michael Schoenfeldt, and Jean Wilson – each of whom read all or part of this study at various stages in its composition, and without whose guidance, encouragement, and criticism the book could never have been written. I would also like to thank the staff at both the *Oxford English Dictionary* and the *Historical Thesaurus* at Glasgow for kindly allowing me to consult their files.

xi

Illus. 1. George Gascoigne, 'The Tale of Hemetes the Heremyte' (*c.*1575), Royal
MS 18 A xlviii, fol. 1, by permission of the British Library

Prologue

In the new year of 1575–6 George Gascoigne made Queen Elizabeth a handsome gift: a lavish manuscript containing 'The Tale of Hemetes the Heremyte' translated into four languages, and embellished with hand-drawn emblems. At the front of the book a picture shows the kneeling poet offering his manuscript to the Queen (see illus. 1), an image which neatly figures the bid for royal favour which the gift as a whole was clearly designed to represent:

fyndyng my youth myspent, my substaûce ympayred, my credytt accrased, my tallent hydden, my follyes laughed att, my rewyne unpytted, and my trewth unemployed/ all wch extremyties as they have of long tyme astonyed myne understanding, So have they of late openly called me to gods gates and yor ma^tye being of God, godly, and (on earth) owr god (by god) appoynted, I presume lykewyse to knock att the gates of yor gracyous goodnes/ hopyng that yor highnes will sett me on worke though yt were noone and past before I soughte service.[1]

Elizabeth had first heard the tale of Hemetes when on progress at Woodstock the previous summer. It is an elaborate, somewhat complicated story about three lovers, each of whom, for different reasons, is barred or separated from his mistress. In the miraculous and activating presence of the Queen, however, each lover is satisfied and restored, and, in inviting Elizabeth to interpret the tale not 'grossely and literally' but, rather, allegorically, Gascoigne alerts her to the obvious correspondence between the happily resolved courtships of his tale on the one hand and his own act of courtship on the other.

Gascoigne's New Year's gift hereby encapsulates many of the issues with which this study is concerned. For this is a book about courtship: both 'courtship' in the sense of wooing or making love to another person, and 'courtship' in the sense of being a courtier, of suing for favour, of behaving as courtiers should behave.

I

The conjunction between the two meanings of courtship and how they came to be related in a particular historical period is the subject of this book, and it is as an obvious and peculiarly suggestive site for the overlap of the two meanings that the court of Queen Elizabeth presents itself as the predominant focus. The study thus aligns itself with much recent and exciting work in which courtship narratives of many kinds (sonnet-sequences, courtly romances, court entertainments) have been shown to relate to the political scenario of Elizabethan England, and in which fictional courtships have been seen as an expression of the self-positioning of male writers within a political system of clientage.

Put thus crudely, this book may seem to offer little that has not already been challengingly introduced and worked over by a number of scholars and critics. But in the pages that follow I hope to show by a series of linked studies how courtship (in every sense) was a highly nuanced and exceptionally complex literary and political procedure. For, on further investigation, it becomes clear that courtship narratives involve much more than a simple reading might at first suggest, and that many of the texts to be studied reveal themselves, like the Tale of Hemetes, to be particularly receptive to a 'double reading over'.[2]

For, although primarily a social exchange, courtship has never been a simple transaction. In the prefatory poem to his Tale of Hemetes Gascoigne describes himself 'In dowbtfull doompes, which waye were best to take', drawing attention to the competing demands of deference and candour and to the profound uncertainty of his self-presentation. A courtier must know how to graduate his behaviour and utterance with a view to attracting favour and winning from the object of his devotion some longed-for token of esteem. Courtship is a delicate, fraught, hazardous procedure which requires constant prudence, tact and subtlety because it depends for its effectiveness upon the appearance of sincerity, an appearance which could (and at times had to be) carefully calculated. Courtship is consequently a mode which puts sincerity and deception in a teasing and often inextricable juxtaposition.

As a game, role, or way of behaving, courtship is often seen to be a highly codified system, a series of signs aimed at reassuring the prince or mistress of the suitor's unquestioning and dutiful service. And these signs must be interpreted and decoded correctly in order to manipulate the prince or beloved into making the desired gesture of return. But a courtier could never guarantee the hoped-for response, of course, and, however circumspect, judicious, rhetorically aware, he could be cruelly spurned, his suit rejected or ignored.

In the texts with which this study is primarily concerned, these well-known vulnerabilities of courtly life are inscribed and formalized within the vicissitudes of fictional courtship and romance. Gascoigne's allusion to the parable of the vineyard ('yt were noone and past before I soughte service') hints ruefully at the difference between human and divine scales of reward, when the divine are shown to be impenetrable if not arbitrary and unfair (Matt. 20: 1–16). His text thus admits quietly of the possibility that Elizabeth might fail to respond altogether, or might do so in such a way as to demean the poet's gift and offer of service. Throughout this book, we will see courtiers and writers suing for favour while also, more subtly, rehearsing their projected failure and meditating upon its implications for their future and for their art.

While a suitor's courtship inevitably laid itself open to misinterpretation and misrepresentation, therefore, the quintessentially courtly strategies of indirection and obliquity could also be exploited as agents of distortion. In *The Adventures of Master F.J.*, for example, F.J. and Elinor conduct their courtship by means of 'secrets' (55) and 'private talk' (57); they share an overwhelming tendency to speak 'in cloudes' (64) and in 'cyphred words and figured speeches' (77).[3] Gascoigne's courtship narrative is thus governed by the need for closed systems of meaning, codings which are comprehensible only to a specific group or pair. As a result, the relationship between the lovers is constantly dogged by misunderstandings, the 'doubtfull shewe' (53) with which their liaison began proceeding little further than the 'doubtfull conclusion' (101) with which it ends.

Gascoigne's sense of frustration and marginalization at court is figured not only in the doubtfulness and perplexity that exists between Elinor and F.J., however, but also in the instability of courtly language itself as a referent of value. For here we find that notions of courtesy, of the proper conduct at court, and of the idealized male–female relations (as sketched by Castiglione) are scrutinized, analysed and, in the end, debunked. So while 'courtesy' is seemingly stabilized at the outset of the story by Gascoigne's courtly setting, the courteous qualities of hospitality, grace, and yieldingness are increasingly disturbed and perverted by the events of the narrative. For the 'courtesy' which Elinor and F.J. show to each other is no more than sexual favour: 'of hir curteouse nature [Elinor] was content to accept bords for a bead of downe' (69); F.J. 'could no lesse do, than of his curteous nature receyve his Mistresse into his bed' (91), and, 'having now forgotten all former curtesies', then rapes her. Although loth 'to use such curtesie' to her jealous lover, Elinor finds herself 'constreyned (for a time) to abandon hir body to the enimies curtesie' (92). 'Courtesy' thus begins to evolve quite different associations until it is shown to be unstable, polysemous, ambiguous, and over-extended.

It will be clear from even these brief examples that Elizabethan courtship narratives raise issues more complicated than might at first be supposed. For courtship is shown to be semantically confusing as well as narratively and politically potent. Furthermore, it will become evident that those who (for whatever reason and in whatever capacity) had to 'court' Queen Elizabeth seemed to display an acute self-consciousness about what they perceived to be their predicament, and about the possibilities that the representation of romantic courtship in fiction granted them. For the structural and semantic ambivalence of courtship provided Elizabeth's subjects with a rich and varied means of exploring relations with their sovereign, allowing them to rehearse alternative and competing experiences: success and failure, domination and subordination, obedience and subversion.

This book focuses most closely, therefore, on the courtship narratives written by a number of men who, like Gascoigne, stood in some kind of client relation with the Queen – Leicester, Essex, Lyly, Sidney, and Spenser – and shows how the internal tensions of courtship allowed them to enact and animate their own positions. It begins by putting this specific focus into the much larger historical and theoretical contexts which the subject demands, considering how the detailed study of a particular period fits into related semantic and historical changes that were occurring across Europe at the same time, and how Elizabethan 'courtship' might fruitfully be compared with medieval romantic terminology and with the preoccupations of so-called 'courtly love'. I draw on recent anthropological models of gift-exchange which stress ambivalence as the governing principle of courtship, and suggest that the uncertain relations between courtier and sovereign can be understood in terms of the relation between courtship and marriage, a theme central to the literary genres of comedy and romance.

After a detailed semantic analysis of 'courtship' and related words in English and other European languages, the book moves on to study selected literary examples of Elizabethan courtship narratives, and begins by looking at a series of pageants and entertainments that were mounted at court. This section considers ways in which issues of manifest political urgency (such as the succession or Elizabeth's marriage) became the focus for a complex and thoroughgoing trial of the participants' own circumstances, and shows how the presentation of courtier–sovereign relations in these texts is more disorientating and polyvalent than first appears.

The textual instability of many of these entertainments (arising largely from the transmission from a manuscript to a print culture) makes for a climate of doubtfulness and uncertainty that is not, in every case, accidental. In *The Adventures of Master F.J.*, for example, Gascoigne exploits the 'doubtful' status of his own text (47), layering different narratives in order to distort perspectives and to confuse his readers. A study of the *Euphues* and *Arcadia* narratives shows how Lyly and Sidney similarly expose courtship as a nexus of particularly difficult interpretative (and therefore moral) questions.

The book concludes by looking at Spenser's meditations on courtship in both the *Amoretti* and *Epithalamion*, and in book VI of *The Faerie Queene*. Superimposing a public courtship upon a private one, Spenser's alternative 'endings' to the sonnet-sequence subtly figure the poet's own aspirations and fears as a courtly hanger-on. Book VI of *The Faerie Queene* is marked by a semantic and practical rupture in which courtesy can no longer be seen to derive simply or directly from the court. Throughout book VI, Spenser is shown to problematize gestures of mutual return, thus hinting that the proper function of courtesy at court is an enticing but an idle dream.

CHAPTER I

The rhetoric of courtship: an introduction

Courtship has been an abiding and compelling subject in human discourse from the most ancient times because it ritualizes elements that are fundamental to social existence: love, sex, marriage, and procreation. In our own age, psychologists have shown how susceptible amorous and sexual behaviour is to change, and how modern courtship, cohabitation, and marriage have all been radically influenced by the changing demographic and ideological patterns of a post-industrial society. And, while courtship rituals naturally vary widely in different cultures and at different times, yet whatever the culture-specific variations in courtship practice, the prioritizing cultural activity which surrounds courting is pretty well a constant in Western culture and civilization.

Courtship clearly presents itself, then, as an enormous subject, with ramifications that veer off into the anthropological, sociological, mythological, historical, and psychological (to name but a few). This book's particular focus upon the rhetoric of courtship in Elizabethan language and literature therefore requires a word of explanation. For to concentrate predominantly on representations of courtship in one historical period might be argued to imply an anteriority, development, and progress through time, all of which conflict with the abiding presence of courtship as a cultural phenomenon. Yet the methodology of this book is such as to allow for a certain specificity. For this study traces the point in history when the word 'courtship' evolved meanings which had a particular political and amorous resonance, and when it came to mean broadly what it does today – the interactive behaviour and ritual between two people who are emotionally and romantically engaged.

The following chapter compares detailed diachronic and synchronic analyses of 'courtship' and cognate words in several languages in order to locate, where possible, the precise historical moment when their meanings changed. But here it is enough to say that 'courtship' first developed a predominantly amorous sense during the Renaissance period. Before then it had little to do with love or marriage at all, and signified, rather, 'being at court' or 'behaving as courtiers behave'. During the sixteenth century, 'courtship' (and the transitive verb 'to court') came to particularize certain aspects of court existence, and, from the proliferation of subsidiary meanings that subsequently developed, the modern amorous sense of the words – 'wooing' and 'to woo' – emerged to supersede the others and to become, in time, their chief designation.

What this book sets out to discover is what love had to do with courts. Why should a verb meaning 'to be at court' or 'to behave as a courtier' come to mean the same thing as 'making love'? If 'being at court' and 'wooing someone' shared a semantic field, what then was the precise relation between them? Does 'courtship' provide an example of how an already patriarchal vocabulary of love adopted the lexis of courtly hegemony? Did the etiquette and social practice of Renaissance court life lend themselves to love in a way that medieval custom did not? Does the semantic shift of 'courtship' and 'to court' post-date the allegedly medieval cult of 'courtly love'? How is it that courtship – a subject that might legitimately, if loosely, be seen as a major focus of attention and anxiety in texts of 'bourgeois' orientation, like the novel – originally had no 'bourgeois' overtones but specified elements of life at court? And, if it did, how valid do such terms as 'courtly' and 'bourgeois' remain?

The court of Queen Elizabeth I is an obvious place to look for the answers to some of these questions. In English, the words 'to court' and 'courtship' both evolved the amorous sense of 'to woo' and 'wooing' during the second half of the sixteenth century. It seems particularly appropriate – an enticing coincidence – that 'being a courtier' and 'playing the lover' should come to mean the same thing during her reign. For Elizabeth's femaleness aroused deep suspicions and anxieties in the male-dominated society she ruled. One of the ways in which her society responded was to mystify and mythologize her virginity, to de-genderize her as the 'prince', and to revive the myth of the King's 'two bodies' – only one of which was mortal, frail, and feminine. Over the last ten years, ground-breaking articles by Arthur Marotti, Louis Adrian Montrose, Leonard Tennenhouse, Maureen Quilligan, Peter Stallybrass, Ann Jones, and others have taught us to reflect on whether the courtship-situation that appears so often in Elizabethan literature figures the political backdrop of late sixteenth-century England; and whether writers like Sidney, Spenser, or Ralegh consciously mirror in the courtships of their poetry and prose their own self-positioning before a female authority.[1]

Much of this study is concerned with such poetic self-positioning. But this is also the place to say that the link between Elizabeth's sovereignty and the contemporary change in meanings of 'courtship' is, however satisfying, potentially misleading. For 'courtship' was (and is) a highly polysemous term, subject, both culturally and linguistically, to fluctuation, transition, and nuance. A mere glance at the dictionaries reveals that the developing meanings of 'courtship' had ramifications which extended far beyond the relatively localized effects of England's having a queen in the second half of the sixteenth century. For the semantic development of 'courtship' to mean 'wooing' was not a random occurrence in the highly volatile language that was Renaissance English. An identical semantic shift took place in the major European languages, and did so – fascinatingly enough – at more or less the same time: around the turn of the sixteenth century. Thus we have the French verb 'courtiser', the Italian 'corteggiare', the Hispanic 'cortejar', even the German 'hofieren', all developing an amorous sense, and all bequeathing that meaning to modern usage. And in each of these cases, of course, the amorous meaning of 'courtship' developed quite independently of any female political rule.

The correlation between 'wooing' and 'acting the courtier', which had been actualized in England by Elizabeth's rule, was therefore, in effect, part of a more profound and far-reaching socio-historical development. For the parallel shifts in the sense of 'courtship' across Europe at this time invite an obvious connection with the contemporary development of court societies. Some historians have designated the fifteenth and sixteenth centuries as a period marked by the intense centralization of power by a small number of European dynasties, one symptom and manifestation of which was the creation of supreme royal courts. And while there is a danger, in any such overview, of underestimating the highly sophisticated court societies of the Middle Ages, there are grounds for seeing a difference in degree (if not in kind) in the growth of Renaissance courts. In the Middle Ages, power was relatively decentralized, and the feudal system of reward by fief proliferated the number of lesser courts, the enclaves of self-styled barons with their retinues of knights.[2] From the fifteenth century, however, the court became a self-conscious model for the exercise – social, bureaucratic, and public – of royal hegemony. As D. A. L. Morgan has recently argued, while the language of courtesy had an indisputably medieval pedigree, extending back at least as far as the troubadours, the language of the court was (certainly in English) a fifteenth-century phenomenon.[3] Perceived as a centre of political and cultural activity, the court became a focus of scrutiny, and its members, the courtier and the prince, were formalized by Castiglione and Machiavelli as rhetorical role-models and categorial types.

So far so good. The rapid development of court society as an area of intense vigilance and scrutiny led to the evolution of a court-related lexis. But such a development does not, of course, explain why 'being at court' should lend itself (of all activities) particularly to love-making.

In an attempt to answer this intriguing question, the present study goes back to the words: 'courtiser', 'corteggiare', and 'to court'. In the next chapter, I analyse in detail the usage of these words in French, Italian, and English in order to ask what they used to mean, how they changed, and what common semantic ground the two senses of 'being at court' and 'making love' shared. The semantic analysis reveals three things: firstly, that each language developed a verb which specified 'being at court'; secondly, that this verb came to particularize a whole range of different courtly activities; and thirdly, that the element of behaviour at court which 'courting' came to denote most insistently was rhetoric – the flattering, dissembling, deceitful, and tactical discursive strategies that existed between individuals who found themselves forced to graduate and adjust their behaviour in the tense and hierarchized milieu of the Renaissance court. Spenser, for example, warns his readers against 'courting masker[s]' when they 'with smooth flattering / Doo fawne on you'; and Donne ridicules the man who must needs 'grin or fawne' on a magistrate, 'or prepare / A speech to court his beautious sonne and heire'.[4]

In shifting its meaning from a social or quasi-political sense ('being at court', 'behaving as courtiers behave') to an amorous one ('wooing'), the words 'courtship' and 'to court' thus demonstrate one of the simpler models for semantic change described by the linguist Stephen Ullmann: 'sense s1 has some features in common with some other sense, s2, lying within its associative field. At a given moment, attention will be focused solely on the common denominator, on the overlap between their semantic ranges, and the name pertaining to s1, n1, will be felt as an adequate designation for s2.'[5]

The 'courting' described by Spenser and Donne connotes a style of discourse which problematizes intention and utterance, sincerity and deception. As a polysemous and volatile word, 'courtship' did not invariably have pejorative overtones: in another poem, for example, Spenser praises the 'rightful Courtier' for his judicious policy and 'courting'.[6] But, as we shall see, it was, on the whole, the broadly negative connotations of courtship – flattery and dissimulation – that lent themselves to the language of love. A simple associative shift from the discourse directed toward a prince–patron to that aimed at a woman–beloved gave a ready-made language of flattery and persuasion a whole new area of specification. It meant, of course, that 'courting' a lady was often understood to mean deceiving or abusing her, as Spenser's cunning Paridell 'courted [Hellenore], yet bayted euery word'.[7]

In the sixteenth century, then, men and women across Europe began to use the word 'courtship' and its equivalents to describe the processes of wooing or love-making. The significance of this development is made more immediately striking if one compares it with an older usage. For, in the Middle Ages, the verb used for 'wooing' in all the Romance languages took its root not from the court but, rather, from the object of that wooing – the lady, or the *donna* (from *domina*). Thus in Provençal we have the verb 'domneirer', in French 'donoier', in Italian 'donneare', and in the Hispanic languages 'doñear'. The great exponents of courtly love did not so much 'court' their mistresses, therefore. Literally speaking, they 'ladied' (or 'idolized'). In troubadour lyrics, for example, 'domneirer' is the commonest and most important word for love-making, as is its equivalent for those great lyricists of the Middle Ages, Chrétien de Troyes, Dante, and Petrarch (none of whom uses 'corteggiare' or 'courtiser', but only ever 'donneare' and 'donoier').

In the fifteenth and sixteenth centuries, however, the donna-centred vocabulary of wooing became obsolete. A new word – 'to court' – took its place in all the Romance languages, and in English and German as well. 'Donoier' covered a wide range of meanings, from Dante's sublime and rapturous wooing of Beatrice in the *Paradiso* to the more frankly sexual behaviour of some of the lovers in the *Roman de la Rose*.[8] But as men ceased 'to lady' – 'donoier' – the female beloved no longer occupied her central, defining role. And (without leaping to premature conclusions about the 'de-pedestaliz-ing' of women) one can suggest that the replacement of 'donoier' by 'courtiser' reveals a radical reconceptualization of the courtship-situation. For, once the donna-centred vocabulary became obsolete, wooing could no longer definitively be a thing that men did to women. Instead, courtship began to be perceived as a shared activity, a behaviour in which both parties, male and female, were subject to a milieu that was figured as external: the court. A lover no longer spontaneously 'ladied'. Instead, wooing was conceived as a rhetorical procedure that was strained, tortuous, and formalized. Strategies of persuasion, knowing, testing were designed to bridge an emotional, epistemological, and psychological gap that had opened up between the two partners in love.

'Courting' lent itself to the art of love-making because wooing a member of the opposite sex came to be regarded as a highly complex, tactical, and strategic rhetorical *procedure*. Partners were perceived as two remote and distanced individuals between whom communica-tion was presented as difficult and highly pressurized. Norbert Elias considers this transformation of emotional and amorous behaviour a direct consequence of the wholesale 'civilizing process' which had, from the Middle Ages, been sponsored and exploited by court societies.[9] Court society, he argues, was the product of centralized power, and, as autocratic rulers maintained their monopoly of force by minimizing spontaneous displays of violence or emotion among their subjects, so those individuals were encouraged to sublimate their desires, lastingly transforming the imperatives of 'civilized' social behaviour into self-constraints. The internalization of desires (which reached an apotheosis for Elias in the court society of the *ancien régime*) therefore created a community of autonomous indivi-duals who became increasingly attracted to sceptical or solipsistic philosophy, and also to 'romantic love both as a real occurrence and perhaps still more as a cult and ideal'.[10]

In tracing the influence of institutional development on moral or psychological change, Elias takes from Emile Durkheim a sense of the primacy of social structures in generating patterns of behaviour and belief.[11] But there are obvious problems with Elias's thesis. In seeking out the theoretical and ideological bases for romantic love, and in drawing his models of sexual and emotional repression

directly from Freud, Elias remains mired within romantic conceptions of interiority. Defending the alliance of history and sociology,
Elias constructs objectivist structures for social behaviour, and
consequently reduces literature (in particular Honoré d'Urfé's romance *L'Astrée*) to documentary 'evidence' for the sexual and
psychological mores of early seventeenth-century French courtiers.

   The following study, by contrast, aims to resist such sociological
and anthropological objectivism, and to consider the presentation of
courtship in literature not as the symptom of closed-off, irreversible,
and mechanical rituals, but as a living and ever-changing exchange
of human desires. For this book is concerned with the structural
ambivalence that is intrinsic to the courtship-situation. Courtship is
manifestly a social transaction – one which involves a complex
interplay of giving and receiving, offering and responding, asking
and replying. There has been a tendency in the past to treat such
gift-exchange as a static manœuvre in which the cycle of reciprocity
that is generated by an act of giving is ritualized and perceived as the
mechanical interlocking of pre-regulated actions. But the (essentially
structuralist) notion that individuals spontaneously proffer gifts and
countergifts according to some unthinking and semi-automatic
societal principle of obligation has recently been questioned by the
social anthropologist Pierre Bourdieu. In his *Outline of a Theory of
Practice*, Bourdieu restores the principle of 'structural ambivalence'
to social interaction by showing that apparently irreversible, mechanical laws of obligation (requiring the recipient of a gift to make some
gesture of return) are, in fact, so designed, so arranged, and so timed
as to give the impression (or illusion) of reversibility. For, Bourdieu
suggests, 'any really objective analysis of the exchange of gifts ...
must allow for the fact that each of these inaugural acts may misfire,
and that it receives its meaning, in any case, from the response it
triggers off, even if the response is a failure to reply'.[12]

   As the properly courteous response to a gift or gesture of generosity, Bourdieu argues, a countergift must be both different from that
first gift and also deferred, as otherwise it would seem like a
downright refusal (the return of the same gift). Over-eagerness to
discharge one's obligations is a sign of rudeness and ingratitude
because it obliterates the time-lag between the receipt of a gift and a
courteous response – one which constitutes a subtle dialectic between
giver and receiver, and which creates an atmosphere of suspense and
uncertainty between them. The operation of courteous gift-

exchange therefore presupposes an act of 'misrecognition', a pretence of reversibility, allowing the recipient of a gift to give the impression that he or she has fully weighed up its value before responding appropriately. The lapse of time that intervenes between the receiving of a gift and giving in return therefore marks a deliberate oversight, a pretence that is collectively maintained and approved of in order to avoid the appearance of rudeness. And, as Bourdieu suggests, these minutiae of social behaviour reintroduce the element of strategy into gift-exchange. For, until he or she has given in return, the recipient is under an obligation to show gratitude to the benefactor. But, until he or she does return that gesture of generosity, the recipient presides over a period of suspense and uncertainty during which the initial giver is forced to wait and see. For Bourdieu, therefore,

cycles of reciprocity are not the irresistible gearing of obligatory practices found only in ancient tragedy: a gift may remain unrequited, if it meets with ingratitude; it may be spurned as an insult. Once the possibility is admitted that the 'mechanical law' of the 'cycle of reciprocity' may not apply, the whole logic of practice is transformed. Even in cases in which the agents' habitus are perfectly harmonized and the interlocking of actions and reactions is totally predictable *from outside*, uncertainty remains as to the outcome of the interaction as long as the sequence has not been completed.[13]

It is precisely such reversibility which operates in the rhetorical exchanges of courtship. The emotional and psychological distancing of the two partners (which, as we shall see, the very word 'courting' implies) engages the individuals in a highly complex, almost choreographed routine of proposal and response. And the longer that the response (which might be positive or negative) is delayed – through the prevarication or equivocation of one party (traditionally the woman) – then the more prolonged becomes the complex social interplay of debt and gratitude that exists between the individuals involved.

Let me take as an example the oft-quoted lines at the beginning of Spenser's Book of Courtesy, in *The Faerie Queene*:

> Then pardon me, most dreaded Soueraine,
> That from your selfe I doe this vertue bring,
> And to your selfe doe it returne againe:
> So from the Ocean all riuers spring,
> And tribute back repay as to their King.[14]

By taking the virtue of courtesy 'from your selfe', Spenser subtly implicates Queen Elizabeth in a cycle of reciprocity which he has activated himself by offering her his poem as a return-gift, a thankyou-present, a token of his esteem and gratitude. Elizabeth's courtesy is not simply some theoretical, inner virtue, therefore, but her active participation in the courteous cycle of receiving and giving – a cycle which Spenser creates with his own disingenuous deference (veiling his otherwise presumptuous suggestion that she should reward him). Spenser thus presents us with a cycle that is, as yet, incomplete. Like the rivers flowing inexorably toward the ocean, the poet has discharged his tribute to Elizabeth. Her task is to reciprocate, but her notorious prevarication and indecision (the traditional prerogatives of the courtly mistress) keep the suitor hanging on, and consequently forge the political and social tension that exists between them.

Spenser thus collapses the strategic practices of amorous and political 'courtship' into a single (and deceptively simple) gesture of request. As we have seen, the word came to describe a lover's behaviour to his mistress precisely because of the affinities that existed between that behaviour and the highly careful, flattering procedures endemic to courtly rhetoric. But there remains a problem. For, since courts were proverbially 'pictures of vice' (as Donne wrote), and since courtly rhetoric was frequently regarded as deceitful, wheedling, and cajoling, then the methods involved in 'courting' a prince or beloved threatened to become equally suspect.[15] As the next chapter shows, a large number of examples of 'courtship' being used in the amorous sense carry pejorative overtones, as 'the common loue in this our age', in which, wrote Lyly, 'Ladyes are courted for beautye, not for vertue.'[16]

The negative connotations of courtship might therefore be seen to lend themselves to a crude polemic which identifies aristocratic sexual mores as illicit – an argument characterized by Robert Greene's words that 'it is a Courtiers profession to court to euerie dame but to bee constant to none'.[17] The kind of conventional, anti-court polemic which Greene's words here detail gives rise, moreover, to a binary or 'scapegoat' mechanism which, while projecting wholesale moral corruption to an out-group ('the court'), attributes a correspondingly pure sexual morality to an in-group ('the country').

As a growing number of sixteenth- and seventeenth-century

historians have been suggesting, however, the polarizing tendencies of this polemic are dangerously over-simplistic and culturally loaded. Revisionist historians are becoming increasingly sceptical about the old 'court/country' divide, and of an essentially 'whig' historiography which perceives the sixteenth- and seventeenth-century aristocracy to be in a more or less permanent state of moral and fiscal crisis.[18]

Contrary to expectation, therefore, the frequently pejorative overtones of amorous 'courting' in the sixteenth century provide little indication of the sexual proclivities of Renaissance aristocrats. For, in describing sometimes illicit liaisons, 'courtship' epitomizes a trend so universal in literature that it sometimes needs to be baldly spelled out. From the earliest Greek novels, through the twelfth-century lyric, Renaissance prose and drama, the eighteenth-century novel, and on to modern cinema, the presentation of courtship in Western culture has almost always projected a love-relation that is, broadly speaking, transgressive. Lovers are perceived to conflict with a basic injunction – social, liturgical, paternalistic – and the joys and trials of their courtship depend, for the most part, upon the obstacles that are put in their way. The obstacles take many different forms: the troubadours, for example, characteristically guard against jealous husbands and the officious scandal-mongers at court; Romeo and Juliet conflict with a paternalistic injunction; Othello and Desdemona with social and racial ones. Yet all are versions of the same fundamental conflict between individual sexuality and a perceived authority.

Courtship has been so abiding a subject in literature precisely because it enacts the tense and problematic relation between individual desire and the laws which set about to govern it; between the impulse to transgress, on the one hand, and those injunctions which normalize, prohibit, and curtail sexual desire, on the other. And because literature resists schematization, literary courtship explores the relation between individual sexuality and the law in a way that is more fluid, open-ended, and, in the end, satisfying than the sociological and psychological 'models' of a Freud or a Foucault. Thus, while Foucault's dialectical model of power-relations may seem at first to be attractively flexible, and a revision of Freud's rigidly 'repressive' model, literary texts, by contrast, do not quantify the unquantifiable, and rarely illustrate sociological models without being themselves distorted or over-simplified. As a particular instance of cultural and narrative practice, the literary texts which this book considers are shown to rehearse and enact the fundamental questions raised by courtship, and explore at every level the ramifications of a highly complex subject.

So a study of courtship in the literature of the sixteenth century does not indicate that court morals were 'decadent' and to be contrasted with 'respectable' bourgeois values. For all its derivation from a court lexis, 'courtship' is not a class issue. Instead, courtship raises questions that have a more general validity, above all in exploring the tense and problematic relation between individual sexuality and law: a distinction which cuts across social and hierarchical boundaries.

Let me take as an example the complex and controversial issue of 'courtly love' – a phenomenon whose misleading nomenclature has produced a wealth of criticism dedicated to finding out why a very specific kind of love-relation flourished in the seigneurial courts of the twelfth century.[19] In what is now one of the most notorious debates of literary history it is recognized that the phrase 'courtly love' conjoins its two elements – courtliness and love – in what can only be called deceptive simplicity.[20] Much of the ensuing critical chaos arises, in fact, because 'courtly love' is a poor translation of the French phrase 'amour courtois', coined by Gaston Paris in 1883 to describe Lancelot's submissive and adoring love for Guinevere in Chrétien de Troyes's *Conte de la charrette*.[21] The English version – 'courtly love' – loses much of the polyvalence of Paris's definition because 'courtois', of course, has the sense of 'courteous' (itself a notoriously polysemous word) as well as 'courtly'. Moreover, scholars have come to be suspicious of a phrase which, however convenient and however suggestive, scarcely appears in the literary texts that it is supposed to epitomize. And, as a result, literary historians increasingly find themselves having to justify the use of the term. While, for some, 'courtly love' remains a useful shorthand, a good translation of the Provençal 'fin'amors', for others it is a misleading anachronism. Among its more virulent attackers, the term has variously been called a 'myth', a 'scholar's hypothesis', and an 'impediment to the understanding of medieval texts'; one critic has called for its ritual purging in a 'grand and purifying holocaust'.[22]

Even at the most preliminary level, then, what Georges Duby judiciously calls 'l'amour dit courtois' appears to create more problems than it solves.[23] And although a growing number of scholars have begun to probe the precise relation between courts and love, they have not yet reached any consensus about whether there was a connection at all.[24] Scholars may concur that the 'fin'amors' of the troubadours and the chivalric novels of Chrétien evolved from the seigneurial courts of twelfth-century Provence and France, but interpretations of this connection vary widely. For some, the love-relation portrayed in these literary forms reflected a real state of affairs, the self-enclosed secular court (in which men and women lived in close domestic propinquity) providing an ideal breeding-ground for civilized notions of amorous play.[25] For others, seigneurial courts were not homogeneous or self-regulating institutions, but collections of often turbulent individuals held together by ties of feudal bondage or kinship that varied in intensity. It has been suggested that the lord of the castle invented and exploited the game of 'amour courtois' in order to give his young vassals something to do, and to minimize tension in the small and intimate feudal court.[26] For others, the yearning for the love of a noble female which characterizes the love-lyric of the period betokens nothing so clearly as the dreams of social advancement in a group of upwardly mobile young men.[27] At the same time, the charge that 'courtly love' rarely looks ahead toward marriage as its object has been met with the suggestion that, in making marriage conspicuous by its absence, the love-lyric in effect prioritizes it. The preoccupation with adultery can therefore be seen to belong to a polemical and misogynistic tradition which alternately satirizes, savages, and penalizes female sexuality and desire.[28]

Amidst all the controversy surrounding 'courtly love', however, there is one subject upon which most scholars seem to be agreed: that the love-relation envisaged in 'fin'amors' is a subversive one. Both the lyrics of the troubadours and the chivalric novels of northern France foreground a love-relation that (if not openly adulterous) is frequently denied a legitimizing conclusion. The love of Tristan for Isolde, of Lancelot for Guinevere, or of the troubadour for his 'dompna' is not generally directed toward marriage: the satisfactions and trials of this passion lie elsewhere. For 'courtly love' traditionally portrays predicament, its typical scenario sketching a love that, for various reasons, is impossible, dangerous, and hedged in by a whole series of prohibitions.

It is a symptom of how intertwined love and marriage have become in modern Western romantic ideology that a literary scenario which drives them apart should present us with interpretational difficulties.[29] For the relation between marriage and a literature which appears to undermine it is a fraught and trenchant one. The attention devoted to adulterous and divisive romantic love in the literature of the medieval period coincided with an ecclesiastical reformulation of sexual and matrimonial codes. Upholding monogamous marriage if not as a human ideal at least as an inviolable sacrament, the Church reflected the wholesale demographic and juridical changes in this period which we call 'feudalization'. The process of feudalization, while not (as Marc Bloch has shown) a regular or consistent one, none the less brought about a radical change in medieval conceptions of the family.[30] One of the most crucial changes was the gradual transformation of the fief from a reward granted at the discretion of a patron, to a hereditary right. As fiefs came to be regarded as valuable assets not to be dispersed but passed down as nearly as possible intact through a dynastic line, notions of the family underwent what R. Howard Bloch calls 'an axial shift'.[31] From a heterogeneous collection of individuals related to each other 'horizontally' by ties of blood and marriage, the *familia* evolved a sense of linearity and reorientated itself 'vertically' or agnatically in an attempt to preserve the patrimony.

The institution of marriage was perhaps the first to feel the impact of this radical reconceptualization of the family. For the conjugal unit came to be regarded as the bedrock of aristocratic perpetuity, a means of uniting families, of producing and legitimizing heirs, of regulating and ensuring the transmission of wealth through successive generations. Every effort was therefore made to guarantee the procreation of legitimate male heirs. An enormous stake was placed upon female virginity and chastity, children were betrothed young, women were jealously guarded, wives discarded or replaced if they failed to produce sons. In the words of Georges Duby, 'the rites of marriage are instituted to ensure an orderly distribution of the women among the men; to regulate competition between males for females; to "officialize" and socialize procreation ... Marriage [therefore] establishes relations of kinship. It underlies the whole of society and is the keystone of the social edifice.'[32]

So the student of 'courtly love' is faced with a seeming paradox. A literature which appeared to privilege illegitimacy flourished at a time when the legitimacy of aristocratic marriage was becoming an intense focus of attention and anxiety. Yet the paradox is, if not resolved, at least put into perspective by shifting one's gaze away from the twelfth century and by regarding the peculiarities that are internal to 'courtly love' as symptomatic of a more universal phenomenon. For almost all Western courtship-literature centres upon the discrepancy between individual sexuality and law. The courtly backdrop of the medieval lyric no doubt provides a rich site for exploring individual sexuality, because the latter was under such vigilance and scrutiny there. But the issue at stake is not whether twelfth-century men and women were really adulterous, or whether seigneurial lords popularized 'courtly love' to restrain their men or to browbeat their wives. Rather, 'courtly love' exemplifies a vir-tually universal tendency in courtship-literature: the portrayal of a tension between individual desire on the one hand, and the demands of societal or liturgical law on the other.

Whether courtship exists outside marriage altogether (as in 'courtly love') or whether it is a prelude to marriage (as in the novels of Jane Austen, for example) the crucial point is that it is never the same as marriage. Courtship stands in a peculiarly ambivalent and indeterminate relation to marriage, for it remains a preliminary process – what happens before marriage, or outside the conjugal unit – and therefore exists temporarily 'outside' the law which that conjugality represents.[33]

The 'courtly love' scenario is of relevance to this study, therefore, not because it took place in courts (a question which remains open to debate), but because the relation between courtship and marriage echoes the structural ambivalence that resides within courtship itself. For amorous courtship represents a period of 'free play' during which the participants are not yet subject to the laws of marriage, and when suits can be granted, delayed, or denied. Of particular fascination in male-dominated societies, courtship contrasts the otherwise mutually exclusive roles of male lover (adoring, submiss-ive) and husband (domineering, authoritative) with those of the female mistress (defiant, cruel) and wife (humble, obedient).

As we have seen, the typical 'courtly' scenario portrays a predica-ment in which the lovers are perceived, in different ways, to be *on the outside* of socializing and legitimizing rules. In literary presentation, courtship traditionally postpones closure, puts off the moment at which the lovers' relation is legitimized and, henceforth, subject to the multifarious laws governing marriage and married sex. Court-ship represents that period of time – in many cases a protracted period – during which men and women stand in a specialized position both to each other, and to the rest of society at large.

While courtship is subject to its own highly formalized rules, then, these are not the rules which dictate social and sexual behaviour in marriage.[34] Courtship bears the same relation to marriage that a game bears to the 'real' world. A game does more than simply mimic or parody the injunctions of that world; it presents an alternative (albeit temporary) culture that stands counter to the laws of everyday. Although courtship exists temporarily outside the law, therefore, it takes its definition from that law, and becomes a kind of sanctioned lawlessness, a licensed mirth, in which the limits of law are explored and exploited if eventually acknowledged and obeyed.[35]

This is why courtship is a staple of comedy – not because the relations between men and women are intrinsically humorous, but because comedy explores the relation of rule to misrule. Comedy presents a carnival world in which the impossible is allowed to happen, and in which rules are deliberately bent, injunctions disobeyed. The curtain traditionally falls at the point when a courtship ends and when the lovers finally marry because the alternative, picaresque world which comedy meditates upon ends abruptly with the re-establishment of law. Nothing remains to write about since, as Congreve put it, courtship is to marriage as 'a very witty prologue to a very dull play'.[36]

I should add a word here about the methodology to be used in tracing the rhetoric of courtship in the Renaissance period. For the kind of lexical material we have been considering is, of course, notoriously difficult to quantify, and can have no real status as scientific 'evidence' for those shifts in understanding and perception that I have been claiming. The cheerful evaluation of the past meanings of words is a hazardous procedure, and one beset with the limits and problems inherent in philological objectivism.

It is a given of post-Saussurean linguistics that, while the practice of courtship might or might not have changed, the language that defines it indisputably has, and, indeed, that the first is merely a symptom of the second. This study therefore takes as its starting-point Saussure's distinction between diachronic and synchronic linguistics. Briefly, diachronic linguistics perceives language to be a historical and temporal construct that is seen to evolve, develop, and change through time; synchronic linguistics, by contrast, studies language when it is hypothetically understood to be a fixed and relatively stable word-system at any given time.[37] Applying the Saussurean categories to semantics, Stephen Ullmann writes that while 'synchronistic semantics is the science of meaning, diachronistic semantics is the science of changes of meaning'.[38]

Since the basis of my inquiry is the change in meaning of a single word, the distinction that Saussure and Ullmann make here has obvious advantages, and the following chapter traces the changing meanings of 'courtship' diachronically before going on to investigate synchronically its semantic and associative field. But, at this stage, it is impossible to proceed any further without addressing the suspicion which the Saussurean categories have aroused in modern theoretical writing, most notably in Derrida.[39] Given the radical instability of language and the fraught relation between a word and what it signifies, Derrida contends that 'meaning' is never something that can be evaluated. He therefore takes issue with Saussure's synchrony as a wrong-headed and inadequately theorized attempt to fix linguistic elements within a system that admits itself to be artificial.

Derrida's radicalism has, in turn, been met with the charge that his happy use of coinages, and his notoriously self-reflexive terminology, are themselves the product of a conservatively trained philological mind. Derrida's words 'itérabilité', 'dérive', and 'différance', for example, depend, for our understanding, on parallel senses in French or Latin usage, or even in Indo-European custom.

Now this fact does not, of course, confute the grounds of Derrida's scepticism. On the contrary, it reinforces his doubts, demonstrating – in the most economical way – that the critic's words are just as susceptible to semantic misprision as the ones he writes about. Considering the fact that no theorist can write about linguistic drift or slippage while separating off his own discourse as stable and authoritative, Derrida's dilemma is not an isolated one.[40] As Montaigne wrote, 'I write my book for few men and for few years ... In view of the continual variation that has prevailed in [our language] up to now, who can hope that its present form will be in use fifty years from now? It slips out of our hands every day.'[41] But traditional philological inquiry does present the problem of objectivism in a particularly acute way. For, in evaluating the meanings of the past, the philologist (like the anthropologist) is in danger of assuming the position of the 'impartial' observer – a position that is fraught with obvious preconceptions, distortions, and critical redundancies.

It is precisely this difficulty that Derrida takes issue with – so powerfully because his scepticism about the referentiality of language is taken to its logical extreme. It is the well-known crux of Derridean scepticism that, if 'itérabilité' is seen to govern every utterance indiscriminately, then language as a system of communication ceases to function. Once set adrift in the errant, arbitrary, and opportunistic linguistic medium, every utterance becomes a free-floating and literally 'sense-less' unit.

This is not the place to explore all the ramifications of Derrida's philosophy of language. But it is appropriate to consider how Derrida's radicalism has been met (and 'rehistoricized') by philologians and literary historians of the medieval and Renaissance periods. Some historians of philology have suggested that Derrida's radical 'itérabilité' can be challenged (as it had been in the past) with an alternative hypothesis. That is to say, extreme nominalism can be taken to be as hypothetical as extreme conventionalism, or, put another way, the radical fissure between signifier and signified to be as hypothetical as the philologist's supposed ability to evaluate meaning historically. In effect, the argument comes down to whether one does or does not accept as a premise that language is a system of communication. If it is taken as such, then its radical drift is arrested and, while remaining unquantifiable and differential, meaning can none the less legitimately be sought.[42]

These arguments do not only have the effect of rehistoricizing Derrida, or of locating him within a Western tradition of linguistic philosophy. More significantly, for our purposes, they restore the ground (theoretically, at least) for traditional, even conservative, philological inquiry. For Derrida's sense of historical relativity and his struggle against 'logocentrism' could be argued to locate him within a tradition that was first initiated by the humanist philological scholars of the fourteenth, fifteenth and sixteenth centuries.

For the historical consciousness which we call modern derives, at least in part, from the perception of change and of periodization which marked off these scholars' historical thinking from the age that preceded them. Petrarch celebratedly derived his 'modern' sense of the past from what Leonardo Bruni called his appreciation of 'the lost style of the ancients', that is, from a primarily philological perception.[43] It was the sense of irrecoverable loss, of what he saw as the decline of the Latin language, that prompted Petrarch, along with Dante, Valla, Poliziano, Erasmus, and others, to devote himself to texts. Philology gave these men a method, however limited, to set about restoring the past, making its axioms and its sentences live again, and inspiring them to embark on the huge process of recovery which their editions, versions, and imitations of biblical and classical texts all represent.[44]

Linguistic mutation – the falling of Horace's famous leaf from its branch – was to the Renaissance humanist mind, therefore, an incontrovertible symptom of change, a taxonomy of history. To study philology, however minutely, was deemed to be part of a heroic (if thwarted) attempt to re-engage with the past, indeed, with historicity itself. If modern Western historical consciousness derives at root from Renaissance philology, then the study of lexical change corroborates that vision of history as anthropocentric, contingent, and mutable.

Now, this argument may seem suspiciously circular: if Dante and Petrarch historicized medieval perceptions of linguistic flux, then to defend philological strategies that derive from their practice as 'evidence' for historical change is tautologous and over-simplistic. To put it another way, if semantic change reflects (locally or generally) a shift in perception, then that act of reconceptualization can only be signalled by semantic change. The problem lies with the old distinction between inductive and deductive reasoning, and was long ago dubbed the 'philological circle' by Leo Spitzer.[45]

There is no obvious solution to the methodological tautology, and it can certainly make for irresponsible philological tail-chasing. There is a very real sense in which philological analysis can only ever present its findings as incomplete, and its totalizing impulse to restore the past as a thwarted one. Yet, as Thomas Greene suggests, it also creates an imaginative environment for the puns and *doubles entendres* that were beloved of Renaissance minds.[46] Whether or not one takes the fluidity of 'courtship' and its cognate forms in the sixteenth century to reflect a renewed focus on courts as centres of power, it certainly reflects a Renaissance taste for wordplay: 'Of Court it seemes, men Courtesie doe call', quizzed Spenser; 'Hee named it not unproperlie that called it first court', wrote a translator of Antonio de Guevara, 'for in Princes courts all things are courtaild.'[47]

The twentieth century might be impatient with such apparently puerile, Hamlet-like punning, but, as Johan Huizinga has cautioned, a rigid dichotomy between the serious and the playful would have been foreign to medieval and Renaissance minds.[48] In its methodology, therefore, the ensuing study attempts to take a middle road between philological inquiry and its questionability as 'evidence' on the one hand, and, on the other, a historical consciousness which is the legacy of the Renaissance, and which takes its origin from philological inquiry. Stressing continuities rather than discontinuities, this study thus attempts to locate itself within the linguistic and historical practices that would not have seemed alien to the subjects about which it is concerned.

CHAPTER 2

The semantics of courtship

Most Romance languages, and all those under consideration here, had a name first for the residence and then for the retinue of a prince – the court.[1] The word derived from the classical Latin words 'cohors' and 'curia', via the medieval Latin 'cortis'. In the Middle Ages, all the languages under discussion formed a verb whose root derived from the word for court – Provençal 'cortejar', the Hispanic languages 'cortejar', French 'cortoyer' (becoming 'courtiser'), and Italian 'corteare' (becoming 'corteggiare'). And, in almost all cases, the verb began with a purely social sense signifying 'being at court', as in the following example from the thirteenth-century *Chanson des Quatre Fils Aymon*, where a mother describes how she sent her sons to serve Charlemagne:

> Jes envoiai en France, à Paris cortoier;
> Charles en ot grant joie, tot furent chevalier.[2]

At this early stage, 'cortoyer' and its equivalents also particularized certain specific aspects of courtly behaviour. In the following extract from Guillaume d'Orange's epic *La Battaile d'Aleschans*, for example, the hero's humble behaviour contrasts with the civilized norms that 'being a courtier' evidently entailed:

> Sire Guillaume, alez-vos herbergier,
> Vostre cheval fètes bien aésier,
> Puis revenez à la cort por mengier.
> Trop pouremant venez or cortoier:
> Dont n'avez-vos serjant né escuier,
> Qui vos servist à voste deschaucier?[3]

Then, in the fifteenth century, a parallel lexical development took place in French and Italian. The French intransitive verb 'cortoyer' developed the transitive 'courtiser' (its medial 's' deriving either from 'courtisan' or from 'courtois'), and the Italian intransitive 'corteare', the transitive 'corteggiare'.[4] From its inception, the new French verb 'courtiser' covered a whole range of meanings. Thus, in the fifteenth century, Olivier Basselin employs it to describe the kind of behaviour appropriate to the wooing of ladies:

> On va disant que j'ai fait une amie,
> Mais je n'en ay point encore d'envie:
> Je ne sçauray assez bien courtiser.
> Moy, j'aime mieux boire un coup que baiser.
>
> L'amour je laisseray faire
> Et les dames courtiser,
> Il ne me faut plus qu'à boire
> D'autant, et me reposer.[5]

The complex publication history of Basselin's lyrics makes precise dating difficult, but it is striking that 'courtiser' was being used in a specialized erotic sense so early. This fact suggests that the verb expanded its semantic parameters very rapidly, and that it developed specialized senses at an early stage. It is possible that fifteenth-century French usage was influenced by the troubadours here, for, although the verb 'cortejar' was relatively rare in troubadour lyrics (the most common verb for wooing being 'domneirer'), when it was used, 'cortejar' almost invariably signified 'love-making' (rather than 'being at court'):

> E car vos am, dompna, tan finamen
> Que d'autr'amar no·m don' Amors poder,
> Mas aize·m da c'ab autra cortey gen,
> Don cug de me la greu dolor mover.[6]
>
> De tals n'i ac que mout si dolgron
> de las dompnas, que ges non volgron
> c'om las vengues trop cortejar;
> lassas foron del cavalgar
> e de la calor c'an ahuda.[7]

In order to see how the French verb 'courtiser' came to include the amorous sense of 'wooing', I'd like to turn to the rich associative field of the word, for which sixteenth-century usage provides more evidence. In the following quotations from Olivier de Magny and Joachim du Bellay, for example, the verb 'courtiser' is used to describe generally ingratiating and flattering behaviour:

Mon Compaignon s'estime et se plaist de se veoir,
Il est dispost, bragard et plein de gentillesse,
Il oste le bonnet, il courtise, il caresse,
Et fait quelque fois que ne veult le deuoir.

Qu'il ayt cet aiguillon qui tout le monde poingt
De vouloir estre grand, qu'il courtise et caresse,
Qu'il blasme ceulx qui ont en eulx quelque finesse,
S'il te plaist en cela il ne me desplaist point.[8]

In each of these examples, 'courting' involves a kind of masking, wheedling behaviour that seems designed to ingratiate and curry favour. Both poets use 'caresser' as a synonym in order to drive the point home. So when, in another sonnet, de Magny employs 'courtiser' in a straightforwardly amorous context, he does so by extension:

Bien heureux est celuy qui la peult courtiser,
Et plus heureux encor cil qui la peult baiser,
Mais plus heureux cent fois qui se voit aymé d'elle.[9]

Describing a scale of amorous encounters in which 'courtiser' comes first, 'baiser' second, and 'd'être aimé' last, de Magny suggests that 'to court' his mistress is a preliminary, rhetorical, flattering procedure – one closely related to the kinds of social 'courting' described above. Likewise, Ronsard demonstrates that flattery is the common semantic field shared by typical courtly behaviour and by amorous love-making. In the first two examples below (1564, 1569), 'courtiser' means to flatter one's superiors, and, in the second two (1575, 1578), to flatter women:

Il fault les grans Seigneurs courtizer et chercher,
Venir à leur lever, venir à leur coucher.[10]

Il faut mentir, flater et courtizer,
Rire sans ris, sa face deguiser
Au front d'autruy ...[11]

Pour vous baiser les mains, embrasser les genoux,
Courtizer, adorer, il ne le sauroit faire.[12]

Courtiser et chercher les Dames amoureuses,
Estre tousjours assise au milieu des plus beaux,
Et ne sentir d'Amour ny fleches ny flambeaux,
Ma Dame, croyez moy, sont choses monstrueuses.[13]

The development of the Italian word 'corteggiare' was, meanwhile, closely related to the French 'courtiser', although the former developed a range of meanings more slowly than the French verb. While the French 'courtiser' could apparently be used from its inception specifically to describe amorous wooing (as well as more generalized flattery), the Italian 'corteggiare' for a long time maintained only a generalized sense – 'accompagnare, far corteggio a un principe o a un personaggio molto importante, accompagnare, seguire, stare intorno a una persona' – which we can see illustrated in the following examples from Giovan Francesco Straparola (1550–3), Girolamo Savonarola (1494), and Torquato Tasso (c.1593):

Ora essendo il giovane Nerino in Padova, ed avendo presa amicizia di molti scolari che quotidianamente il corteggiavano, avenne che tra questi v'era un medico che maestro Raimondo Brunello fisico si nominava.[14]

Chi non lo corteggia [il tiranno], e chi non si presenta alla casa sua, o quando è in piazza, è notato per inimico.[15]

Ma s'io ragionava d'arme e d'imprese e de la bellezza di questa nostra lingua e de'nostri poeti, o pur di cortesia e di quel ch'appertiene al corteggiare e al cortesaggiare, era alcune volta udito non mal volentieri.[16]

It was around the turn of the sixteenth century that 'corteggiare' evolved the specialized sense of 'wooing a lady' that was already current in France. In the following example from *Gli Asolani* (1505), for example, Pietro Bembo neatly demonstrates how the verb shifted from a generalized social sense to a more specialized amorous one:

Perchè gran senno faranno i tuoi compagni, se essi questo prence corteggieranno per lo innanzi, si come essi fatto hanno le loro donne per lo adietro ...[17]

Bembo suggests that courting the prince involves precisely the kind of behaviour that is requisite in courting ladies. And, from early in the sixteenth century, we find Italian writers beginning to use 'corteggiare' directly to mean the wooing of women. Thus Ariosto (1509–20), Ludovico Dolce (1541), and Matteo Bandello (1554) write:

> Ma in quali case essere
> sentite donne voi, ch'abbiano grazia,
> che tutto il dì non vi vadino i giovani
> (essendo o non essendovi i lor uomini)
> a corteggiar?[18]

Io dico, padrone, che egli ha una sorella che lo avanza di signoria e ha maggior copia di cavalieri che la cortégiano.[19]

Erano stati alcuni che, non conoscendo intieramente la qualità de la donna, s'erano messi a corteggiarla e far seco a l'amore, i quali ella, poi che di dolci sguardi aveva un tempo pasciuti, or con una or con un'altra beffa in modo si gli levava d'intorno, che gli incauti amanti restavano miseramente scherniti.[20]

In contrast with its continental equivalents, 'courtiser' and 'corteggiare', the English verb 'to court' evolved relatively late. It does not appear in Middle English, where 'to woo' (from OE woȝian) remained the chief verb for love-making. There is no Middle English equivalent of 'cortoyer' or 'corteare', meaning 'to reside at court', and it is not until the fifteenth century that one finds even the noun 'court' being used as the accepted term for the royal residence. The first recorded example of the verb 'to court' in English comes from Alexander Barclay's *Certayne Egloges* (a translation of Aeneas Silvius's *Miseriae Curialium*), which were published in 1516:

> Thus all those wretches which do the court frequent,
> Bring not to purpose their mindes nor intent.
> But if their mindes and will were saciate,
> They are not better thereby nor fortunate.
> Then all be fooles (concluding with this clause)
> Which with glad mindes vse courting for such cause.[21]

Barclay employs the gerund 'courting' several times in the *Egloges*, in each case using it to mean simply 'being at court' – a predominantly social sense which persisted, incidentally, throughout the period. In an undated letter to Sir Christopher Hatton, for example, a court lady laments 'how unjustly I am afflicted with [the Queen's] disgrace and indignation. It shall make me less careful than I have been . . . for that life of courting.'[22] In 1601 John Chamberlain was still using the gerund 'courting' in this social sense: 'Our frend the sherriffe of Barkeshire was almost out of hart at the first newes of the Quenes comming into the country', he wrote, 'because he was altogether unacquainted with courting, but yet he performed yt very well and sufficiently, being excedingly well horsed and attended.'[23] Two years later, Henry Chettle used the same verb to describe his life as a member of Elizabeth I's court: 'when I was yong, almost thirtie yeeres agoe, courting it now and than: I haue seene the Ladies make greate shift to hide away their looking glasses if her Maiestie had past by their lodgings'.[24]

As monarchs and their courts developed greater monopolies of power, thereby fundamentally altering the socio-political picture of Europe in the fifteenth and sixteenth centuries, the language associated with those courts naturally developed and expanded. Earlier in the sixteenth century, Castiglione had set himself the task of defining 'cortigiania' – the behaviour particularly fitting to the Renaissance courtier – and, in the course of *Il Cortegiano*, the term assumes something of the status of a keyword. Translating Castiglione into English in 1561, Sir Thomas Hoby brought the words 'courtiership' and 'courting' into general usage, and it is evident that court-related words were rapidly evolving from the middle of the sixteenth century. In his *Arte of Rhetorique* (1553), for example, Thomas Wilson introduces the verb-phrase 'to court it' in order to describe a certain type of behaviour evinced at court: 'when we see one gaye and galaunte', he writes, 'we vse to saye, he courtes it'.[25] In Marlowe's *Edward II* (1594), the same verb-phrase connotes further peculiarities of court behaviour. Baldock is told 'to court it like a Gentleman ... be proud, bold, pleasant, resolute, / And now and then, stab as occasion serves'.[26]

As court government became increasingly centralized, and as life at court (as both a profession and an occupation) came under new scrutiny, 'court' cognates therefore rapidly expanded their semantic parameters to particularize certain facets of court behaviour. Throughout the century, the words 'courtship' and 'to court' were applied not simply to 'being at court' or to 'behaving as a courtier', but to highly specific courtly activities. In *Polyhymnia* (1590), for example, George Peele praises the valour of Anthony Cooke, who was 'For Armes and Courtship equall to the best'.[27] In the second part of *Tamburlaine* (1591), Marlowe associates 'courting' with the production of 'maskes and stately showes' at court.[28]

But what 'to court' particularized most often, however, was courtly rhetoric, and in this the English verb closely followed the French and Italian. In his poem 'The Will', for example, Donne ironically bequeaths his 'best civility / And Courtship, to an Universitie', where he assumes the art of civil conversation is wanting.[29] Richard II observes Bolingbroke's obsequious 'courtship to the common people', his 'familiar courtesy' and 'craft of smiles'.[30] Bolingbroke's greasy rhetoric here might be compared with the so-called 'noble, and subtile science of courtship' which is understood by the traveller Amorphous in *Cynthia's Revels* (1601). And when Tiberius finally dismisses debate and speculation in *Sejanus* (1603) –

'Leaue our courtings' – he employs the word to mean 'deliberations' or 'conversation'.[31] Thomas Nashe almost invariably associates the word with fraudulent rhetoric, summarizing, in *Pierce Pennilesse* (1592), that 'the Frenchman (not altered from his owne nature) is wholly compact of deceiuable Courtship'. In *The Unfortunate Travel-ler* (1594), Jack Wilton is warned against seemingly hospitable Italians, 'when in kindnes and courtship thy throat shall be cut'.[32]

So the kinds of rhetoric which 'courting' specified most precisely were devious, ingratiating, and wheedling attempts to impress and to curry favour. In *Have with yow to Saffron Walden* (1596), Nashe cruelly mocks Gabriel Harvey for attempting to win the patronage of Sir Philip Sidney: 'I haue perused verses of his, written vnder his owne hand to Sir Philip Sidney, wherein he courted him as he were another Cyparissus or Ganimede.'[33] Spenser warns the reader against this kind of flattery in *The Ruines of Time* (1591):

> When painted faces with smooth flattering
> Doo fawne on you, and your wide praises sing,
> And when the courting masker louteth lowe,
> Him true in heart and trustie to you trow.[34]

In book VI of *The Faerie Queene* (1596), the Hermit's plain speech contrasts with 'such forged showes, as fitter beene / For courting fooles, that curtesies would faine', while, in the House of Holiness, Reverence 'Does faire entreat; no courting nicetie, / But simple true, and eke vnfained sweet.'[35]

Translating della Casa's courtesy book *Galateo* in 1576, Robert Peterson writes that when men 'find themselves cunningly courted, they be soone weary of it', while the flatterers themselves 'doe plainly shewe, they count him, whom they court in this sorte, but a vaine, and arrogant bodie'.[36] In the *New Arcadia* (1590), the evil queen Cecropia recalls the flattery and tribute that had once been paid to her: 'I came into this country as apparent princess thereof, and accordingly was courted, and followed, of all the ladies of this country.'[37] Donne again suggests that, in its flattering mode, court-ing epitomizes fraudulence and dissimulation:

> Nor come a velvet Justice with a long
> Great traine of blew coats, twelve, or fourteen strong,
> Wilt thou grin or fawne on him, or prepare
> A speech to court his beautious sonne and heire,

and, in another poem:

> I durst not view heaven yesterday; and to day
> In prayers, and flattering speaches I court God.[38]

Given that 'courtship' and 'to court' denoted flattery so frequently throughout the period, only a simple associative shift was necessary (from suing a prince or superior to wooing a woman) and a ready-made language of flattery and persuasion lent itself to the lover. In *As You Like It* (1599), for instance, Rosalind tells Orlando of 'an old religious uncle of mine . . . one that knew courtship too well, for there he fell in love'.[39] John Florio shows how the contiguity of the social and the amorous senses in Italian could equally be illustrated in English. In his Italian–English dictionary (1611), he defines the word 'corteggiare' as 'to court one with attendance and obsequious-nesse', and the word 'cortesaggiare' (a near synonym in Italian) as 'to shew curtesie, louingnesse or kindnesse, to fawne vpon one'.[40]

It is necessary, therefore, to locate the moment when this import-ant associative shift took place. As we have seen, the English noun 'courtship' and verb 'to court' had rapidly developed a wide semantic field from the early decades of the sixteenth century, one that covered a whole range of different activities at court. It was not until the 1560s, however, that we find the words beginning to evolve the specifically amorous sense of 'wooing'. A text that is of particular interest, therefore, is Sir Geoffrey Fenton's *Certaine Tragicall Discourses* (1567) (a translation of François de Belleforest's *Histoires tragiques* (1564–5)), in which the words occur in the amorous sense over twenty times. Fenton frequently translates 'to court' directly from the verb in the French text, 'courtiser':

besides what example of vertue is it, to see one of our reuerend religious fathers and gouernou[r]s of conuentes, more geuen to courte the dames with requestes of sensualitie, then to torne ouer the leaues of the new testament.

From Belleforest:

C'est un exemple notable pour le peuple de voir ces reuerends s'amuser plus à courtiser les Dames, qu'à feuilleter les sainctes lettres.

Likewise, Fenton describes the Spaniard in his seventh tale, Don Piero de Cardonne, as a man who was 'so ignoraunt in the pursute of this queste, [that it was] as if he had neuer made courte to any Lady of reputacion or honor', using the verb-phrase to translate Belleforest's 'comme iamais il n'auoit courtisé ny serui dame qui fust de grand maison'. The argument to the tenth tale exalts the virtues of a gentleman who, 'hauing longe courted a young and faire damesell', finally preserves her honour, translating from the French source, 'ayant courtisé une ieune & belle femme'.[41]

Far more often, however, Fenton employs the verb 'to court' where there is no 'courtiser' in the source-text, suggesting that he had fully assimilated the word and was able to use it freely where context and association made it possible. One curious peculiarity of Fenton's usage is that the word frequently appears with a set cluster of other words, implying that his associative field was very closely defined:

he Imployed his time to court her continually with his company.

So being the chiefe courtier that hawnted the companie of Ladyes ... he failed not to court wyth a contynual proffer of his seruice.

so was she more courted wyth the contin[u]all haunte and companie of the Gentlemen and Princes of ITALY.

... some tyme he visited the hauntes and assemblies of ladies, courtyng suche of theym as he founde to giue most eare to hys ydle talke.[42]

While the verbs 'frequenter' and 'hanter' are to be found in Belleforest's text, they do not cluster around 'courtiser' with such formulaic regularity. This implies that Fenton had a very clear idea of what courting entailed, and that primarily this was the propinquity of young men and women in society at large. Elsewhere, it is possible to see the range of Fenton's associative field, as he frequently uses the verb 'to court' to translate a different word in the source. Twice, for example, 'to court' substitutes for the French 'amouraicher', and on another occasion 'caresser'.[43] 'To court' also replaces the synonymous 'faire l'amour', together with the more elaborate 'offrir service'.[44] Often Fenton expands Belleforest's text, the latter's simple 'langage' being rendered 'courtlike wooing', for instance, his 'services' being transformed to 'seruices of court', and his 'estant recueilly' to 'proffers of court', in each example expanding the semantic range of the word in his source-text.[45]

Fenton not only introduced the amorous sense of the word 'to court' by means of translation, therefore, but also by grasping its associative possibilities. More often than not in Fenton, 'courting' connotes physical or sensual love. In the argument to the sixth tale, Fenton attacks a worldly friar who is more given 'to courte the dames with requestes of sensualitie' than to reading the Bible. Later in the same tale, the friar recalls that women generally yield 'to him that courts theim with the offer of loue' and attempts to assail the innocent Parolyna with 'thuttermost of his forces'. In another tale, one of the promiscuous Pandora's many lovers, finding her not to be a virgin, 'fayled not to courte her with a contynuall haunte of his companye, in suche sorte, that his chiefe exercise and tyme was employed in the supplye of her gredy desyre'.[46]

With its thorough assimilation of the amorous sense of 'courting', Fenton's *Certaine Tragicall Discourses* therefore marks an important moment in the semantic development of the word in English, and, from this period, the incidence of the word in this sense increases dramatically. And, as the 'new' amorous sense gradually came to be established, writers in the 1560s and 1570s can be shown to use the word with a degree of uncertainty and hesitation, as they explore the semantic overlap between 'being at court' and 'wooing'. In a later chapter we shall see how John Lyly experimented with these competing senses of 'courting' in *Euphues* (1578) and *Euphues and his England* (1580). In *The Palace of Pleasure* (1566–7), likewise, William Painter writes of 'the condition of courting flatterers' and of the extravagance and vanity of 'Courtyng Ladyes' (in both cases describing generalized aspects of behaviour at court), while also describing a 'Nymphe, and earthie Goddesse, who with courtinge countenaunce imbraced the place where I did stande' (employing the same participial adjective in the amorous sense).[47]

George Gascoigne is particularly sensitive to the unstable meanings of 'courtship' that were developing in the 1570s. We have already seen how he problematizes the meaning of 'courtesy' in *The Adventures of Master F.J.* (1573). In the following poem, 'Pride of Court', the poet homes in on the word 'courting' to similar effect:

> In country first I knew hir, in countrie first I caught hir,
> And out of country now in court, to my cost have I sought hir.
> In court where Princes reign, hir place is now assignd,
> And well were worthy for the roome, if she were not unkind.
> There I (in wonted wise) did shew my self of late,
> And found that as the soile was chang'd, so love was turn'd to hate.
> But why? God knowes, not I: save as I said before,
> Pitie is put from porters place, and daunger keepes the dore.
> If courting then have skill, to chaunge good Ladies so,
> God send ech wilful dame in court, som wound of my like wo.[48]

The poet's bewilderment here centres on the ambiguity of 'courting', a word which can be understood either in its generalized sense ('being at court') or in its specialized sense ('wooing').[49] For the poet's mistress has either been distracted from his love simply by being at court, or she has been lured away from him through the flattery and persuasions of another.

The ambiguity in Gascoigne's poem arises because of the contiguity of sense between the social and amorous meaning of the word. We have already seen that a common specialization of 'courtship' signified flattery, and have suggested that, by a simple association, this word came to be applied to the discourse directed by men toward women. In his *Palace of Pleasure*, for example, Painter describes one lover who was accustomed to addressing his mistress in those terms 'sutch as gentlemen commonly vse in company of Ladies'. Indeed, he 'became so famyliar with the Lady, and talked with hir so secretly, as vpon a day being with hir alone, hee courted in this wise'.[50] It is clearly the lover's calculated and tactical rhetorical strategy that makes his behaviour qualify as 'courting'. The wooing of women was therefore perceived to be a delicate, potentially hazardous rhetorical procedure. The ladies in *Love's Labour's Lost* (*c.*1595) justly account the courtiers' blandishments for what they are, 'courtship, pleasant jest, and courtesy', and in Chapman's *Homer* (1614–16), Penelope's suitors clearly regard their wooing as something of a rhetorical feat: 'Their speeches given this end, Eurymachus / Began his Court-ship, and exprest it thus.'[51] In *The Duchess of Malfi* (1614), Ferdinand warns his sister against 'varietie of Courtship; / What cannot a neate knave with a smooth tale, / Make a woman beleeve?'[52] By contrast, a soldier-lover in one of Barnaby Rich's tales is 'so blunt and plaine, aswell in his gesture, as in his tearmes' that he clearly has 'little skill in the courting of Gentlewomen'.[53] In *Pierce Pennilesse* (1592), Thomas Nashe presents us with a 'vagrant Reueller [who] haunts Plaies, and sharpens his wits with frequenting the company of Poets: he emboldens his blushing face by courting faire women on the sodaine'.[54]

In the following passages from his autobiography (*c.* 1576), Thomas Whythorne introduces the word 'courting' as something of a neologism, and, in his attempt to come to terms with the semantic range of the word, draws a fascinating associative field around it:

another thing was then in me, which hindered such actions very much, the which was bashfulness towards women, and chiefly in the affairs of wooing of them; the which fault hath continued in me ever since. And yet when time served to be in company with women, to talk with them, to toy with

them, to jibe and to jest with them, to discourse with them, and to be merry
with them (all the which some do call courting), I could use the time with
them somewhat aptly and fitly. But and if it came to making of love by
word, sign or deed, especially in deed . . . I had no more face to do that than
had a sheep.

As far as courting remained a rhetorical performance, somehow
removed from the real business of winning affection, Whythorne
could evidently play his part with satisfaction. A little later in the
autobiography, he recounts a conversation that he had with a lady
of the court. Again, 'courting' is closely identified with some of the
peculiarities of behaviour at court:

Sometimes she would talk of the court, with the bravery and vanities
thereof, and of the crouching and dissimulation, with the *bazzios las manos*
that there is used by one courtier to another. And sometimes she would
minister talk of the courting of ladies and gentlewomen by the gallants and
cavaliers. And sometimes she would talk pleasantly of the love that is made
and used in all places between men and women.[55]

Whythorne's refusal to read between the lines of the court lady's
manifestly flirtatious speech, moreover, itself provides a neat illustration of the very courtship-rituals which she is describing. For
nothing expresses so clearly the distancing of the two partners, the
need to bridge an emotional and epistemological gap between them,
and the problems of interpersonal communication (all implied by
'courting') than Whythorne's own (apparently ingenuous) incom-
prehension of the general thrust of his interlocutrix's words. George
Puttenham was later to call allegory the 'Courtly figure' because in
it 'our wordes and our meanings meete not'.[56] When, in the sixteenth
century, the amorous behaviour between men and women assumed
the vocabulary of courtship, the two partners in love similarly
subjected themselves to a world of teasing hints, innuendoes, and
indirections, sometimes with comic results. In his translation of
Stefano Guazzo's *La civile conversatione* (1581–6), for example, George
Pettie describes men who 'if a woman shewe but a merry countenance, make some signe by chaunce, or use any other jesture, they
apply it all to themselves, as done in their favour, and filled with a
thousande vaine pleasures, oftentimes make court to suche a one,
whose minde is farre of both from them, and their purpose'.[57]

Until this point, then, our broadly diachronic analysis has considered how the words 'courtship' and 'to court' changed their senses

in a number of languages during the sixteenth century. Following their continental equivalents, the English words developed quickly in the first half of the century from meaning simply 'being at court' (as in Barclay) to specifying whole areas of courtly experience, particularly courtly ways of speaking and behaving. The amorous sense of the words appeared in the 1560s through a combination of translation and association (as seen in Fenton), and, after an experimental period in the 1560s and 1570s, gradually stabilized as an accepted usage in the 1580s and 1590s.

The following section goes on, then, to attempt (as far as is possible) to evaluate the full range of meanings possessed by 'courtship' and 'to court', and to trace still further the subtle nuances that the words possessed for the language-users of the time. Our method now moves, therefore, from diachronic to synchronic semantics.

We have already seen in passing that the morally pejorative overtones of 'courting' (in the sense of courtly rhetoric) carried over into the new, amorous sense, thus casting aspersions on the potentially devious language of lovers. Many contemporary uses of the words in their amorous sense therefore equate the courting of women with the unscrupulous use of flattery for personal advancement at court. In Thomas Lodge's prose romance *A Margarite of America* (1595), for example, the treacherous Arsadachus is allowed 'to court' the heroine.[58] The deceitful lover in Robert Greene's *Mamillia* (1583) 'framing a sheepes skin for his woolues backe, and putting on a smooth hide ouer his Panthers paunch, vsed first a great grauitie in his apparell, and no lesse demurenes in his countenaunce and gesture, with such a ciuil gouernment of his affection, as that he seemed rather to court vnto Diana, then vow his seruice vnto Venus'.[59] In *The Faerie Queene* (1596), Duessa entertains Sansfoy with 'courting dalliaunce', while Sansloy woos Una: 'With fawning wordes he courted her a while.' As well as courting Hellenore, Paridell 'did court, did serue, did wooe' the false Florimell, and in book II Phedon attacks his treacherous friend Philemon, who 'Did court the handmayd of my Lady deare'.[60] In Thomas Heywood's *Troia Britanica* (1609), Paris is said to 'court' Helen with 'Louetrickes', while in George Peele's version of the Troy story (1589), Paris 'strives to court his Mistres cunninglie'.[61] In *The Complaint of Philomène* (1576), George Gascoigne lampoons those 'comely courting knights' who abuse their rhetorical skill and 'use al arte to marre

the maidens mindes' and 'win al dames with baite of fonde delights'.[62] And, in Marlowe's *Hero and Leander* (?1593), Mercury – the
god of rhetoric – exploits his powers in order to cajole his earthly
mistress:

> Maids are not woon by brutish force and might,
> But speeches full of pleasure and delight.
> And knowing Hermes courted her, was glad
> That she such lovelinesse and beautie had
> As could provoke his liking.[63]

In the *New Arcadia* (1590), Sidney uses the verb 'to court' to
describe the dubious courtship offered by Phalanthus to the vain
Artesia:

> many times it falls out that these young companions make themselves
> believe they love at the first liking of a likely beauty, loving because they
> will love for want of other business, not because they feel indeed that divine
> power which makes the heart find a reason in passion, and so, God knows,
> as inconstantly lean, upon the next chance that beauty casts before them.
> So therefore, taking love upon him like a fashion, he courted this Lady
> Artesia ...[64]

Artesia makes Phalanthus pledge to defend her beauty over all
other women, although he has little faith in the enterprise and
eventually the 'courtship' is called off for mutual convenience. This
kind of courtship has little to do with real affection. In *Euphues and his
England* (1580), Lyly's narrator rebukes women for picking out
'those that can court you, not those that loue you', and, in Giles
Fletcher's sonnet-sequence, *Licia* (1593), the poet disarmingly admits how 'Court I did, but did not love.'[65] As a purely rhetorical
performance, courtship could therefore be used to hoodwink any
number of women: in *The Diall of Princes* (1568), for example,
Thomas North describes an 'amorous courtier, that so dearely
seemed to loue his lady, will now make court a fresh to others, and
dislyke that heretofore hee loued, and fly from her whom erst he
folowed, abhorring that hee once delyted in.'[66] And, divorced from
love or affection, such courtship could equally be performed on
another's behalf. In *The Spanish Tragedy* (?1585–7), Balthazar
quizzes Heironimo: 'what, courting Bel-imperia?' 'Ay, my lord', he
answers, 'such courting as, I promise you, / She hath my hart, but
you, my Lord, haue hers.'[67]

'Courtship' thus accrues a host of negative associations. The unscrupulous courtier is often shown to make his advances under cover of night, like the gentleman described by Thomas Lodge who 'walks the streets and the Exchange, to spy out faire women; by night he courts them with maskes, consorts, and musicke'.[68] George Whetstone anticipates the dire consequences of such courtship when, in his *Heptameron of Ciuil Discourses* (1582), he describes a young girl who would

manie times walke, vnto the Piatso Richio, a place where the brauest Gentlemen assembled, and where the fynest deuices were sould: she taking this liberty to walke, bound the gallant yong Gentlemen, in curtesie to Court her: curtuous seruice, is to be accepted with thankes: acceptance of seruice, inlargeth acquaintance: acquaintance ingendreth familiarytie: and famyliaritie, setteth al Folies abroach.[69]

In his collection of tales, *A Petite Pallace of Pettie his Pleasure* (1576), George Pettie describes one lover who 'sought all meanes possible to insinuate himselfe into [his mistress's] familiaritie, and courted her continually with dutiful service and secret signes of sincere affection ... she could not looke out at her chamber window, but that she saw him walke solitarily underneath'.[70]

When used in these contexts, then, 'courtship' was frequently understood to lead not to legitimate marriage but, rather, to a fatal 'familiarity'. For John Lyly, 'woemen that delight in courting, are willing to yeelde', and the same 'woemen yeelde when they are courted'.[71] In Brian Melbancke's prose romance *Philotimus* (1583), a father asks his son to dedicate his life to three mutually exclusive alternatives: 'Whether the firste of all to Pallas, and to liue at the Vniuersity, there to attaine the profound and sound knowledge of the liberall artes. Or honour sacred Iuno with solemnizing her mariage ... Or if none of these will fit thy fancie, wilt thou vow thy self to Venus, and court it awhile?'[72]

In these terms, 'courtship' becomes an irresponsible pursuit and is most commonly associated with lust, or with those fleeting sexual encounters described by Lyly's Euphues as 'begunne in an houre and ended in a minuit'.[73] Philip Massinger equates 'boystrous courtship' with 'loose language and forcd kisse', and John Florio defines 'amoreggiare' in his Italian–English dictionary (1611) as 'to court with lust', hinting that the act of persuasion and the sexual intention are indeed synonymous.[74]

So, when Sir John Davies addresses some lines to his mistress, his

use of the verb 'to court' sits comfortably with the obscene undertones of the poem:

> Faith (wench) I cannot court thy sprightly eyes,
> With the base Viall placed betweene my Thighes . . .
> I am not fashioned for these amorous times,
> To court thy beutie with lascivious rimes.[75]

For other writers, the word is virtually synonymous with gross
displays of physical affection. In Michael Drayton's *Endimion and
Phoebe* (1595), for example, Jove spies Endimion and 'courted him,
inflamed with desire'.[76] Those lovers who lie 'lulde in Ladies lappes
. . . that plaie with womens paps', are described by Barnaby Rich as
'courtyng mistres mince', while one of the characters in George
Wilkins's play, *The Miseries of Inforst Marriage* (1607), lists all the
'degrees of loue' as 'either to Court, kisse, giue priuate fauours, or vse
priuate meanes'.[77]

'Courting' is equated with wantonness in the sober, religious
context of George Herbert's poetry.[78] Sir John Harington makes a
similar association of ideas in his translation of the *Orlando Furioso*
(1591):

> If so I may a paradise it name
> Where love and lust have built their habitation,
> Where time well spent is counted as a shame,
> No wise staide thought, no care of estimation,
> Nor nought but courting, dauncing, play, and game,
> Disguised clothes, ech day a sundrie fashion,
> No vertuous labour doth this people please,
> But nice apparell, belly cheare, and ease.[79]

A scandalized George Peele catalogues 'courting' in a similar way:

> To wish, to dallie, and to offer game,
> To coy, to court, and caetera to doe:
> (Forgive me Chastnes if in termes of shame,
> To thy renowne, I paint what longs thereto).[80]

All the examples considered so far, therefore, load 'courtship'
unequivocally with negative associations: a rhetorical performance
which, being aimed at deception or seduction, conflicts flatly with all
the domestic ideals of chastity, constancy, and continency. But this is
not the whole picture. As we shall see, for all the citations which
divorced 'courtship' from sincerity or love, as many can be found

which restore the word to a morally as well as socially acceptable definition. In *The Faerie Queene*, for example, Spenser frequently redeems 'courting' from its otherwise lascivious connotations. Thus, while Redcrosse mistakenly entertains Duessa ('Yet goodly court he made still to his Dame'), Arthur emerges as the virtuous archetype a few stanzas later by correctly recognizing Una and entertaining her 'With louely court', just as he later questions Sir Guyon with 'gentle court'.[81] In each case an approbatory epithet condones the verb or verb-phrase. Similarly, Medina welcomes Guyon and 'comely courted with meet modestie', and Alma makes 'gentle court and gracious delight' to him.[82] Indeed, 'courting' is here used invariably in a favourable sense:

> A louely beuy of faire Ladies sate,
> Courted of many a iolly Paramoure.

> Whom when the knights beheld, they gan dispose
> Themselues to court, and each a Damsell chose.

> Thus they awhile with court and goodly game,
> Themselues did solace each one with his Dame.[83]

In certain contexts, then, 'courting' was regularly sanctioned and approved. In his *Arte of English Poesie* (1589), for example, George Puttenham writes that

because our chiefe purpose herein is for the learning of Ladies and young Gentlewomen, or idle Courtiers, desirous to become skilful in their owne mother tongue, and for their priuate recreation to make now and then ditties of pleasure, thinking for our parte none other science so fit for them & the place as that which teacheth beau semblant, the chief profession aswell of Courting as of poesie ... we haue in our owne conceit deuised a new and strange modell of this arte, fitter to please the Court then the schoole.[84]

In the complimentary atmosphere of Puttenham's self-advertis-ingly courtly text, 'courting' is here given implicit approval as a kind of model eloquence, just as George Whetstone's *Heptameron of Ciuil Discourses* (1582) opens with a gathering of 'sundrie well-Courted Gentlemen and Gentlewomen' who make it a proviso of their entertainment that 'euery Gentleman was bounde to Court his misterisse with Ciuill speaches'.[85] Such gallant speeches might be illustrated by Greene's Cicero, whose mistress, 'swilling downe the nectar of his diuine eloquence', modestly blushes, 'as did the fayre

queene of Carthage courted by Aeneas'.[86] And a song from the
entertainment for Queen Elizabeth performed at Cowdray in 1591
gives some hint of what the ideal lover might say: 'And when to us
our loves seeme faire to bee, / We court them thus, Love me and Ile
love thee.'[87]

In *A Courtlie Controuersie of Cupids Cautels* (1578) Henry Wotton
laments a decline in the standards of courteous wooing, for 'nowadays', he says, 'women are ... courted for mariage, without any
enquirie but for welth, and as the match is made for What haue you?
so al other things depend vpon What will you giue me? in such wise,
as vertue is despised and amitie vtterly decaied'.[88] It was in order to
restore the proper eloquence of such 'amitie' that Nicholas Breton
wrote his *Arbor of Amorous Deuises* (1597), 'Wherin, young Gentlemen
may reade many plesant fancies, and fine deuises: And theron,
meditate diuers sweete Conceites, to court the loue of faire Ladies
and Gentlewomen'.[89] Greene describes a contemporary lover who
will 'court a Lady with amor[e]trs' and cause 'Poets to write them
wanton Eligies of loue', for the language of courtship was required to
be learned.[90] The proper gentleman should be able to 'court / His
mistris, out of OVID', or, like Flavius, one of Barnaby Rich's
inamoratos, to 'court' her 'with suche nice termes as woers be
accustomed'.[91]

Translating Stefano Guazzo's *La civile conversatione*, George Pettie
writes that women 'love to be courted and tried, that by their honest
aunsweres, they may be knowne to the world to be honest women'.[92]
Such is the virtue of Barnaby Rich's heroine Clarinda, whom Don
Simonides 'had oft courted, yet neuer conquered', or of Perseda in
Thomas Kyd's play *Soliman and Perseda* (?1592).[93] Overcome by her
constancy and virtue, the Soliman refrains from raping her, and begs
leave only 'in honest sort to court thee, / To ease, though not to cure,
my maladie'.[94]

'Courtship' thus detaches itself from some of the more negative
associations of courtly rhetoric that we traced in earlier examples.
Apparently missing the sarcastic tone of his source, George North
translates a passage from Philibert de Vienne's *Philosophe du cour*,
warmly approving those 'yong gallants' to be found, 'some braue
and in good order, and others smothly combed for the purpose,
courting and woing their Ladies'.[95] In his *Golden Aphroditis* (1577),
John Grange diagrammatizes the courtly love-situation, and, in
order to present the parts of paramour and paragon in a lively

fashion, he makes '(F) stande for the Courtyer, and (G) for the Courtresse'.[96] A 'courtress' is specifically a virtuous court lady here (as opposed to the more meretricious 'courtesan'), and Greene makes a similar distinction between the common 'stale slut' of the day on the one hand, and the virtuous 'courtresse' on the other.[97]

In some settings, then, 'courtship' could denote sincere affection, for, as Thomas Campion notes, 'Courtship and music suit with love.'[98] Thus, in Drayton's *England's Heroicall Epistles* (1599), Queen Katherine writes to her lover, Owen Tudor, of their 'Courtship and Discourse', and later of their 'perfect Court-ship'.[99] In *Menaphon* (1589), Greene's hero

vsed euerie day to visite [his mistress] without dread, and courte her in such shepheards tearmes as he had; which howe they pleased her I leaue to you to imagine, when as not long after she vowed mariage to him solemnly.[100]

And, in the epithalamion which he wrote to celebrate the wedding of Princess Elizabeth to Frederick the Elector Palatine in 1613, George Wither explicitly links 'courting' with marriage:

> Revellers, then now forbeare yee,
> And unto your rests prepare yee:
> Let's a while your absence borrow,
> Sleep to night, and dance tomorrow.
> We could well allow your Courting:
> But 'twill hinder better sporting.[101]

A synchronic analysis of the words 'courtship' and 'to court' in English, therefore, shows them to be semantically highly flexible – capable of denoting model eloquence and etiquette on the one hand, and dissolute or licentious sexual behaviour on the other. The semantic fluidity of the word arises, moreover, from the fact that 'courtship' evolved its amorous sense from an associative field which originally denoted a particular kind of behaviour, a way of talking and acting that could be identified as 'courtly'. Thus George Puttenham notes that it is required of every 'Courtly Gentleman to be loftie and curious in countenaunce, yet sometimes [to be] a creeper, and a curry fauell with his superiors'.[102] The lover finds himself approaching his mistress with precisely the same tokens of regard and favour when he 'courts' her, and his expression of love consequently becomes a series of gestures and utterances which she, in turn, is obliged to decode, interpret, and return.

In the sixteenth century, then, 'courting' (in every sense) refers

essentially to those external and observable signs – deferential behaviour, fawning gestures, flattering talk – which signal to the
outside world that a relationship between two people (be they queen
and courtier, courtier and courtier, lover and mistress, or lover and
queen) exists.[103] Yet those gestures and tokens of regard can never be
more than extrinsic signs. The talking, jesting, and discoursing
between lovers ('all the which some do call courting', says Thomas
Whythorne) only ever remain external tokens of love, incapable by
themselves of indicating the 'real' or 'inner' intention of the lovers
any more than other social formulae, and, like them, therefore,
equally open to misunderstanding and misrepresentation.[104]

The words 'courtship' and 'to court' could as readily describe
liaisons of the most egregiously lascivious kind as the most upright
and exemplary relationships because 'courting' simply meant going
through the motions, putting on an act, playing the part, and
showing the rest of the world that one knew and understood the rules
of social and amorous etiquette. Whether suitors were sincere or not
is neither here nor there, for, as a kind of *behaviour*, 'courting'
uniquely problematizes the relation of sincerity to appearance, and
makes the 'truth' of a courtship-situation difficult, if not impossible,
to judge.

Courtship becomes so fascinating a subject in sixteenth-century
literature, therefore, precisely because of its semiotics – its tableaux
of gesture, utterance, and behaviour which bristle tantalizingly with
multiple and contradictory meanings, which are open to interpretation both by the participants of a courtship and by the people
outside it. It is to the semantic and structural ambivalence inherent
in Elizabethan courtship narratives, therefore, that we now turn.

CHAPTER 3

Courtship at court: some pageants and entertainments at the court of Elizabeth I

Looking back over the reign of Elizabeth I, Francis Bacon recalled how the Queen had 'allowed herself to be wooed and courted, and even to haue love made to her', grudgingly admitting that these 'dalliances detracted but little from her fame and nothing at all from her majesty'.[1]

As Bacon observes, courtship proved one of Elizabeth's most effective tools of policy – the wavering, prevaricating, and normally dismissive behaviour of the conventionalized mistress providing her with an obvious role-model for political manipulation and manœuvre.[2] Elizabeth clearly capitalized on the political potential that was granted to her by virtue of her gender. In what was to be her first public appearance as queen, for example – the coronation pageant through London in January 1559 – Elizabeth made a point of wooing the crowds, who remained 'wonderfully rauished with [her] louing answers and gestures'.[3] Later, Elizabeth is said to have complained that 'I have been courted by some who would rather marry the kingdom than marry the queen', and, in the scurrilous pamphlet, *Leicester's Ghost*, the Earl of Leicester is made to say that 'I assaid Queen Elsabeth to wedd, / Whome diuers princes courted but in vaine.'[4] Sir Robert Naunton was to recall how Elizabeth 'loved martial men', and how consequently she would 'court [Sir Francis Vere] as soon as he appeared in her presence'.[5]

The development of the amorous sense of 'courting' in this period did not, of course, in any way depend upon England's having a female sovereign in the sixteenth century. As we have seen, the word developed the specialized amorous meaning across Europe from the turn of the sixteenth century quite independently of any female rule, and cannot, therefore, be attributed solely to the historical accident of Elizabeth's gender. All the same, the courtship-situation which Elizabeth made use of so effectively has provided modern historians (as well as Bacon) with a convenient and highly economical coda for the political backdrop of sixteenth-century England, and for the overall system of clientage which characterized monarchical government at large across Europe in the Renaissance. As David Norbrook writes, 'Elizabeth's cult of courtly love actualised a metaphor that was always latent in monarchical systems of government: relations between individual and authority were not those of citizen and state but those of a subject, a dependent, to a single individual whose favour had to be "courted".'[6] 'Courting was a metaphor for the desire for power and authority', writes Jonathan Goldberg, and, for Wallace MacCaffrey, 'the stability of the system demanded the arduous and constant wooing of the body politic'.[7]

By identifying courtship-rituals with the actual practice of politicking at the court of Elizabeth I, these historians give the relation between Queen and courtiers a central place in the overall government of the kingdom, and thus critique an older tradition of English historiography which minimized the role of the court aristocracy in government, and which drove a wedge between court and state, between foppish, sycophantic courtiers, on the one hand, and 'professional' bureaucrats, on the other.[8] For Norbrook, Goldberg, MacCaffrey, and others, by contrast, the whims and vagaries of the court – exemplified nowhere more strikingly than in Elizabeth's relation with her male courtiers – are the very stuff of power, not mere distractions somehow removed from the serious business of government.[9]

These new interpretations of court historiography call for new interpretations of the relation between Elizabeth I and her male courtiers. For, although Francis Bacon had felt the need to defend the Queen's dubious amorous stratagems with her suitors against charges of frivolousness and vanity, he was forced to admit that, in the end, such stratagems served her political purposes very well. Even when one acknowledges that the political relation between Queen and courtiers was, almost by necessity, highly sexualized, 'courtship' at court was, in practice, extremely restricted. For by far the majority of Elizabeth's courtiers, courting the Queen was first and foremost a metaphor. Only in the tiniest number of cases was courtship a prelude to an offer of marriage. Archetypally, the relation between Elizabeth and her courtiers reflected a moment in which a courtship had been artificially frozen – in which the 'lover' and 'beloved' stood permanently on the threshold of a sexual relationship which would never be realized; and in which the cycle of reciprocity between an offer and its acceptance was arrested and suspended, creating the tense network of social, sexual, and political ties that is illustrated for us at the beginning of Spenser's Book of Courtesy in *The Faerie Queene.*

All the court shows and entertainments which I consider below ritualize the tense and difficult relation that existed between Elizabeth and her male courtiers. Time and time again, the rhetoric of sexualized desire (which lent itself so naturally and automatically to the condition of these men) is shown to be problematic. Virtually all the texts reveal the figure of a courtier-lover who is forced to re-examine, reinterpret, redraw his relation to the Queen, and to readjust a potentially sexual relation into 'a love purified of physical desire'.[10]

That these men should have returned so repeatedly to the same problems, the same necessity to reposition and relocate themselves toward the Queen, betokens a deep anxiety. In writing, performing, and sponsoring court shows, men like the Earl of Leicester, Philip Sidney, and the Earl of Essex allowed themselves to rehearse and to re-enact their predicament, to reveal to Elizabeth how difficult it was for them to overcome the sexual stereotyping of their age. And they did not always do this by simplifying the courtship-situation, or by reducing it to parody or absurdity. All the pageants which I discuss here self-consciously exploit the internal ambivalence of courtship which the contemporary usage of the word reveals.

As a style of civilized rhetorical and sexual behaviour, 'courtship' could, as we have seen, be approved within the idealized milieu of the court. At the same time, 'courtship' derived its amorous sense from the flattery and cajolery that were employed by courtiers at court, and, as a style of behaviour, it also implied the emotional and affective distancing of the two partners, the intervention of stratagems, devices, persuasions, even deceptions between them. Amorous courtship was not simply the obvious model for male courtiers who found themselves subservient to Elizabeth I. The ambivalence that we have seen to be inherent in the language and gesture of the courtship-situation allowed them to ritualize their own condition, and to enact their marginality, their uncomfortably subordinate roles.

The present chapter therefore explores the very practice of

courtship at court, and considers how courtiers capitalized on the courtship-situation in order to express sensitive issues at court, to manipulate or to advise the Queen, to propagandize questions of domestic or foreign policy, to pursue their own private interests, to proprietize and legitimize sexual desire, and, overall, to handle their subordination to a female prince.

THE INNER TEMPLE REVELS (1562)

As one critic has recently pointed out, entertainments that were sponsored by courtiers and performed at the court of Elizabeth I were 'primarily concerned with affirming a new and special accord between absolute monarch and certain members of her aristocracy', a relationship which was defined 'in terms of the *desire* of courtier for monarch'.[11] Since almost all of the entertainments to be considered here allegorize the relation between Queen and courtier in terms of sexual passion, I would like to begin by considering two allegories of Desire with which Robert Dudley – Elizabeth's long-time favourite – presented to the Queen in 1562 and 1575. Not only do both shows include figures of Desire, but both reveal the allegorization of sexual love to be fundamentally problematic at the court of a female sovereign. This section also considers ways in which Dudley altered what were traditional representations of desire in court pageants specifically in order to create a figure more puzzling and ambiguous for his courtly audience.

Robert Dudley's allegories of Desire had a particular significance in the first two decades of Elizabeth's reign because they provided him with a means of articulating national anxiety over the delicate question of Elizabeth's marriage and the royal succession: both highly sensitive issues which required the utmost tact and discretion. As Elizabeth's long-acknowledged favourite, Dudley naturally found himself at the forefront of these sensitive probings. In 1564, for example, Dudley had entertained the Queen with an allegorical debate between Juno and Diana, that was 'founded on the question of marriage', and in which Juno had the last word. This particular show met with a hostile response from Elizabeth (if one is to believe the interpretation of the Spanish ambassador), but in the two shows to be considered here, Dudley proves himself fully capable of exploiting a culture of indeterminacy in order both to flatter

Elizabeth and to meditate upon his own position as a subject of her formidable and emasculating power.[12]

In 1562 Robert Dudley (then Master of the Horse) took part in the annual Christmas disguising at the Inner Temple. The Revels formed a series of dramatic pieces which had an urgent bearing on the issue of the succession. The first – *Gorboduc* – explored the hazards that attend a disputed succession. The second – and the one in which Dudley himself participated – was a masque in which a group of young initiate knights were sworn in as servants to the goddess Pallas by her emissary Pallaphilos (this was the part played by Dudley). An account of the latter Revels survives in Gerard Legh's popular heraldry manual *The Accedens of Armory*, and, although it is some- what confusingly related there, the entertainment seems to have fallen into two distinct halves.[13]

The first part takes the form of a narrative allegory of Beauty and Desire – its plot largely based upon Stephen Hawes's late-medieval dream-poem, *The Passetyme of Pleasure* – and it dramatizes a tradition- al tale of courtship and chivalry. The story begins when a young man named Desire is inspired by 'yᵉ breth of fame' to seek Beauty. He sets off with his companions, Governance and Grace, to be prepared for his amorous quest in the Tower of Doctrine. While imbibing wisdom there, Desire sees Lady Beauty and falls in love with her, although he is forbidden to woo her until he has fully learned the *ars amandi* and proved himself in chivalrous combat. Desire is then dubbed a knight – 'Awdacitee bare his helme, Cur- raige the brestplate, Speede helde his spurres. And Trouth gaue him yᵉ charge' (210) – and, thus armed, he confronts and eventually kills a nine-headed beast which represents the sins of dissimulation, misreport, envy, detraction, and so forth. He is finally granted the hand of Lady Beauty in marriage, and he embarks on a 'ioyfull lyfe' with her until, after his death, he achieves his apotheosis in the heavenly Chamber of Felicity.

In Legh's text, this allegory of desire is, in turn, embedded in the dramatic action which forms the second of the two plots in the Christmas Revels. The scene for this second part of the show is set in the temple of Pallas – the goddess of learning and warfare, and a symbol (as Bacon was later to show) of 'how kings are to make use of their counsel of state'.[14] Pallaphilos (Dudley) here appears as the chief officiator at the temple, and his task is to initiate a group of

twenty-five knights into the order of Pegasus, in what is clearly a
romantic rendering of the Garter ceremony. In Legh's account,
Pallaphilos delivers a long speech to the initiate knights on 'thonour
of thorder', on their loyalty to each other, and on their obedience to
the sovereign, Pallas (215). He explains each item of the knights'
paraphernalia (including the 'targe', which depicts the head of the
Gorgon), and an allegorical arming ceremony follows, in which each
knight is armed 'wyth the brest plate of Currage ... ye sword of
Iustice ... the Spurres of spede' (224). The young knights then
proceed to pray and to offer sacrifice to their goddess, Pallas.

The two parts of the Inner Temple Revels are intimately related.
For it is the figure of Pallaphilos who narrates the story of Desire and
Beauty, and there are clear parallels between the allegory and the
arming of the twenty-five knights. Desire, for example, is inspired by
Fame and rewarded at the end by Fame's epitaph. Likewise, the
initiate knights are reminded of their duty to 'auncient Fame' and
enjoined to preserve their 'liuing fame' (217, 223^v). Pallaphilos tells
them that fame alone is everlasting, and the only honourable motive
in dynastic or epic ambition. Moreover, both Desire and the knights
are encouraged to attain wisdom. Desire has to learn the arts and
sciences before he can proceed to serve Beauty, while Pallaphilos'
twenty-five knights are exhorted to be worthy members of Pallas'
temple, a latter-day Helicon in which the 'liberall Sciences [flow] so
abundantlye' (204).When Desire is dubbed a knight, he is welcomed
into a 'felowshippe of Knighthoode' (210) just as the other knights
are initiated into 'so honorable a felowship' (216^v). And, finally,
there are obvious parallels between the two passages which describe
the ceremonial arming of both Desire and the young knights. In
Desire's arming ceremony, as we have seen, 'Curraige [held] the
brestplate, Speede helde his spurres' (210). Likewise, each of Pallaphilos' knights is given 'the brest plate of Currage ... the Spurres of
spede' (224).

Marie Axton suggests that the two distinct halves of the Revels
disguising specifically conflate different parts of the Perseus myth, a
legend which forms a consistent theme throughout Legh's text.[15] In
legend, Pallas punishes Medusa for defiling her temple by transforming her into the monstrous Gorgon. When Perseus defeats the
Gorgon, Pallas grants him the virgin Andromeda and blesses their
marriage. For Axton, the Revels therefore involve a complex
interplay of mythical and allegorical roles. Pallas represents Eliza-

beth's 'political body' as queen, a figure worthy of the deeply reverent and loyal commitment of Pallaphilos and his knights. Lady Beauty, on the other hand, figures her 'natural body' as Andromeda, a virgin who is to be wooed and won. The material of the Revels therefore reflects the old medieval distinction between the monarch's two bodies, and also, by implication, between the 'two bodies' of Robert Dudley – posing as both hopeful suitor to Elizabeth (Desire) and as a loyal subject of the Queen (Pallaphilos).

One thing which Axton does not venture, however, is why Desire remains so surprisingly uncomfortable a figure. For hints and inconsistencies throughout the text of the Inner Temple Revels suggest that the show cannot in fact be treated as a simple allegory of Dudley's own matrimonial ambitions, and that the well-known favourite was not merely promoting himself as the young queen's obvious choice of a husband. Beauty – Desire's long-promised prize – is a generalized, undifferentiated figure, and yet she possesses some surprisingly unpleasant attributes. There are clear parallels between descriptions of Lady Beauty in the allegory of Desire, and the monstrous Gorgon, depicted on the 'targe' of Pallas which each of Pallaphilos' knights carries. In the allegory, for example, Desire begins with a survey of 'dame natures deckinges' and praises Beauty as 'all ornamentes of Nature' (207, 209). Legh later describes the shamed and metamorphosed Medusa in disturbingly similar terms: 'she was by ye goddes decree for her so foul a faut, berefte of all dame Bewties shape, with euerye comely ornament of Natures deckinge' (221–221^v). In the allegory, Desire is told that when his amorous suit succeeds, 'then shall ye see the glyding lokes steale foorth, and shewe themselues the Messengers of loue' (209). Yet it is precisely Medusa's 'gliding eye framed to fansy amoruse luste, [that] turned was to wan and deadly beholding' (221^v).

Beauty's precarious similarity to the Gorgon here strikes a discordant note, and would be out of place if the allegory of Desire were a simple tale of successful courtship. As if to emphasize this discrepancy, Legh's text makes an interesting departure from his source in Hawes in order (it would appear) to drive the point home. When Desire is being tutored in the art of love by the figure of Counsel, he is invited to consider the cases of previous lovers, including that of Troilus. In *The Passetyme of Pleasure*, Hawes presents Troilus as an icon of the long-suffering and finally rewarded lover. But Legh's text betrays a somewhat more sophisticated interpretation of Chaucer's poem. In the Inner Temple Revels, Counsel warns Desire: 'Let Troylus bee to you herein a Myrrour, how oft he languished wrapt in Venus bandes, yet [in] Time obtained loue of thuntrue Creside' (208ᵛ). Why should Counsel thus draw attention to the treachery of Cresseid, if Troilus is to inspire a newly minted lover as an exemplar? Similarly, what is the purpose of the aspersions on Beauty – so likely to be treacherous, or to turn into a Gorgon at any time? These questions remain unanswered, and have the effect of seriously compromising Desire's status as a courtly lover. It has to be admitted that, if the Revels show did conflate the two parts of the Perseus myth – the defeat of the Gorgon, and the marriage to Andromeda – then it did so in a very confusing way. And if Desire's conquest of Beauty was meant to reflect Dudley's hopeful wooing of England's young queen, then Legh's hinting parallels between Beauty and the Gorgon were, to say the least, unfortunate and extremely tactless.

The allegory of sexual desire in the Revels show is therefore severely compromised if one attempts to decode it simply as an indication of Dudley's hopes of marrying the Queen. One reason for this, I suggest, is that the figure of Desire – a favourite masque-persona in the Henrician court, as we shall see – was somehow out of place in the court entertainments of a young, virginal queen. Robert Dudley was constrained from presenting himself outright as a possible husband and sexual partner for the Queen, and thus found himself consciously having to reformulate and refashion a figure (familiar from earlier court shows) in order to reassure Elizabeth that he was fully aware of the complexities of their very public relationship. At the same time, Dudley seems to hint that Lady Beauty may not be all that she seems, and that, in wooing Elizabeth, he was just as likely to be turned to stone as he was to be accepted, honoured, and cherished as a husband.

In 1501, Henry VII had mounted a masque to celebrate the wedding of Prince Arthur to Katherine of Aragon. The show included a pageant ship out of which descended the figures of Hope and Desire, emissaries of the 'Knights of the Mownte of Love'. Hope and Desire attempt to persuade a group of intransigent court ladies to accept the knights, and they eventually do so, in a typical emblem of sexual conquest.[16] Later, in 1511, Henry VIII presented a spectacular series of pageants to celebrate the birth of a son. Henry himself took part as 'Ceure loyall' and his companion Sir Thomas Knyvet as 'Valliaunt desyre'. Henry, Knyvet, and other participants were all dazzlingly arrayed, and 'every persone had his name in letters of massy gold'. It was probably no accident, therefore, that Knyvet's codpiece was adorned with the single word 'desyre'.[17] Henry frequently appropriated the persona of Desire himself in court disguisings. In 1512 he entered a tournament accompanied by 'ladies all in White and Red silke' (the traditional colours of desire), and, in a device mounted by Wolsey in 1522, he played the part of Ardent Desire, dressed 'all in crimosin sattin with burnyng flames of gold'.[18]

The allegory of desire in the 1562 Inner Temple Revels is embedded in the same medieval tradition as these earlier Henrician disguisings. But the joyous celebrations of royal libido which characterize many Henrician shows would have been manifestly out of place in the court of Queen Elizabeth. Dudley's allegory of desire in the Inner Temple Revels provides an indication of how the figure of Desire had to be reinterpreted and transformed at the court of a virgin queen. For the purpose of the strange aspersions on Beauty in the Revels allegory is, on one level, to play down Desire's sexual conquest, and to lay greater emphasis on his apotheosis in the Chamber of Felicity as a tried and trusted knight than on his prowess as a courtly lover. The figure of Desire in the Inner Temple Revels is therefore an early version of the restrained, legitimized figures of desire which were to appear, on and off, in pageants throughout Elizabeth's reign.[19]

On a second level, however, the predicament of Desire reflects the hazards that manifestly attended any male courtier who aspired, like Dudley, to use the language of courtship to his own advantage. In a device that was planned to be performed during the year which followed the Inner Temple Revels, for example, the figure of Desire, so compromised in the Revels allegory, reappears.[20] The show presents an allegory of Peace, in which two ladies, Prudentia and Temperantia, imprison the wicked figures of Discord and False Report. As reward for their action, the two ladies are permitted to live with Peace in the Court of Plenty: a court that is guarded by two porters – Perpetuity and Ardent Desire – 'signifyinge that by ardent desyer, and perpetuitie, perpetuall peace and tranquillitie maye be hadd & kept throughe the hole worlde'.[21]

In this entertainment, Ardent Desire is a wholly marginal figure – a very different character from the energetic Desire of Henrician mummings. And while there is a more active hero in the masque –

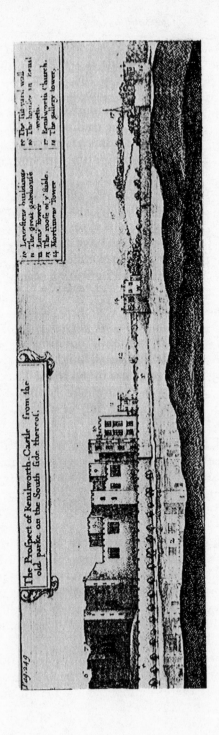

Illus. 2. View of Kenilworth Castle, from Sir William Dugdale's *Antiquities of Warwickshire* (1765), by permission of the Syndics of Cambridge University Library

the valiant figure of Hercules who defends the two ladies and their establishment of peace – the character who represents sexual desire is here stripped of any erotic stirrings and relegated to a porter's job.

The allegory of Peace was prepared for a projected meeting between Elizabeth and Mary Queen of Scots that was planned to take place at Nottingham Castle between May and July 1562. In the event this meeting never took place. But the preparation of the masque of Peace coincided with that somewhat peculiar (and temporary) decision of Elizabeth's that Robert Dudley should be offered as a possible husband to the Scottish queen in return for an assured succession. Whether or not the deviser of the masque was familiar with Dudley's role in the Inner Temple Revels of 1562, the emasculated and marginalized figure of Desire in the summer show hints that, in the company of queens, sexual desire played a very lowly role, and that Dudley had consciously to restrain and suppress any tendencies to present himself as a sexually active suitor.

KENILWORTH (1575)

Dudley's second major allegory of Desire formed a part of the lavish and spectacular entertainment which he laid on for Elizabeth at his castle of Kenilworth, in July 1575. Here we find Dudley acting as host to the Queen, entertaining her day after day with shows and displays remarkable for their variety and seeming spontaneity. No individual courtier had ever entertained Elizabeth so expensively before, and, as one critic writes, 'in few other places in English Renaissance literature do we find the Elizabethan dramatic impulse given such extravagant and spontaneous expression'.[22]

Dudley (now the Earl of Leicester) seems to have exploited the ambivalence of his position as Elizabeth's host and subject from the very outset of the Queen's visit.[23] When Elizabeth arrived at Kenilworth Castle on Saturday, 9 July 1575, she and her retinue made their way to the castle by the newly built tiltyard (still the entrance for modern visitors), and passed under a construction called Mortimer's Tower (see illus. 2). Carved into this tower was a curious engraving which would have signified to Elizabeth (if she had had her wits about her) the kind of 'functional ambiguity' with which Dudley was planning to entertain her for the next few days.[24] For the carving (as the antiquarian William Dudgale notes) showed 'the Arms of *Mortimer* ... cut in stone'.[25] Dudley seems to have added the engraving to his tower in order to make a very specific allusion to Roger Mortimer, the Earl of Wigmore and former owner of Kenilworth Castle, who had given a famous and historic tournament there in 1279. Dudgale describes the event as follows:

a great and famous concourse of noble persons here at Kenilworth, called the Round table, consisting of an hundred Knights, and as many Ladies; whereunto divers repaired from forreign parts for the exercise of Arms, viz Tilting, and martial Tournaments; and the Ladies, Dancing.[26]

John Stow also refers to the historic Kenilworth tournament as a 'knightly game' and Drayton was frequently to recall it as one of the greatest achievements of the Mortimer family.[27] The purpose of Leicester's carving in 1575, then, was presumably to draw an affinity between himself and Wigmore, as a former owner of the castle. In so doing, Leicester was appealing to a sense of historical continuity of which Elizabeth's visit was presented as the climax and culmination (the castle clock stood still for the duration of Elizabeth's visit). Moreover, his allusion to Mortimer's great tournament anticipates the Arthurianism that was to be a recurrent feature in the Kenilworth entertainment as a whole, with its *dramatis personae* including such figures as the Lady of the Lake and Sir Bruce sans Pity. At the same time, Leicester alludes to the fact that the Earl of Wigmore had been a loyalist and a supporter of the Crown during the Barons' Wars of the thirteenth century, and, in identifying himself with such an illustrious historical figure, he was able to reassure Elizabeth of his own continued loyalty and service.

The full significance of the engraving on the Mortimer Tower at Kenilworth comes to light, however, when we turn again to Dugdale. For Dugdale mistakenly identifies the specific Mortimer to whom Leicester alludes not as the Earl of Wigmore (the initiator of the great tournament of 1279) as one would expect, but, rather, as another, younger, though equally famous Mortimer – the Earl of March.[28] The latter, of course, was the Mortimer who was renowned in history for having once loved a queen – Isabel, the wife of Edward II. In other words, Dugdale confuses Mortimer, the Earl of Wigmore, with Mortimer, the Earl of March (the former's grandson). But his apparent slip of the pen alerts us to the (perhaps deliberate) ambivalence of Leicester's own self-presentation: for, as Mortimer the Earl of Wigmore, Leicester presented himself as a loyal supporter of the crown, but as Mortimer the Earl of March, he alluded to a man who was notorious for having once loved a queen.

So, even before a word had been spoken at the Kenilworth entertainment, Dudley had already set the tone for subtle allusion and inference that was to characterize the shows of the next few days: and nowhere more so than in an allegory of Desire which picks up on the ambiguities surrounding sexual desire that he had already explored in the Inner Temple Revels of 1562.

The allegory of Desire at Kenilworth falls into two parts, both written, devised, and performed in person by George Gascoigne. Returning to the castle after a successful day of hunting, Elizabeth was accosted by Gascoigne, dressed as a Salvage Man, and gripping an 'Oken plant pluct vp by the roots'.[29] In Renaissance iconography, the 'wodewose' or 'green man' was familiar as an overtly sexual figure, the lover driven to distraction. In surviving Henrician court songs, for example, the 'greenwood' is a recognized locale for dalliance, and the 'jolly forester' ditties occasions for risqué *doubles entendres*.[30] It was therefore entirely in keeping with his 'Hombre Salvagio' character that Gascoigne should address Elizabeth in erotic terms: 'Can no cold answers quench desire?', 'Had I the bewties blase? / which shines in you so bright', 'But comely peerelesse Prince, / since my desires be great: / Walke here sometimes in pleasant shade, / to fende the parching heate.'[31]

The Salvage Man's overt allusions to sex and sexual desire were to be repeated in the second part of the allegory of Desire, which was performed (again by Gascoigne) on the day of Elizabeth's departure from Kenilworth. As she was leaving the castle to continue her progress, she was again accosted by Gascoigne, disguised this time as Sylvanus – the god of woods and satyrs – and a figure equally if not even more strongly associated with sexual desire than the Salvage Man. Sylvanus acts as a spokesman for desire, and, as an emissary from the gods, he has been sent to entreat Elizabeth to delay her departure, and to 'commaunde againe / This Castle and the Knight, which keepes the same for you'. Sylvanus moves the Queen to 'have good regard to the general desire of the Gods' because 'the whole earth earnestly desireth to keepe you' and because he himself is 'thorowly tickled with a restlesse desire'.[32]

Sylvanus then leads Elizabeth toward a grove – an enchanted forest, he tells her, of lovers who have been mysteriously metamorphosed into trees by their cruel mistress, Zabeta (clearly a figure for

Elizabeth herself). Gascoigne thus allegorizes a typical courtship-
scenario in terms of an ancient and familiar romance motif. For
Zabeta's 'rare giftes have drawne the most noble and worthy
personages' to woo her, and yet they have each been 'rigorously
repulsed . . . and cruelly rejected'. Sylvanus weeps bitterly at the fate
of the arborified lovers, and points out to Elizabeth a number of
individual trees (which quake as she approaches), among them, a
holly bush and a laurel tree – once 'two sworne brethren which long
time served [Zabeta], called *Deepe desire*, and *Dewe desert*'.³³

Deep Desire is, as one might expect, a highly eroticized figure.
Like the Salvage Man and Sylvanus (and like the most frankly
sexual 'Ardent Desire' of Henrician disguisings), he is an emblem of
overt male sexual longing. In Gascoigne's words, Deep Desire was
'such a one as neither any delay could daunt him: no disgrace could
abate his passions, no tyme coulde tyre him, no water quench his
flames'.³⁴ Gascoigne's Sylvanus thus contrasts sharply with another
appearance of the satyr-god in a later entertainment that was
performed for Elizabeth at Elvetham in 1591. As a part of this later
show, Sylvanus pledged himself the servant of Elizabeth ('beauties
Queene'), but his desires are deemed to be improper and he is
ducked in a pond for his pains – 'water will extinguish wanton fire'.³⁵
Gascoigne's Sylvanus, by contrast, suffers no such punishment and is
permitted to address Elizabeth familiarly as 'dame pleasure' and 'my
deere delight'. And, metamorphosed into a holly bush, Desire
naturally lends himself to crude Mercutian bawdiness and gross
phallic symbolism. For he is, of course, equipped with pricks: 'to
prove the restlesse prickes of his privie thoughts'.³⁶

A number of critics have interpreted Desire's sexual bid for Zabeta
as a version of the Earl of Leicester's long-term ambitions to win
Elizabeth in marriage. Muriel Bradbrook and Bruce R. Smith, for
example, both identify the figure of Deep Desire with Elizabeth's
host, and Marie Axton argues that Gascoigne's devices were
designed to press Dudley's suit.³⁷

The enclosed world of topicality and in-jokes which characterizes
coterie writing certainly makes courtly texts (more than others)
invite such identifications. And yet to link allegorical figures directly
with real individuals risks ignoring all the subtleties and ambiguities
that lie embedded in Dudley's allegory of Desire. For the figure of
Deep Desire is here (as in the Inner Temple Revels of 1562) deeply
problematic and ambiguous, since he includes attributes that

are equally unworthy and worthy. Arborification is in itself a highly ambivalent symbol. In Virgil, Dante, Ariosto, Tasso, and Spenser, for example, being transformed into a tree tends to be a punishment for surrender to physical passion: it is generally lovers and suicides who are thus metamorphosed. But in Ovid's *Metamorphoses*, the arborified victims are virgins; and, in Daphne's celebrated case, being turned into a tree is the direct consequence of her refusal to give in to sexual desire. When the Queen visited Sudeley in 1592, for example, she was entertained with a pageant in which the metamorphosed Daphne was magically released in Elizabeth's presence: 'whether should chastety fly for succour, but to the Queene of chastety?', Daphne asks.[38]

Dudley therefore exploits all the ambiguities of the tree-metamorphosis in his Kenilworth show. For, metamorphosed into an evergreen holly bush, Desire becomes a phallic symbol *par excellence*. But, again as a holly bush, he also becomes a traditional symbol for constancy:

> As the holy grouth grene
> And never chaungyth hew,
> So I am, ever hath bene,
> Unto my lady trew.[39]

Sexual desire and constancy were normally considered antithetical in the Renaissance, yet Deep Desire combines constancy and lust in equal proportions. When Sir Henry Lee entertained Elizabeth at Ditchley in 1592, he led her to a forest which not only contained both inconstant and constant lovers, but one single tree which itself emblematized the paradox of courtly love:

> we knights are trees whome roots of faith doe bynd
> our ladies [leaves] who sometyme give us grace,
> but fall awaie with everie blast of wynd.[40]

Like Henry Lee's tree, Leicester's self-presentation as Desire in the Kenilworth show is also highly complex and paradoxical. Deep Desire is described, in the euphuistic register of antithesis and antimetabole, as 'that wretch of worthies, and yet the worthiest that ever was condemned to wretched estate'. Moroever, another of the metamorphosed lovers whom Gascoigne points out to Elizabeth in the enchanted forest is an oak – once 'a faithfull follower and trustie servant of hyrs, named Constance'.[41] And if one is going to identify Deep Desire with Dudley, then the oak (in Latin, *robur*)

contains an equally obvious allusion to Dudley's given name
(Robert).

The enchanted forest is not, therefore, as straightforward an
allegory of the typical 'courtly-love' scenario as it first appears. For it
is less individual trees than the forest as a whole – mixed, hybrid,
polyvalent, as it is – which figures Leicester's various personae as
host, courtier, lover, and servant. The Kenilworth forest contains a
courtly 'cocktail' of different types of lover: some (like Constance,
Deep Desire, Due Desert), the victims of a cruel, wilful mistress who
fails to recognize true service and who consequently punishes them
unjustly; but others who are quite rightly punished. For in addition
to Constance, Deep Desire, and Due Desert, the forest contains a
poplar (representing Inconstancy), an ash (Vainglory), a briar
(Contention), and ivy (Ambition).

Was Dudley complimenting Elizabeth on her merciless treatment
of flatterers, or was he presenting himself as a loyal servant who had
been cruelly and unjustly punished? The answer is not obvious, for
Zabeta's motives themselves remain deeply equivocal. Like Deep
Desire himself, Zabeta's presentation is problematized by a register
of antithesis in which opposites are held in stark and static contrast –
'this courteous cruell, and yet the cruellest courteous that ever was' –
but never resolved.[42] We remain uncertain whether she acts wilfully
and irresponsibly in failing to recognize true service, and thus
unjustly penalizes Desire; or whether she is a righteous judge,
someone who 'countervaile[s] this cruelty with a shewe of justice',
and who is capable of identifying unacceptable courtly conduct
(Ambition, Contention, and so forth) and of punishing it appropriately. If the first, then Zabeta's treatment of Deep Desire is presented
as unmotivated and cruel; if the second, then she is thoroughly
justified in reining his overweening ambition.

Presumably, Dudley was being diplomatic. For he was, in effect,
complimenting Elizabeth on two different attributes: her justice and
her chastity. The first of these enabled her to identify flattery and
ambition at court; the second, effortlessly to transcend the sexualized
desires of her male courtiers. But by casting Deep Desire in a
_ subordinate (and metamorphosed) role, Dudley was also able to
articulate (however faintly) his own sense of marginalization. And in
his Kenilworth show the sexually active lover (the holly as Deep
Desire) combines with the respectful and proper lover (the oak,

Constance) to conflate Dudley's 'two bodies', as suitor and subject, with the same teasing ambivalence as the Inner Temple Revels of 1562.

THE LADY OF MAY (1578–9)

Dudley's nephew, Philip Sidney, was almost certainly one among the courtly audience of the spectacular Kenilworth show in 1575. Four or five years later, no doubt inspired by the artful spontaneity of Dudley's *al fresco* entertainments, Sidney was to write a dramatic pastoral which was perfomed before (or, more accurately, around) Queen Elizabeth when she visited Dudley's house at Wanstead during the spring of 1578 or 1579.

Sidney's entertainment – nowadays generally called *The Lady of May* – concerns a simple courtship-scenario, and centres around folkloric associations between Maying and the choice of suitors. In Sidney's device, the Lady of the May finds herself wooed by two suitors, a forester (Therion) and a shepherd (Espilus). As she cannot decide which is the worthier of the two, her mother (the Suitor) seeks the advice of the Queen, who thus enters into the pageant in a teasing interplay of fact and fiction.

The Lady of May is loosely concerned with the political issues which preoccupied the English court in the 1570s. And, if the debate between the respective merits of the active forester and the more contemplative shepherd does not allude specifically to active Protestant militancy, nor the theme of a choice of lovers figure Elizabeth's own long-looked-for choice of husband, then, in the words of Louis A. Montrose, Sidney certainly attempts in *The Lady of May* to 'define and advance his place in the Elizabethan body politic, and his relationship to the queen in the light of those recent and ongoing developments'.[43]

Both the date and the text of the piece remain unstable. Like all the shows we have already considered, *The Lady of May* was designed for a single performance only, making for obvious discrepancies between actual, private performance and the polished and public presentation text. Moreover, the text of the entertainment preserves two alternative endings. When first published in the 1598 edition of Sidney's works, a cryptic and impenetrable statement tells us that 'it pleased her Majesty' to opt for Espilus. A surviving manuscript version of the show, on the other hand, concludes with an eclogue in which 'Master Robert' (identified by most critics with Leicester) appears to be vindicated and given the last word.

The Lady of May therefore exemplifies the critical problems that arise when dealing with shows which, as we have already seen, belonged categorically to a culture of obliquity and indirection.[44] *The Lady of May* is a dramatic pastoral, and its debates take the form of eclogues – the oldest form for what George Puttenham calls 'disputation and contentious reasoning'.[45] The very structure of the entertainment thus creates an environment for decision, resolution, and judgement, leading many critics to regard the argument of *The Lady of May* as weighted one way or the other, steering the audience or reader toward a destined outcome. And yet, as I shall argue, Sidney deliberately makes a point of *not* weighting his argument on either side, but, rather, on preserving the baffling and bewildering equality of the two suitors.

Most critics identify the active forester, Therion, with the Earl of Leicester, and all claim that he is by far the more attractive suitor. Sidney certainly exploits the semiotics and associations of his setting, for *The Lady of May* takes place in what Bruce R. Smith calls the 'middle distance' – that ambiguous space that lay between the highly formal Elizabethan garden and the wilderness of Wanstead Forest which lay all around. Wanstead Forest had been preserved as a royal game park from the days of Henry VII, and would therefore have been redolent with associations of aristocratic hunting and sport for Elizabeth and her courtly retinue.[46] Unlike the lowly Espilus, Therion is presented as an indisputably aristocratic figure, and he therefore had obvious affinities with the generations of courtiers who had hunted in Wanstead Forest from the days of Elizabeth's grandfather. Moreover, as a hunter, Therion is also akin to the 'jolly forester' figure, familiar from Henrician disguisings, and to both the Salvage Man and Sylvanus in Leicester's Kenilworth show. While the properties and delights of the hunt had, for decades, been a commonplace in courtly shows, the appearance of shepherds such as Espilus would, in the 1570s, have appeared somewhat novel. *The Lady of May* was to popularize the form of dramatic pastoral in court shows for years to come; but in 1578–9 its only precedent was an entertainment performed at Reading in 1574 (involving 'shepherdes hookes' and 'Lambskynnes').[47]

But to say that Elizabeth and her courtiers might have identified more readily with the familiar forester-figure than with a shepherd is not, of course, to argue that Sidney was weighting the argument toward Therion. For Espilus and his companions anticipate those personal and well-known associations with shepherds which Sidney fashioned for himself, both in the fiction of the *Arcadia* and in the semi-fiction of court tournaments, and for which his contemporaries were later to memorialize him. In the *New Arcadia*, for example, the shepherd-knight, Philisides, enters the lists with 'a dozen apparelled like shepherds' who sing an eclogue, 'one of them answering another' to the sound of their rustic recorders. Philisides wears armour that is 'dressed over with wool', perhaps as one would have expected Espilus (meaning 'woolly or hairy one') to appear.[48] By the time of his death, Sidney's guise as the Shepherd-Knight was so established that both Spenser and the Earl of Essex mourned him as 'Sweete Sydney, fairest shepheard of our greene'.[49]

For Sidney proves to be just as sensitive to the ambivalences and ambiguities of the courtship-situation as his uncle had been at Kenilworth. Sidney does not court Elizabeth directly in *The Lady of May*. He displaces the Queen as an object of personal or sexual desire, and, instead, invites her to act as an impartial judge in a case of sexual politics. And he thus enacts in trivial or play form the relation between a queen and her subject. By presenting Elizabeth with a simple situation which it is entirely (and exclusively) within her power to arbitrate, Sidney figures his own self-positioning before her, and, more significantly, the ultimate arbitrariness of her power over him. Sidney had to fashion a text that was capable of accommodating either judgement: Therion or Espilus. *The Lady of May* therefore provided him with a means of expressing ruefulness that a courtier's independent advice often had little influence over royal decision. Indeed, Sidney rehearses the fact that a courtier's direction and counsel could be (and in Sidney's case manifestly was) utterly, wilfully, whimsically disregarded by the Queen, if she so chose; and he thus reflects, to some degree, the pointlessness of trying to offer the monarch unsolicited advice.

Despite a critical consensus that he loads the argument toward Therion, therefore, Sidney insists, in the very structure of *The Lady of May*, that the two suitors are in essence exactly the same, and, indeed, that it is impossible to choose between them. Therion is sometimes identified as representing the active life (privileged over the contemplative in the Renaissance). Yet foresters had no intrinsic moral superiority over shepherds, and, traditionally, pastoral or romance made no differentiation, social or otherwise, between the two. In Thomas Lodge's *Rosalynde*, for example, and in *As You Like It* (perhaps Shakespeare's most 'Sidneian' play), shepherds and foresters happily coexist in the temporarily non-hierarchical, undenominational world of the pastoral.[50] In the *Old Arcadia*, moreover, the forest becomes the venue not of 'active' citizens but of withdrawal, retreat, and contemplation, each of which belongs more to Espilus than to Therion:

> O sweet woods, the delight of solitariness!
> O how much I do like your solitariness!
> Here no treason is hid, veiled in innocence,
> Nor envy's snaky eye finds any harbour here,
> Nor flatterers' venomous insinuations.[51]

Here (as in another poem, *Dispraise of a Courtly Life*) the forest provides courtiers with the same refuge that the pastoral world provides for the shepherds in *The Lady of May*: a haven from 'envy' and 'servile flattery' (28).

Moreover, the chief reason why the argument of *The Lady of May* extends through a myriad different debate-forms is simply that there is no appreciable difference – quantative or qualitative – between the two rivals. And while the dualistic debate-structure of the entertainment invites us to read the argument as aggressively combative, the use of the comparative form – 'Espilus is the richer, but Therion the livelier' (25) – in fact suggests a stalemate or impasse. Therion's merits are not privileged over those of Espilus, or vice versa: for the one's virtues cancel out the other's vices. Only as 'the beautifullest lady' (24) does Elizabeth reintroduce the superlative form (and with it a hierarchy of values) in a version of the judgement of Paris that was to form so popular a motif in other court entertainments to come.[52]

The static, euphuistic structure of the Suitor's opening words therefore sets the tone for the whole performance of Sidney's device. She first addresses Elizabeth by confessing herself to be 'as deeply plunged in misery, as I wish you the highest point of happiness' (21). Sidney's use of *compar* and *contentio* here expresses the Suitor's frustration and predicament rather than any logical progression of argument. In 'The Supplication' – a highly formal poem, which carefully counterbalances thesis with antithesis – images of Elizabeth's dazzling face and mind in the first sestet are re-presented as merciful in the second, the rhetorical question 'How dare I?' becoming 'So dare I' in the second. The poem's balanced, static structure is then dramatically actualized as two 'sestets' of foresters and shepherds enter quarrelling, their tug-of-war creating a striking emblem of the impasse that has been reached by the two parties. In the singing competition that follows, the two rivals' verses interweave with each other's, but the issue is still unresolvable. And when both parties proceed to debate the question in an eclogue on the merits of their respective 'professions' they get no closer to concluding their debate.

The rhetorical structure of *The Lady of May* is thus based upon a 'comparison of contraries', a device described by John Hoskins in his *Directions for Speech and Style* as when 'contraries are sometymes arranged togeither by payres one to one, as compare the ones impatience to the others myldnes, the ones impenitency with the others submission, the ones humility with the others indignacon'.[53] The purpose of exaggerating the 'few small services and no faults' of Espilus with the 'many great services and many great faults' (29–30) of Therion in *The Lady of May* is therefore simply to make the argument impossible to resolve, for, as Hoskins explains, the rhetorical device is an ornamental, courtly trope which amplifies argument but which does not help to answer it.

Unlike the 'judicial' orations of accusation and defence which we find in book v of the *Old Arcadia*, *The Lady of May* approximates, rather, to the second main category of rhetorical speech – 'deliberative' oration. The *Rhetorica ad Herennium* defines deliberative speeches as 'either of the kind in which the question concerns a choice between two courses of action, or of the kind in which a choice among several is considered'.[54] In Thomas Wilson's words, a judicial oration ensures that 'the earnest trial of al controuersies, rest[s] onely vpon iudgement'. In a deliberative oration, on the other hand, 'we doe not ... determine any matter in controuersie'.[55]

The Lady of May does conclude with judgement, of course, when Sidney invites Elizabeth to arbitrate the as yet unresolved dilemma of the May Lady. But the text of Sidney's entertainment is presented as an open-ended debate, which, like a deliberative oration, relentlessly argues two alternatives *in utramque partem*. *The Lady of May* thus accretes new opinions, polishes and sophisticates old ones, yet scarcely develops the central argument. By endlessly rehearsing the same issues, and by repeatedly deferring the moment of decision, Sidney hints strongly that he is writing in a deliberative vein – one for which he had an obvious and well-known rhetorical model: the courtly *questione d'amore*.

The tradition of courtly debate, which went back to the platonic dialogues and which lies embedded in texts like *The Book of the Courtier*, is too well-known to need lengthy reiteration here. With its choice of lovers, the informal garden setting, the call for female (especially royal) arbitration, *The Lady of May* clearly signals its affiliation to this courtly form. Indeed, Sidney's plot closely resembles an archetypal courtly debate in Boccaccio's *Filocolo* (an English translation of which had appeared in 1566).[56] In Boccaccio's text, a lady who is being courted by two suitors is asked to indicate which of the two she intends to accept. In response, she bestows on one of the lovers a rose-garland that she is wearing, while taking from the second lover a garland of laurel which he has been wearing. A formal *questione d'amore* then arises: which of the two lovers did the lady choose? The one to whom she gave, or the one from whom she took? The issue is debated by a group of courtiers, but in the end their arbitress, Fiammetta, acknowledges that the lady's action was designedly ambiguous, and that either lover could have been her elected husband. 'We know very wel', she concludes, 'that in these our reasonings much might be obiected agaynst this our definition, & much also answered to the contrary reasons.'[57]

The purpose of Boccaccio's debate is less to decide which of the two had been chosen, than to argue on both sides various urgent questions of love and sexuality. The courtiers' debating techniques are essentially the same as those of academic inquiry, but their subject-matter is different – 'feminine', and courtly. The distinction between academic and courtly modes of discourse was a commonplace in the period, George Puttenham claiming to write in a style 'fitter to please the Court then the schoole', for example. And, while 'in vniuersities vertues and vices are but shadowed in colours, white and blacke', comments a courtier in Lyly's *Sapho and Phao*, in courts they are 'shewed to life, good and bad'.[58]

Like Puttenham and Lyly, Sidney also prioritizes courtly methods of debate over academic argument in *The Lady of May*, nowhere more clearly than in his merciless debunking of Rombus (a prototype for the dusty scholars he was to attack in the *Apology for Poetry*). For Rombus' fussy Ramist logic is both misplaced and misinformed.

He instructs Dorcas, for example, that 'you must divisionate your point . . . for prius dividendum oratio antequam definiendum' (27). But Rombus makes what Sidney's educated audience would have recognized at once as an elementary mistake, for, in formal rhetorical argument, the definition always comes first.[59] Rombus also confuses 'species' with simple divisions, when they are technically 'the kinde, or sorte of any thyng (comprehended vnder a worde more vniuersall)'.[60] More significantly, Rombus proves (for all his training) to be incapable of conducting even an academic debate properly. For, at the end of Rixus' speech on the pastoral life, Rombus takes the argument back to where it began by quoting the May Lady's initial question – 'whether the many great services and many great faults of Therion, or the few small services and no faults of Espilus, be to be preferred' (29–30) – instead of giving a conclusion as would be technically required in a formal oration.[61]

By ridiculing Rombus as a figure manifestly incapable of conducting a formal oration (and, instead, unwittingly adjusting himself to the courtly mode of the debate), Sidney emphasizes still further that *The Lady of May* revolves around a *questione d'amore* that Elizabeth would eventually arbitrate, and therefore presents his audience with a pre-eminently courtly way of handling a courtly problem.

For the courtship-situation enacted in *The Lady of May* enabled Sidney to explore the real effectiveness of a courtier's attempt to persuade, manipulate, or advise the Queen. Courting the prince was a tense and hazardous procedure, and, in 1580, Languet was urging Sidney to use judicious caution in his dealings with Elizabeth: 'you must take care not to go so far that the unpopularity of your conduct be more than you can bear . . . when you find that your opposition only draws on you dislike and aversion, and that neither your country, your friends, nor yourself derive any advantage from it, I advise you to give way to necessity, and reserve yourself for better times'.[62]

In deliberately leaving the outcome of *The Lady of May* open-ended, Sidney models his show on those traditional courtly debates which resist decision and, like the pastoral eclogue, conclude with the characters breaking up and going home. For, since 'it pleased her Majestie to judge', Sidney could not afford to be seen to steer her one way or the other. All he could do was to devise a show which – in keeping with the apparent jest and triviality of court entertainments – was capable of reflecting his own ineffectualness.

The wit and ambivalence of *The Lady of May* appear all the greater when contrasted with a similar and nearly contemporaneous show written by Thomas Churchyard. Churchyard's device was designed for the Queen's visit to Norwich in August 1578, and was to have been performed before Elizabeth and the French ambassadors who had come over to England in order to negotiate her proposed marriage to the Duke of Alençon. In the event, bad weather prevented Churchyard's show from being performed. But, had she seen it, Elizabeth would have recognized at once its similarities with *The Lady of May*:

The Shew of MANHODE was inuented to be playde in a Garden, or wheresoeuer had bene found a conueniente place, the Prince then being in presence. And vnto hir Highnesse shoulde there haue come a Lady called Beautie, humbly on knees, requiring ayde and succoure, or else iudgemente, in a matter disputable, and in greate controuersie, vpon whose sute and humble intercession, the disputation was to beginne.[63]

Churchyard's garden-setting and call for the Queen's arbitration of the 'controuersie' closely follow *The Lady of May*. And, like Sidney's entertainment, Churchyard's putative Show of Manhood centres around a simple courtship-scenario: a suit for Lady Beauty's hand, which is debated between her three hopeful lovers – Manhood, Desert, and Good Favour. In the course of the entertainment, however, all three find themselves challenged by the figure of Good Fortune (Beauty's elected lover), who, having easily demolished their arguments, finally wins the lady.

The endings of *The Lady of May* and of Churchyard's show are therefore strikingly different. Gearing his show for an audience which included the French Commissioners, Churchyard seems to imply that Elizabeth (like Beauty) is not for the taking, except by a suitor of her own choice. Indeed, as a statement of nationalistic pride, Churchyard's show is particularly unsubtle. *The Lady of May*, by contrast, remains teasingly ambiguous. For, in the final song of Sidney's show, the two former rivals join together in song. The triumphant shepherd Espilus invokes Sylvanus – the god of his forester-rival; while Therion calls upon Pan – the patron and god of shepherds. The effect of the song is to create a wonderful (and, I argue, quite deliberate) sense of ambivalence. On the one hand, the two lovers seem palpably to be singing words prepared for each other in anticipation of a different result. On the other, their song represents a still moment of reconciliation and harmony akin to the resolution of the debate between the 'reasonable shepherds' and the 'appassionate shepherds' in the *Old Arcadia*.[64] Neither interpretation in itself betrays which of the two rivals (if either) Sidney was championing. And the fact that critics continue to argue over the meaning of the final song of *The Lady of May* testifies eloquently – even conclusively – to the skill with which Sidney constructed an event of warrantable ambiguity.

THE FOUR FOSTER CHILDREN OF DESIRE (1581)

In *The Lady of May*, then, Sidney had presented Elizabeth with a simple courtship-situation and had then invited her to step in and arbitrate it. As an impartial judge of the May Lady's predicament, Elizabeth herself was displaced as the object of desire. For Sidney was not courting the Queen directly, but, rather, exploring the limits of expression at court, and meditating upon the courtier's apparently helpless position before what he portrayed to be a wilful and wholly arbitrary power.

In May 1581, on the other hand, Sidney was involved in a full-blown pageant which made no bones about centralizing Elizabeth as an object of desire.[65] This entertainment is traditionally called *The Four Foster Children of Desire*, and, with its mock-siege of a castle of love, the show clearly harked back to an older tradition of Burgundian and Henrician court extravaganzas. In a scenario typical of earlier tournament fictions, Elizabeth was metamorphosed into the allegorical figure of Beauty, and her gallery in the Whitehall tiltyard into the 'Fortresse of perfect Beauty'. *The Four Foster Children of Desire* was a splendid show. Robert Carey describes the pageants that were mounted for the Duke of Alençon later that year as 'such as the best wits and inventions in those days could devise to make the court glorious, and to entertain so great a guest', and there is no evidence to suggest that courtiers scanted courtesy in May.[66] On the contrary, the participants in the May show were 'desirous to shew them al courtesie ... and to sporte them with all courtly pleasure' (66).

The Four Foster Children of Desire took the form of a tournament, and began with a challenge issued some weeks earlier by a herald, who represented the figure of Desire.[67] The challenge recounted how four foster-children of Desire had laid claim to Beauty as their 'desired patrimonie', and announced their intention to besiege her fortress if she refused to yield (66). The foster-children also pledge to fight at tilt and tourney with any of Beauty's knights who might enter in her defence.

A two-day encounter followed, on 15 and 16 May. The parts of the four foster-children were played by Philip Sidney, Fulke Greville, the Earl of Arundel, and Lord Windsor. When they entered the tiltyard on 15 May, they brought with them a pageant car designed to impress Beauty with their firm purpose to conquer her fortress: a 'Rowling trench' concealing a hidden consort of musicians. Their herald reappraised Beauty of the children's claim, and a pair of sonnets (possibly written by Sidney) led to the 'affectionate Allarme' and the 'desirous Assaulte'. The fortress of Beauty – Elizabeth's tiltyard gallery – was then bombarded with sweetmeats, perfume, and flowers in the traditional manner of a courtly mock-siege.

At this point in the show Beauty's defendants entered, in a medley of public and private symbolism. Sir Thomas Perrott and Anthony Cooke were announced by the figure of an angel who introduced them with the story of a Frozen Knight, melted by the sunlike favour of the Queen. Perrott and Cooke themselves assumed the roles of Adam and Eve. Thomas Radcliffe, another defendant, entered as a 'desolate Knight' who had retired to a meditative and enchanted life in a mossy cave by a 'Cliffe adjoining to the maine Sea' (presumably punning on his real identity). The four Knollys brothers came into the tiltyard disguised as the sons of Despair – the traditional enemy of Desire.

Their differences unresolvable by parley, the challengers and defendants then proceeded to tilt with staves, and both sides 'performed their partes so valiantly ... that their prowesse hath demerited perpetuall memory' (80).[68] The tournament continued on the second day. This time, the four foster-children entered the tiltyard in a pageant car drawn by horses 'apparelled in White and carnation silke, beeing the colloure of Desire' (82). Seated on the pageant car was a female figure representing Desire, to whom the four challengers longingly turned their gaze.

Desire's party submitted at the end of the fighting on the second day, their herald approaching Elizabeth in the ash-coloured garments of repentance, and carrying an olive-branch in token of peace. The foster-children humbly admitted defeat, acknowledging 'the blindenes of their error, in that they did not know desire (how strong so ever it be) within it self to be stronger without it selfe then it pleased the desired' (83).

Included among the courtly spectators in Whitehall that May were the group of French Commissioners who had come to finalize the delicate negotiations for the proposed marriage between Elizabeth and the Duke of Alençon. *The Four Foster Children of Desire* is usually regarded, therefore, as a direct policy-statement outlining the hostility of the English court to the French match. The day before the Commissioners arrived in London, Elizabeth had apparently warned Leicester and Walsingham that she felt repugnance at 'the ardent desire of so young a man as Alençon'.[69] Most critics agree that the device identifies the defeated figure of Desire with the French prince, and that it was designed to prepare the Commissioners for a similar failure.[70]

Indeed, for some scholars, 'the meaning of the pageant was obvious'.[71] But, on the evidence of the court devices we have already considered, it seems extremely unlikely that English courtiers ever felt themselves in a position to say anything 'obvious'. In the Inner Temple Revels, the Kenilworth shows, and *The Lady of May*, Dudley and Sidney had exploited ambiguity and ambivalence so as to present issues that were highly sensitive and delicate. On inspection, *The Four Foster Children of Desire* proves to be equally devious, subtle, and equivocal in its presentation of Desire. For the tournament turns out to be less anti-marriage propaganda than a meditation on courtiers' self-presentation and self-preservation at the court of a female sovereign.[72]

Certainly, the French match with Alençon was unpopular in England. When negotiations began again in earnest in 1578 there was a flurry of activity on the part of courtiers and writers to make this point to Elizabeth.[73] But the match also had its supporters – among them Lord Burghley and the Earl of Sussex. And while Greville and Sidney of the challengers, and Perrott, Knollys, Henry Grey, and Edward Denny of the defendants, can all be associated with the anti-marriage faction led by the Earl of Leicester, Lord Windsor (another challenger) was a Catholic, and the Earl of Arundel (the fourth foster-child) had Catholic sympathies. They, like Anthony Cooke (a cousin of Lord Burghley's) or Thomas Radcliffe (a relation of the Earl of Sussex), may all have been supporters of the French match.[74]

That the participants of *The Four Foster Children of Desire* – both challengers and defendants – should have represented so diverse a political spectrum necessarily compromises the traditional reading of the entertainment as straightforward anti-marriage propaganda. Instead, it seems more likely that the show was designed to suppress faction, and to present a picture of Anglo-French concord by subsuming real differences under romantic battles with that 'sweet enemy, France'.[75] Later that year, the Duke of Alençon came to the English court himself, his chief motive being to secure Elizabeth's backing for his exploits in The Netherlands. At New Year 1581–2 he mounted a 'royall Combat and fight on foote before her Maiestie' which included a similar mix of political opinion.[76] The challengers included Alençon himself, the Prince Dauphin, together with those arch-rivals of the English court the Earls of Leicester and Sussex. In other words, political differences were suspended under the fictional and romantic guise of court entertainments, Frenchmen co-operating with Englishmen, and former supporters of the French marriage appearing alongside its most virulent opponents.

So *The Four Foster Children of Desire* is by no means as 'obvious' as it first appears. Like the other entertainments we have considered, it exploits the internal ambivalence of the courtship-situation with subtlety and complexity. Most strikingly, *The Four Foster Children* departs from the normal Beauty–Desire motif by making the figure of Desire a woman. In the 1581 entertainment, the Desire who courts Beauty is not the 'Ardent Desire' of Henrician shows, or the 'Deep Desire' we saw at Kenilworth. Instead, she is female – a foster-mother. When the four foster-children entered the lists on the second day of the tournament, they turned their eyes longingly and lovingly toward the figure of Desire who accompanied them. In other words, Desire becomes a Beauty-figure, not an emblem of male sexuality but, rather, a version of the object of that sexuality.

Paradoxically, the femaleness of Desire desexualizes desire. For, as a woman, Desire represents sexuality which is non-violent, and neither aggressive, appropriative, nor patriarchal. Indeed, the four foster-children finally come to admit that they have perverted the 'true' desire which their foster-mother represents 'in making violence accompany Desire' (83).

The foster-children are therefore presented as men whose understanding of desire in the court of Elizabeth I is overly crude and aggressive. As the entertainment proceeds, constant emphasis is placed on the children's need to be educated in the proper expression of desire at such a court. Like Astrophil, or like the *giovani* of whom Bembo speaks in *Il Cortegiano*, the four foster-children are presented as juveniles who need to be tutored in the art of courtship at court. And just as Astrophil learns (reluctantly) to read from the legend of Beauty written in Stella's face, so the foster-children of Desire learn that 'the whole storie of vertue is written with the language of Beautie' (70–1). In the pageant, the figures of Beauty and Desire merge to assume Stella's role as 'step-dame Study', the 'school mistress' of love.[77]

The Four Foster Children does not conclude with the defeat of Desire, therefore. It ends with the four children recognizing their error and adopting a style and rhetoric more fitting at the Elizabethan court – the Desire represented by their foster-mother. In a sense, Desire is vindicated, triumphant, because the truant children eventually admit that they have learned their lesson. And although the challengers lose the tournament and approach Elizabeth in the pose of submission, they do not cease to desire her. Indeed, 'they acknowledge Noble Desire shoulde have desired nothing so much, as the flourishing of that Fortresse [of Beauty]' (84). Far from being defeated by their failure to conquer Beauty, the foster-children continue to adore her. Desire has not been extinguished but merely taught a lesson.

By presenting a tableau of how men should position themselves before a female monarch, *The Four Foster Children of Desire* appealed not only to Alençon's Commissioners but to all courtiers at the court of Elizabeth I. As Louis Montrose writes, 'the politics are internal as well as international, concerned with the queen's relationship to her courtiers as well as with her relationship to Alençon'.[78] For the defendants of Beauty are as well-versed in the language of Desire as their young rivals. As the Desolate Knight, for example, Thomas Radcliffe admits that Beauty is 'of every one to be desired, but never to be conquered of Desire' (78). He offers Elizabeth a shield made of rock and covered in moss, 'a double signe of his desire, thinking that nothing could manifest Beawtie so well as Pithagoras wallnut, a tender ryne and a hard shell' (78). As the sons of Despair, the Knollys brothers admit that 'Desire is the most worthie to woe, but least deserves to win Beawtie, for . . . when Beawtie yeeldeth once to desire, then can she never vaunt to be desired againe' (79–80). In the speech introducing the entry of Thomas Perrott and Anthony Cooke, an angel describes how the Frozen Knight dissolved because 'Desire, (ah sweete Desire) enforced him to behold [Elizabeth] the Sun on the earth' (73). And, as Adam and Eve, Perrott and Cooke themselves enact a long, involved allegory in which the original parents of sexual desire have now become the exponents of a new kind of virtuous desire: 'For as they were before driven from their Desire, because they desired to knowe the best, so now shall they be driven to their Desire whiche they covet to honour most' (74).

The defendants of Beauty may persist in using the language of Desire because they have learned something which the foster-children have yet to learn: how desire might suitably be expressed at Elizabeth's court. The challengers, on the other hand, appropriate Beauty by laying siege to her in a way that would immediately have struck an audience of 1581 as old-fashioned. As part of the pageants devised to celebrate the wedding of Prince Arthur to Katherine of Aragon in 1501, for example, a group of castle-bound ladies were besieged by the 'Knights of the Mownte of Love' until they finally yielded themselves and 'descendid from the seid castle'.[79] In 1522, Cardinal Wolsey mounted a device involving a mock-siege which also looked ahead to the assault of Beauty's fortress in 1581. In Wolsey's show, the castle under attack was called the 'Schatew Vert' – a three-turreted construction within which eight court ladies (including Princess Mary, the Queen of France, and Anne Boleyn) were imprisoned. After an assault in which the castle was battered with dates, oranges, sweetmeats, and rose-water, the ladies were rescued by Ardent Desire (Henry VIII) and his team of knights.[80]

The scenario of the allegorical siege – so popular in late-medieval and early sixteenth-century courts – emblematized erotic male desire and sexual conquest.[81] In both the examples mentioned above, the siege concluded with the ladies yielding to the men and agreeing to dance with them – an emblem which, as Sir Thomas Elyot wrote, commonly 'signified matrimony'.[82] Such allegories of sexually appropriative male desire were manifestly out of place in the court of a virgin queen. There, desire necessarily had to be expressed in a different way, as loyal commitment, or as adoration that was stripped of erotic stirrings. *The Four Foster Children of Desire* therefore appealed to a much wider audience than the French Commissioners who happened to be there at the time. The entertainment mused on the subordination of all male courtiers to a female monarch, and ways in which that subordination might be animated, modified, and expressed.

There is evidence to suggest that this, at least, was the way in which Alençon interpreted the tableaux of Beauty and Desire with which his Commissioners had been entertained in May 1581. In the New Year pageants he put on at the English court a few months later, Alençon entered the tournament 'sur vn chariot fait en forme de rocher. L'Amour & le Destin le menoient lié de grosses chaisnes d'or ver sa Maiesté.'[83] In a song sung jointly by the figures of Love and Fate, the former turned to Elizabeth and addressed her in terms which strongly recall the May tournament: 'Invaincu, mais Vainqueur des plus Grands de la terre'. She presented Elizabeth with the chained Alençon, who hoped

> Non pour sentir l'orgueil de vostre cruauté;
> Mais afin qu'adorant vostre chaste beauté,
> Vous changiez sa prison en franchise honorable.[84]

Like the four foster-children of the earlier show, Alençon pledges to worship Elizabeth's chaste beauty and not to desire her as a sexual object.

The device which concluded Alençon's New Year Revels reinforces the point by presenting a remarkably unconventional castle of love. In this final masque, a group of *knights* are presented, imprisoned within an enchanted castle. After a tournament, the castle opened to reveal a staircase and 'vn lampe ardente'. The prisoners descended having been delivered 'par le moyen d'vn plus excellent & magnanime Prince, & le plus constant en amour qui fut iamais' (Alençon), and by 'la plus chaste, vertueuse & heroique Princesse qui fut au monde' (Elizabeth).[85] Gone is the sexual innuendo of the early Tudor allegorical sieges. Here the victims of love are not helpless court ladies waiting for deliverance by lusty knights, but a group of male courtiers. And their rescue is presented as a joint effort between the still chaste Elizabeth and her permanently adoring servant Alençon.

So *The Four Foster Children of Desire* – like Alençon's New Year show – recast the sexual politics traditionally embedded in the topos of the besieged castle-of-love. More than a policy-statement on the proposed French match, the May entertainment allowed English courtiers to enact in public and in exaggerated fashion the roles enforced upon them as subordinate members of a female-governed court.

LOVE AND SELF-LOVE (1595)

I would like now to turn to a lavish display that was presented at court by the Earl of Essex in 1595, over a decade after *The Four Foster Children of Desire*. The show – which Essex is said to have called his 'darling piece of love, and self love' – is based round a debate between two figures: Erophilus (the lover of desire) and Philautia (self-love).[86] The part of Erophilus was – predictably enough – played by Essex himself, dressed (like the four foster-children) in 'innocent white and faire carnacion' to indicate his affinity with Desire.[87] The device of *Love and Self-Love* formed a part of the Accession Day celebrations in Whitehall, a feast which had (by 1595) become an annual feature of the Elizabethan court calendar.

By 1595 Elizabeth was well past child-bearing age, and speculations about her marriage were thus less urgent than before. None the less, the language of desire evidently proved as powerful a tool as ever in a courtier's self-promotion. In *Love and Self-Love*, Essex continued to draw upon the courtship-situation that had become a commonplace in Elizabethan courtly shows. And he uses the courtship-model to meditate upon issues very similar to those of *The Four Foster Children*: how the male courtier could present himself at Elizabeth's court, how he was enforced to transmute ambition, suggestion, counsel, and even critique into a palatable form.

It is uncertain who wrote *Love and Self-Love*, and the device may well have been a collaborative effort between Essex and his secretary, Bacon.[88] The entertainment began in the tiltyard at Whitehall, and opened with a debate between Philautia and Erophilus' squire on the kind of devotion that could most suitably be expressed to Elizabeth. Philautia advocates a wholly de-eroticized kind of love and seems confident that Elizabeth has always preferred the same, 'for your Majesty has ever rejected the pleadings of love, and given credence to Philautia'. Erophilus, she says, 'proves that no love is worthy of your entertainment' for love is 'an empty trade, a dream, an intoxication, and he who seeks another self loses himself'. Philautia warns the Queen against the 'stratagems' of lovers, and instead counsels her to accept 'the love of those whom one can either serve or be served by, and that only as long as their service avails, and till others can be found cheaper'.[89]

Philautia's words propose a model for sovereign–courtier relations in which all the exigencies of courtship – flattery, cajolery, service,

devotion, self-abasement – are ruthlessly reduced to the barest func-
tionality. She encourages Elizabeth to support only those courtiers
who are any use to her and to discard them as soon as their usefulness
is passed.

Good advice, no doubt. But Philautia's words conflict with the
whole courtship-situation which, as we have seen, both Elizabeth
and the men of her court exploited to the full. In presenting himself
as Philautia's rival, Essex–Erophilus therefore aligns himself with the
tradition which required courtiers to play the lover and to eroticize
their day-to-day dealings with the monarch. In a speech spoken by
his squire (which unfortunately has not survived), Erophilus defeats
Philautia's arguments and extracts a submission from her: 'I will no
longer be an obstacle to the servant of Erophilus, but will entreat the
Queen to take the devoted offer of love, if neither for the sake of
Erophilus nor for that of love, yet for the sake of Philautia.'[90]

Philautia's retraction vindicates Erophilus' ambition to express his
relation to the Queen in sexual terms. In a further extension of the
debate, Philautia tries a second time to wean Erophilus from his vain
commitment to love, by sending three emissaries to him: a Hermit, a
Soldier, and a Secretary. In a dumbshow that follows, each of these
figures presents Erophilus with a book. They proceed to argue with
him in a continuation of the device which took place after the
Accession Day tournament, and after supper.

As figures who represent selfless service to the state in various
forms, the Hermit, Soldier, and Secretary each attempt to dissuade
Erophilus from eroticizing courtly service, from pandering to the
courtship-situation which was occasioned by Elizabeth's femaleness.
But Erophilus wins the debate for the second time, ingeniously
reversing each of the arguments as presented to him by these three
worthies. The Hermit, for example, advises Erophilus to cultivate
the Muses rather than royal favour – more fame is to be found that
way. Erophilus replies by arguing that the Muses are 'tributarie to
her Majestie ... What library can present such a storie of great
accons as hir Majestie carrieth in her royall breast by the often
returne of this happie daie?'[91] By relocating the matter of epic in
Elizabeth's Accession Day Tilt, Essex exaggeratedly defends his
loving devotion to her.

Erophilus defeats the arguments of the Soldier and Secretary in a
similar way. The Soldier advises Erophilus to seek fame in war, not
love, but for Erophilus, 'can all the exploytes of warr winne him such

a title, as to have the name favorite and selected seruante to such a Queen?'[92] The Secretary urges that if Erophilus' real desire is 'to make the prince happie whom he serues' then his study should be statecraft and policy. Erophilus' response is the perfect justification of the humanist-turned-courtier:

can any insolent politique promise to himself such a fortune by making his own way, as the excellency of her nature cannot deny to a careful, obsequious, and dutiful servant? And if he could, were it equal honour to attaine it by a shape of cunning, then by the guifte of such a hand?[93]

As the obsequious and dutiful servant *par excellence*, Erophilus exemplifies the Elizabethan courtier who has fully learned the art of courtship at court: an art that depended upon overtly offering the Queen service in the form of sexual submission.

Essex's device of *Love and Self-Love* therefore seems to reverse the theme of *The Four Foster Children of Desire*. In the earlier show, the expression of a courtier's dedication in terms of sexual desire was shown to be unacceptable. Desire could only be ratified when it had been desexualized. In promoting himself as the figure of Erophilus, on the other hand, Essex was explicitly endorsing the sexualization of courtly service, and most critics see the device as a bid for royal favour couched in terms of the most hyperbolic compliment. G. B. Harrison relates the whole entertainment to Essex's need to reassure Elizabeth after the publication of a seditious pamphlet that had been dedicated to him. And although Elizabeth does not seem to have suspected his collaboration, he may have felt it wise to put her in no doubt of his loyalty in the tiltyard that November.[94]

Most critics who read *Love and Self-Love* as a straightforward expression of loyalty to Elizabeth base their interpretation on the description of the device that survives in a letter from Rowland Whyte to Robert Sidney. In Whyte's account of 'thafter Supper' – the debate between Erophilus and the Hermit, Soldier, and Secretary – Erophilus' squire indisputably has the last word, therefore apparently vindicating his master's particular brand of courtly service. As in all the shows considered, however, Essex's device evades simple interpretation, while any reading of this particular entertainment must be tempered by the tantalizing fragmentariness of the evidence. For no straightforward text of *Love and Self-Love* survives, only a scattered (and often self-contradictory) series of fragments, drafts, and eye-witness accounts.

One might therefore contrast Whyte's record of events with a fragment in Bacon's hand which may represent an alternative ending to the show. Describing the entry of the Hermit, Soldier, and Secretary, Bacon notes that the last (representing Experience) should 'begin to the Squire, as being the master of the best behaviour or compliment, though he speak last'.[95] Bacon's note is only a draft, and might represent an initial plan which was then changed. But the fragment suggests that the Secretary, and not Erophilus' squire, might have had the last word of the argument. As the 'master of the best behaviour', the Secretary is the most powerful of the three orators of Self-Love (perhaps Bacon had himself in mind). And in his speech to the wayward Erophilus, the Secretary comes up with a formula for the ideal courtier whose service to the prince is irreproachable in every respect:

when his mistress shall perceaue his endeavours are to become a true supporter of her, a discharge of care, a watchman of her person, a scholar of her wisdom, and instrument of her operation, and a conduit of her virtue, this with his diligences, accesses, humility and patience, may move her to give him further degrees and approaches to her favour. So that I conclude I have traced him the way to that which hath been granted to some few, *amare et sapere*, to love and be wise.[96]

If these words – rather than those of Erophilus' squire – had concluded the device, then we are forced to revise the accepted reading of the show. For *Love and Self-Love* may have been intended not to vindicate the lover-of-love, Erophilus, but, rather, Philautia. Alongside the words 'The time makes for you' in one of the manuscripts of the device, there is a marginal note addressed to Essex in Bacon's hand: 'That your Lordship knoweth, and I in part, in regard of the Queen's unkind dealing, which may persuade you to self-love'.[97] There are various suggestions as to what Elizabeth's 'unkind dealing' might have been. But it remains possible that Essex intended to deflate Erophilus as the doting courtly lover and instead vindicate self-love which – while serving the Queen, could also allow him to serve his own interests.

Clearly, a reappraisal of *Love and Self-Love* along these lines cannot depend upon anything as uncertain as a manuscript fragment of an earlier draft of the show. It is possible, of course, that Bacon did not mean to give the Secretary the last word altogether, but just that he should speak after the Hermit and Soldier. None the less, in a further account of the 1595 Accession Day Tilt – George Peele's *Anglorum*

Feriae – there is evidence to suggest that Erophilus was not left the *amans triumphans* in the end. In his account, Peele makes much of the Soldier and Secretary who solicit Erophilus to follow their exemplary lives, but he makes no mention at all of Erophilus' expression of love to the Queen. Peele was evidently more impressed by the arguments of Philautia than those of Erophilus. It would naturally be a mistake to read too much into what amounts to a poetic rendering of the Accession Day Tilt, but it is possible, none the less, to interpret Peele's version of events as a discreet omission. Rowland Whyte records that Elizabeth's reaction to the device was mixed: 'if she thought there had been so much said of her, she would not have been there that night'.[98] If Erophilus had had the last word, and had not pleased Elizabeth, there would be an argument for excluding him from the account in *Anglorum Feriae*. If not, then all the more reason for dwelling on the virtue of the Secretary, a man who applied himself dutifully to the care

> Of common weale affaires and showe the way,
> To helpe to underbeare with grave advice,
> The waightie beame whereon the State depends.[99]

Peele's text typifies the problem of interpreting courtly devices like *Love and Self-Love*. In effect, either reading is possible – one which vindicates Erophilus and the eroticization of court service, and one which vindicates Philautia and the kind of 'proper' desire we saw in *The Four Foster Children*. In the case of Essex's device, the difficulties are largely created by unavoidable textual instability. But I think we can also see an element of wilful obliquity in the texts that have survived. I have been arguing that courtly shows resist simple identifications and, in most cases, exploit ambivalence and ambiguity in order to explore the sensitive, delicate, and uncomfortable characteristics of Elizabethan court life. And just as two alternative endings survive for *The Lady of May*, seriously compromising any political interpretation of that device, so Essex's show of *Love and Self-Love* seems deliberately to leave the debate open-ended.

For even if we disregard the evidence of Bacon and Peele and admit that Erophilus did have the last word of the argument, we should ask why he is given so strenuous a time of it. If Essex had simply intended to avow eroticized desire for the Queen as a hyperbolic compliment, why did he not leave the debate after

Philautia's initial submission to the Squire? Why, in other words, did he extend the debate after the tilting, and reintroduce Philautia, this time armed with such a formidable battery of defence? The Hermit, Soldier, and Secretary are mouthpieces for the ideal, humanist-trained courtier, and they amalgamate his roles as thinker, defender, and counsellor as effectively as Castiglione or Sir Thomas Elyot. There were certainly elements of this role with which Essex would have identified himself – above all that of the soldier.[100]

So if Philautia was destined to lose the argument, one wonders why Essex has her re-enter with the considerable rhetorical force of her three emissaries, and why Erophilus has to argue all over again the aim and purpose of his devotion. It seems likely that, like Sidney in *The Lady of May*, Essex did not feel that the ramifications of the debate could be contained within a pat dialogue. Instead, he presented a device in the tiltyard that November which was as equivocal and open-ended as each of the shows we have been considering.

The same ambivalence presents itself in another tiltyard device which internal evidence links closely with Essex's show of *Love and Self-Love*. An account survives of a speech that was performed at the tiltyard by a page representing an Indian Prince.[101] The Prince, we are told, was born blind. Having been advised by an oracle, his father has sent him to England where 'reigns a Queen in peace and honour true'. The Prince himself is 'armed after the Indian manner with bow and arrows', and, although attired decently for the occasion, he is 'in his ordinary habit an Indian naked, or attired with feathers'.[102]

Now, this description of the Indian Prince hints that he was more than he seemed. In Renaissance iconography, a naked, feathered, blind boy, armed with a bow and arrows could only be one person – Cupid. In *Anglorum Feriae*, George Peele describes one of the 1595 tilters attired 'Lyke Venus sonne, in Mars his armor clad', perhaps alluding to this Cupid-figure, normally naked but dressed for the occasion in tournament armour.[103] The identification of the Indian Prince with the god of love is given greater force when, in Elizabeth's miraculous presence, he suddenly regains his sight, and is presented to the Queen as a figure of 'Seeing Love'.[104]

The Prince's page begs Elizabeth to accept his master, now transformed into this figure of a seeing Cupid:

though Philautia hath hitherto so prevailed with your Majesty, as you
would never accept of him while he was an unperfect piece, yet now he is
accomplished by your Majesty's grace and means, that you will vouchsafe
him entertainment.[105]

The page lists several arguments against love – including the fact
that lovers often presume too high, while the Queen would have to
stoop in accepting them – which had been among Philautia's objec-
tions to Elizabeth's acceptance of Erophilus. And yet those arguments had all depended on the proverbial blindness of love. Now
restored to sight, he urges, Cupid may be welcomed at court.

If the speech of the Indian Prince did form part of Essex's
elaborate tiltyard device in 1595, then the vindication of Seeing
Love might at first be seen to strengthen the case of Erophilus.
Again, we see Elizabeth being urged to endorse and accept an
eroticized expression of desire. But in fact Seeing Love conflates the
roles of Erophilus and Philautia, of love and self-love. For the Indian
Prince presents himself as both the god of love and as a spokesman
for those humanist values upheld so eloquently by the Hermit,
Soldier, and Secretary. In his advice to Erophilus, the Prince urges
him to give over the erotic connotations of his self-presentation: 'Let
him consider whom he serves, since in his blindness he hath chanced
so well as to fix his affections in the most excellent place, let him now
by his sight find out the most ready way.'[106] Erophilus must learn his
lesson exactly as the four foster-children of an earlier show had to
learn theirs.

Seeing Love then turns to Elizabeth and advises her on how to
handle courtship at court, how to distinguish between genuine
service and the empty flattery that was sometimes a surrogate for it:

Your Majesty shall obtain the curious window into the hearts of which the
ancients speak; thereby you shall discern protestation from fullness of heart,
ceremonies and fashions from a habit of mind that can do no other,
affection [affectation?] from affection. Your Majesty shall see the true
proportion of your own favours, so as you may deliver them forth by
measure, that they neither cause surfeit nor faintness ... And to conclude,
your Majesty may be invested of that which the poet saith was never
granted, *Amare et sapere*.[107]

These words are one of the clearest statements on the proper
expression of courtship at court that exist in the period. Seeing Love
concludes his speech with the same tag – to love and to be wise –

which the Secretary was to propose to Erophilus in the 'after Supper' later that night.

So, far from vindicating Erophilus' sexualized bid for royal recognition and favour, Seeing Love sides with the men who successfully subsume the inherent sexuality of the courtship-situation under selfless service and proven loyalty. At the same time, Seeing Love is a version of that icon of desire – Cupid – and is therefore another version of the lover of love, Erophilus. The various fragments which go to make up what we know of Essex's device of *Love and Self-Love* therefore serve, in the end, to present a highly complex interplay of ideas. The device resists simple interpretation, and, instead, explores the versatility in role-playing that was evidently demanded of Elizabethan courtiers in the last decade of the reign.

ENDIMION (1591)

Although performed and published before Essex's device of *Love and Self-Love*, Lyly's play *Endimion* encapsulates many of the themes and characteristics of courtship at court that we have been discussing, and therefore seems an appropriate place to conclude this chapter.[108] Like all the shows considered so far, *Endimion* meditates upon the exigencies of serving the Queen and on the proper expression of devotion and duty at court. As a wooer of the queen-goddess, Cynthia, who is first rejected and finally rewarded, Endimion typifies the figure that has been so central in the court devices under discussion. And, although attempts have been made in the past to identify Endimion – 'the flowre of my Courte' (v. iii. 36) – with the Earls of Essex or Oxford, Lyly's play firmly resists such schematization.[109] Endimion emerges instead as a generalized figure, an amalgam of the courtier-lover, and a man who characterizes the peculiarities and pressures demanded by courtship at the court of Elizabeth.

Lyly's play demonstrates the same subtlety and equivocation that we have seen to be so central in handling this difficult and sensitive subject. Like so many of the courtier-lovers figured in these court shows, Endimion is forced to desexualize his love for his queen before he can win her favour. And, as in the other entertainments, courtship at court proves to be highly nuanced, the subject of a teasing fluctuation between satire and approval, criticism and acceptance. Moments of high seriousness lie alongside some of the most hilarious scenes Lyly wrote. *Endimion* therefore remains puzzlingly tentative, open-ended, and equivocal in its handling of courtly desire.[110]

The most important fact about Endimion is that Lyly presents him as a perjured lover: a man who has transferred his affections from his mistress, Tellus, on to his queen-goddess, Cynthia, and who therefore conforms to the sexual stereotype of the inconstant courtly lover. Tellus pledges to trick Endimion into wasting his youth in a hopeless and irresolvable passion: 'in flattering of my face, and deuising Sonnets in my fauour. The prime of his youth and pride of his time, shall be spent in melancholy passions, carelesse behauiour, vntamed thoughts, and vnbridled affections' (I. ii. 58–61). As her name suggests, Tellus is an icon of earthly, sexual, 'burning desire', a woman 'whose desires are so desperate' (I. iv. 13, 29) that she craves Endimion 'burn' for her (I. ii. 44). It is a direct result of Tellus' intervention that Endimion makes his fatal mistake. For he courts Cynthia as if she were his courtly mistress:

Sweet Cynthia, how wouldst thou be pleased, how possessed? ... Desirest thou the passions of loue, the sad and melancholie moodes of perplexed mindes, the not to be expressed torments of racked thoughts? Beholde my sad teares, my deepe sighes, my hollowe eyes, my broken sleepes, my heauie countenaunce. (II. i. 4–12)

Lyly highlights the obvious discrepancy in Endimion's behaviour. Cynthia is not merely a queen but a mythological being of a higher order than her earthly subjects. Yet Endimion approaches her with all the paraphernalia of courtly love, and desires her as Astrophil desires Stella, or Orlando, Angelica – that is, sexually. His 'amorous desires' thus trivialize the tense and complex relation that exists between queen and courtier (II. iii. 9). Instead, Endimion desires to 'possesse the Moone herselfe', to 'rauish' her (I. i. 14–15, 60). He is incapable of envisaging his relation to this spectacular female except in sexual terms. 'Diuorsing himself from the amiablenes of all Ladies, the brauerie of all Courts, the companie of al men' (II. i. 39–40), Endimion assumes the sexual attributes of the stereotypical courtly lover so frequently parodied in the literature of the period: inconstancy and melancholy. Indeed, the failure of his attempt to court Cynthia casts him into a 'deepe melancholy' (II. iii. 22) which Lyly figures in its most extreme form as an irrecoverable sleep.[111]

Endimion's sleep is an emblem of his failure to court Cynthia in appropriate or decorous terms. It is Tellus who bewitches Endimion – for his tendencies toward earthly, sexual love are the very cause of his failure to win the favour of the queen. Although Endimion has wooed Cynthia 'in most melancholie and desperate termes, cursing hys starres, his state, the earth, the heauens, the world' (v. iii. 126–7), all that emanates from the queen is a resounding silence. In the very first scene of the play, Eumenides had warned his friend that 'sleepe woulde doe thee more good then speech: the Moone heareth thee not, or if shee doe, regardeth thee not' (i. i. 67–9). Predictably enough, Eumenides' words come true. The courtier's submissions go unheard, putting paid to any dialogue between the queen and her suitor. Endimion finds himself facing the same intransigence as the four foster-children of Desire in 1581, or Erophilus in 1595.

While Endimion sleeps, Eumenides searches the world for some means to rescue his friend. It is fitting that, in a play full of enchantment and fantasy, Eumenides should find the answer to his quest at the bottom of a magic well. Gazing into the mysterious waters with the eyes of a faithful lover, Eumenides is granted a single wish. And, although his thoughts turn first to winning his mistress, Semele, he soon recalls the plight of his friend. Having debated the claims of love and friendship (in the traditional manner), Eumenides decides that he owes more to his friend than to his mistress, and determines to use his power to release him. Eumenides clearly makes the right choice. Geron, the guardian of the well, contrasts the fleetingness of sexual love with human friendship 'in which there is nothing moueable, nothing mischeeuous' (iii. iv. 125–6). Indeed, Geron castigates sexual love in terms of the familiar topos of Beauty and Desire: 'Desire dyes in the same moment that Beautie sickens, and Beautie fadeth in the same instant that it flourisheth' (iii. iv. 131–2). Eumenides replies that 'Vertue shall subdue affections, wisdome lust, friendship beautie' (iii. iv. 143–4), thus replacing the traditional conqueror of Beauty (Desire) with a love from which sex has been removed – friendship.

By putting friendship in the place of sexual desire, Eumenides restores what Endimion has lost: the ability to woo the queen in terms other than the erotic. Lyly emphasizes this by making it necessary for Cynthia to kiss the sleeping Endimion before he can fully reawaken from his silent sleep. Cynthia's kiss is a platonic emblem of desexualized desire, the one sexual gesture which (as Castiglione's courtiers discuss) may be allowed within the proper parameters of courtly love: 'for this doe all chaste lovers covet a kisse, as a coupling of soules together'.[112] Eumenides' friendship and Cynthia's kiss therefore represent devotion which has been purged of sexual longing, and between them they restore the blind and sleeping Endimion to his senses.

Endimion's sleep and reawakening thus emblematize the difference between unacceptable, thwarted courtship and the productive, rewarding dialogue that could exist between queen and courtier. Endimion's problem had been that he approached his queen with the vocabulary of sexual desire, therefore making light of the complex and subtle relation between them. Endimion's courtly wooing, with its excesses and melancholia, is rendered at times conventional, laughable, even parodic. By contrast, the restored and reawakened Endimion addresses Cynthia in acceptably desexualized terms:

The time was Madam, and is, and euer shall be, that I honoured your highnesse aboue all the world; but to stretch it so far as to call it loue, I neuer durst ... Such a difference hath the Gods sette between our states, that all must be dutie, loyaltie, and reuerence; nothing (without it vouchsafe your highnes) be termed loue. My vnspotted thoughts, my languishing bodie, my discontented life, let them obtaine by princelie fauour impossibilities: with imagination of which, I will spende my spirits, and to my selfe that no creature may heare, softlie call it loue. And if any vrge to vtter what I whisper, then will I name it honor. (v. iii. 162–75)

Duty, loyalty, and reverence are the very virtues learned by the four foster-children of Desire in 1581, and by Erophilus and Seeing Love in 1595. Like so many of the courtly shows we have been considering, Lyly's *Endimion* therefore suggests that desexualized desire is the only suitable means for male courtiers to abase themselves before their queen, and the only successful way to sue her for her 'princelie fauour'.

It is only at this stage in the play, therefore, that Endimion's devotion to Cynthia is rewarded. She tells him that 'this honorable respect of thine, shalbe christned loue in thee, & my reward for it fauor' (v. iii. 179–80). Endimion had failed to woo Cynthia or even to attract her attention when he was embroiled in the conventionalized peculiarities of courtly love. But now that the scales have fallen from his eyes, he becomes another 'Seeing Love', a revitalized Cupid whose properly hesitant expression of desire can be endorsed, approved, and rewarded by the queen.

The central enigma of *Endimion* therefore rests upon the complexities that were inherent in courting a real queen. The devotion (which Cynthia deigns to christen 'loue') is a subtle and paradoxical amalgam – a love that is not strictly love, a desire that is not properly desire. Like so many of the courtier-lovers we have seen presented in these court shows, Endimion is a highly problematic figure. He is portrayed as equally worthy and unworthy; his love for Cynthia at one moment the highest affection humans are capable of, the next, behaviour that is clearly blasphemous, idolatrous, 'ridiculous', 'mad', and 'peeuish' (I. i. 8, 16, 19). Endimion is the flower of Cynthia's court, and yet a perjured lover, someone who abandons one mistress for another, and who tells lies. He claims, for example, that his love for Cynthia contains 'no flatterie, nor deceipt, error, nor arte' and yet proceeds in the next breath to dissemble with Tellus and assure her that he continues to love her. Not only does this compromise his love for Cynthia; it demonstrates how firmly his notions of love and desire are embedded in the earthly.

Lyly infuses the central symbol of the play – Endimion's sleep – with deep ambivalence. For Endimion's collapse is, in one sense, the direct consequence of his unacceptable courtship of Cynthia. Cynthia later tells the reformed Endimion that she 'seemed strange' specifically in order 'to bring thy thoughts within the compasse of thy fortunes' (IV. iii. 78–81), and it is precisely her lack of response to his courtship which feeds both his 'deepe melancholy' and the physical depletion which results in his deep sleep. In this sense, therefore, Endimion has been justly punished by the queen for his presumptuousness in addressing her as a sexual object. But, on the other hand, Endimion is also the passive and wholly sympathetic victim of the fiendish Tellus and her evil witch, Dipsas. His enchantment is figured as a kind of demonic possession which only the good offices of his friend and queen can break.

Endimion therefore becomes as ambivalent and ambiguous a figure as Dudley's Deep Desire in 1575 – a figure justly metamorphosed into a holly bush for the 'restlesse prickes of his privie thoughts' – and yet cruelly and unfairly punished for his abiding devotion and constancy to Zabeta.

In Lyly's play, Cynthia is certainly capable of judging inappropriate rhetorical behaviour among her courtiers and of punishing it harshly. Both Tellus and Semele are penalized for their sharp tongues. Yet Cynthia does not mete out the same treatment to

Endimion, suggesting that, although unacceptable, elements of his sexualized courtship were not, in fact, so unpleasant to her. Cynthia's actions – her aloofness to Endimion followed by her mercy – are therefore as paradoxical as those of Zabeta, the mistress of the enchanted forest in the Kenilworth entertainment. Both queen-figures are presented as worthy judges of court behaviour. Yet both contain elements of the wilful, prevaricating, and defiant courtly mistress of sonnet convention.

The perplexing two-sidedness of Cynthia is symbolized in Endimion's mysterious dream, which is performed in dumbshow as he sleeps. When recounting his dream later on, Endimion recalls a female figure who had threatened to stab him; but 'after long debating with her selfe, mercie ouercame anger', and she throws aside the knife (v. i. 96). He describes this figure in terms of transcendent beauty which clearly align her with Cynthia herself: 'in her heauenly face such a diuine Maiestie, mingled with a sweete mildenes, that I was rauished with the sight aboue pleasure, and wished that I might haue enioied the sight without end' (97–100). The figure's paradoxical nature is further figured in the two women who accompany her – one of whom represents 'vnmoueable crueltie', and the other, 'constant pittie' (101–2).

Lyly here portrays Cynthia's dual aspect – an object of both veneration and execration, who remains, paradoxically, both cruel and merciful, both inconstant and constant: a fitting symbol for that difficult, complicated, and changeable queen, Elizabeth I. And although Endimion's courtship of Cynthia is dogged by fears and uncertainties, he is none the less accepted and rewarded in the end. Endimion thus becomes an image for the condition of the Elizabethan male subject, who found himself, like Lyly, faced with the problem of how to present himself before such a monarch, and how to win her favour with guaranteed success.

CHAPTER 4

'Courtly courtesies': ambivalent courtships in Euphues, Euphues and his England, *and the* Arcadia

Endimion's love for Cynthia – flattering yet desexualized, amorous yet not appropriative – compounds all the paradoxes of courtship at court, and sketches the complex and convoluted relations that existed between members of the court of Elizabeth I. What both the Queen and her courtiers exploited was the sexual indeterminacy of the courtship-situation. Courtiers were permitted to love without loving, and to desire without desiring; the Queen, to be flattered without in any way diminishing her fame or her majesty. At the court of Elizabeth, then, courtship was frequently separated off from its nuptial function and became an end in itself, a convenient way of expressing political loyalty and devotion in desexualized and depersonalized terms. As a form of ritualized love-lore, courtship at court resisted the laws and codes of marriage, and allowed the partners an illusion of temporary liberty, the freedom to explore their sexual roles.

In his great speech on love at the end of *Il Cortegiano*, Pietro Bembo advises his courtly audience on the kinds of amorous behaviour that were permitted at the court: a courtly lady is allowed to grant her lover 'mery countenances, familiar and secret talke, jeasting, dalying, hand in hand, [and] may also lawfully and without blame come to kissing' (all gestures which, as Thomas Whythorne wrote, 'some do call courting').[1] Bembo makes a crucial distinction between 'l'amor razionale' and 'l'amor sensuale', insisting that the latter is mere lechery and has no place in the civilized milieu of the ideal court, while rational love represents the highest passion that human beings are capable of, and is therefore to be cultivated by all educated and sensitive courtiers, male and female alike.

The point of Bembo's speech, and its reception among a somewhat sceptical audience, is this: that while, for the participants of a courtship, there is all the difference in the world between a kiss bestowed in innocence and a kiss bestowed in lust, there is no way of telling that difference from the outside. And while Bembo's 'amor razionale' valorizes human love and attempts to maintain sexual propriety and decorum at court, in fact (as the more cynical Magnifico points out) the most gross improprieties might easily pass under the cover of ingenuousness. For while Bembo's courtly lady might legitimately grant her lover smiles and kisses, another, altogether less scrupulous lover might indulge in the same with nothing else but pleasure in mind.

When the amorous relation between men and women came to appropriate the language of courts in the sixteenth century it took its definition, as we have seen, from external and visible displays of affection – the touching of hands, indulging in conversation, kissing. As the lover ceased 'to lady' (donneare) and began 'to court' ('corteggiare') his wooing was no longer centred linguistically on his mistress but, rather, on the formal etiquette of love such as Bembo describes. The reason why Bembo's courtly love becomes so ambivalent is that its legitimacy, its status as 'rational love', remains a matter of pure speculation. His ideal lovers internalize their passion and may indeed aspire to the highest flights of platonic musing. Yet, to the outside world, their gestures remain open to interpretation. The externalities of their love signal a relation the licit or illicit nature of which remains to be determined. And those gestures (in being merely the external signs of some inner desire) can be interpreted either way: either sensual or rational, either illicit or licit.

This central ambivalence is the key to courtly love. The gestures which men and women knew they could perform at court under the licence of 'l'amor razionale' became titillatingly infused with eroticism when every gesture could be interpreted as a sign of sexual desire. Whether those men and women actively engaged in sex is, in a sense, neither here nor there. The point is that courtship at court derived its fantasy and eroticism from a central uncertainty. And when the relations between men and women are seen as being something uncertain, something open to interpretation, then those relations become a particular focus of attention and anxiety.

Especially ambivalent, of course, was the 'familiar and secret talke' ('ragionamenti domestici e secreti') that Bembo allowed his lovers. For not only was such talk susceptible to misinterpretation and misrepresentation from the outside. It could equally be abused from within a relationship, one lover (usually the man) using his 'dialect and different skill' to hoodwink and deceive his mistress.[2] And while 'luf-talkyng' had provided English poets with a rich site for sexual *doubles entendres* from at least as early as *Sir Gawain and the Green Knight*, what is important here is that the 'ragionamenti' Bembo speaks of comprise those very rhetorical procedures which gave courtship (in the amorous sense) its name.

Roger Ascham highlights the special ambivalence of courtly 'ragionamenti' between lovers in his popular treatise *The Schoolmaster* (1570). In the anti-Italian tirade with which he concludes the first part, Ascham singles out for withering attack the very courtship-practices which Pietro Bembo had described. Impressionable young Englishmen commonly return from Italy, he says, as

contemners of marriage and ready persuaders of all other to the same, not because they love virginity nor yet because they hate pretty young virgins, but being free in Italy to go withersoever lust will carry them, they do not like that law and honesty should be such a bar to their like liberty at home in England. And yet they be the greatest makers of love, the daily dalliers, with such pleasant words, with such smiling and secret countenances, with such signs, tokens, wagers purposed to be lost before they were purposed to be made, with bargains of wearing colors, flowers, herbs to breed occasion of ofter meeting of him and her and bolder talking of this and that, etc.[3]

In Ascham's polemic, these courtship-rituals are as serious as sedition against the state, and one senses that his exasperated 'etc.' encapsulates whole areas of sexual perversion and depravity otherwise unknown to polite English society. And yet Ascham's words betray a deep sensitivity to the ambivalence of the courtship-situation. For in the next breath, he goes on half to approve those very practices which his polemic has obliged him to condemn:

And although I have seen some, innocent of all ill and staid in all honesty, that have used these things without all harm, without all suspicion of harm, yet these knacks were brought first into England by them that learned them before in Italy in Circe's court, and how courtly courtesies soever they be counted now, yet if the meaning and manners of some that do use them were somewhat amended, it were not great hurt neither to themselves nor to others.[4]

Ascham recognizes (exactly as Bembo's courtly audience had done in *Il Cortegiano*) that the external gestures of courtship – touching, kissing, and, above all, talking – are not in themselves sufficient indication of inner and innocent intention. And that mistakes can be made. Entirely innocent love can be made with the very same gestures as the most perverse and sinful passion: the same gestures both licit and illicit and neither (as Sidney might have said) justly.

Although Ascham admits that there are certain circumstances in which 'courtly courtesies' might be wholly legitimate, he does not hazard what those circumstances might be. Instead, his text strives to subsume the troubling ambivalence of courtship under a mounting tide of moral indignation and nationalistic pride. But an uneasiness remains, and provides us, in turn, with a model for the treatment of courtship in the prose romances of John Lyly and Philip Sidney. In the *Euphues* and *Arcadia* narratives, Lyly and Sidney constantly create situations in which we are invited to ask whether 'courtly courtesies' are legitimate or not; whether they invariably lead to illicit sexual encounters, or whether courtship can only be legitimized by marriage; whether courtship is permissible at court (where educated men and women have been trained to distinguish between rational and sensual love), or whether the court is a place where innocent love-making merges inevitably with the sexual.

The depiction of young, heterosexual love has been a staple of romance fiction from the earliest times. But in the Elizabethan period writers consciously borrow the terminology of the court to describe the love-relation between men and women. In the prose fictions of Lyly and Sidney, 'courtly courtesies' serve to externalize inward passion, and to render that passion at times baffling, indeterminate, indecipherable.

Neither Lyly nor Sidney was a successful courtier. Lyly never achieved the court post he aspired to, and his reproachful begging letters to Elizabeth stand alongside Fulke Greville's *Life of Sidney* as testaments of talent that failed to be recognized and rewarded. In the last chapter, we saw how Lyly and Sidney both rehearsed in their court plays the paradoxes involved in courting the Queen – Lyly, in the problematics of Endimion's expression of love; Sidney, in the despairing picture of a courtier's powerlessness to advise his prince in *The Lady of May*. In *Euphues* and the *Arcadia* Lyly and Sidney move away from the localized effects of courtiership and obvious presentations of Elizabeth to consider amorous play in more general terms. But courtship remains an abiding and compelling theme for them both.

The plots of *Euphues* and *Euphues and his England* centre around courtships, but (like their author himself), Lyly's lovers never achieve what they desire: although intense and passionate, their courtships invariably end in failure. The central issue of Sidney's *Old Arcadia* is whether the sexual liberties which the young princes take with the princesses (before being formally legitimized by marriage) are permissible or not. And although the princes' actions and accusations lead up to the great arraignment scene in the final book, the ambivalence of courtship is not something which can satisfactorily be resolved by human justice. Instead, the princes' dubious sexual exploits with Pamela and Philoclea are forgiven in the general outcome of Sidney's comic dénouement. But the sinister questions of legitimization remain lurking below the surface (to be explored further in the *New Arcadia*), for the moral ambivalence and sexual indeterminacy of courtship have not gone away.

EUPHUES AND EUPHUES AND HIS ENGLAND

Lyly was clearly preoccupied with hammering out a definition of courtship in *Euphues* and *Euphues and his England*, for he uses the verb 'to court' some eighteen times in the two tales, constantly returning to the word, holding it up for examination, qualification, and critique.[5] In many ways, Lyly shows an Aschamite predisposition to link 'courtly courtesies' with the perverse and lewd sexual practices of Italy. Near the beginning of *Euphues*, for example, Lyly's cunning protagonist declares that 'if I be in Crete, I can lye, if in Greece I can shift, if in Italy I can court it' (*E* 186), while toward the end of the tale, he writes (now chastened) that he chooses rather 'to dye in my studye amiddest my bookes, then to courte it in Italy, in the company of Ladyes' (*E* 242). At the beginning of the sequel, *Euphues and his England*, Euphues regales his companion, Philautus, with a cautionary tale about a young man who in his youth could 'court it with the Italian, carous it with the Dutch-man' (*EE* 24).

Throughout his texts – especially *Euphues and his England* – Lyly uses the insistent dichotomy of euphuistic syntax to draw a negative associative field around 'courting'. Thus Philautus accuses his friend of a treacherous volte-face when he finds that paragon of new-learned virtue all too soon in love again: 'I see thou art come from thy booke to beastlines, from coting of ye scriptures, to courting with Ladies' (*EE* 93). Here courting presents itself as a shameful surrogate for learning and study, made all the more heinous by Euphues' faint resolve. In a later passage, Lyly's narrator berates women for accepting as lovers 'those that can court you, not those that loue you', driving a wedge between the specious and the sincere (*EE* 121). Later still, Euphues congratulates the newly married Philautus by advising him to 'forget all thy former follyes . . . then there was no pleasure to bee compared to the courting of Ladyes, that now there can be no delight greater than to haue a wife' (*EE* 227). In contradistinction to marriage, courtship becomes a 'folly', a danger-ous, temporary phase now thankfully legitimized by Philautus' wedding.

In all these examples, Lyly uses the endemic parallelism of his dichotomous syntax to define courtship as sensual, devious, illicit, and extra-marital. Some of Lyly's earliest readers reacted to the didacticism of his tone by assuming that (like Ascham) he was attacking courtship as a species of dubious sexual behaviour that could be legitimized only by marriage. Lyly's contemporaries, Thomas Lodge and Robert Greene, for example, both propagated misreadings of *Euphues and his England* by jumping to the conclusion that, if Philautus courted Camilla, then he must have become her husband. In the second edition of *Rosalynde* (1592), for example, Lodge inserted an explanatory 'schedule' supposedly written by the now-retired Euphues to his friend Philautus:

The vehemency of my sicknes (*Philautus*) hath made mee doubtfull of life, yet must I die in counsailing thee like *Socrates*, because I loue thee. Thou hast sons by *Camilla*, as I heare, who being yong in yeres haue green thoghts: & nobly born, haue great minds . . . I haue bequeathed them a *Golden legacie*, because I greatly loue thee.[6]

Lodge also addresses another of his tales, *Euphues Shadow, the Battaile of the Senses* (1592), to Philautus' 'Sonnes liuing at the Courte'. In 1589, Robert Greene published *Menaphon: Camilla's Alarum to Slumbering Euphues*, in answer (or 'requitall') to his own *Euphues his Censure to Philautus* (1587). Both Greene and Lodge therefore link Philautus with Camilla, and assume, in their own euphuistic continuations of Lyly's highly popular tales, that Lyly's portrait of courtship in *Euphues and his England* concluded respectably with marriage.

The point, of course, is that both Lodge and Greene are wrong. They both misread Lyly's text by following an Aschamite tendency to assimilate Philautus' 'courtly courtesies' within a matrix which silently 'legitimizes' courtship by marriage. For although Philautus courts Camilla, he does not end by marrying her. Camilla remains faithful to Surius, and, in a valedictory epistle, Euphues declares that 'they both will lyue well in mariage, who loued so well before theyr matching' (*EE* 223). Philautus, meanwhile, turns his amorous affections elsewhere and eventually marries a different woman, Frauncis.

The mistake that Lodge and Greene make here signals to us a common problem in the interpretation of Lyly's texts. It is clear that *Euphues and his England* cannot be made to fit the didactic pattern which Lodge and Greene impose upon it. And while Lodge and Greene attempt to legitimize the courtship of Philautus and Camilla by assuming that it ends in matrimony, their quest for propriety inadvertently (and quite humorously) deconstructs itself: for, in effect, they give Philautus the 'wrong' wife. And, in addressing *Rosalynde* to Philautus' 'sons by Camilla', Lodge unwittingly directs his tale to young men who, if they were to exist at all, would have to be illegitimate.[7]

For this part of Lyly's text in fact veers in the opposite direction from Lodge and Greene. In *Rosalynde*, wooing and wedding are inseparable, and all the amorous courtships in that tale conclude with marriage. But both *Euphues* and *Euphues and his England* resist the pull toward legitimization (although they are all passionate and intense, few of Lyly's courtships conclude with marriage). Instead of presenting his readers with simple, cautionary tales about the dangers of sexual desire, Lyly intermixes his stories with open-ended courtly debates and questions of love. And he therefore allows his readers to explore on either side trenchant and incisive questions about courtship and human sexuality.

In the prefatory letter to Lord Delaware at the beginning of *Euphues*, for example, Lyly admits that 'a naked tale doth most truely set foorth the naked truth' (*E* 181), and apologizes in advance for the 'superfluous eloquence' that he feels constrained to use: 'Though the stile nothing delight the dayntie eare of the curious sifter, yet wil the matter recreate the minde of the courteous Reader' (*E* 180). Characteristically, Lyly dichotomizes didactic and courtly responses to his text, posturing as a polemicist *manqué* who finds himself obliged to feign a curious style because his courtly readers 'desire to heare finer speach then the language will allow' (*E* 181). But (like the notoriously ambivalent narrators of Gascoigne's *Adventures of Master F.J.* and Sidney's *Old Arcadia*) Lyly poses alternately as an arbiter of moral values and as a courtly entertainer specifically (it seems) in order to problematize our moral judgements.

One of the first things Lyly's Euphues does is to argue down the admonitory warnings of Eubulus. With his care for the *sensus germanus* of words, and his educational precepts culled from Roger Ascham and Sir Thomas Elyot, Eubulus (or 'good counsaile') personifies the humanist pedagogic tradition. But Euphues aims a blow at the very root of Eubulus' deliberative oration by repudiating the power of words to persuade at all:

Infinite and innumerable were the examples I coulde alleadge and declare to confirme the force of Nature, and confute these your vayne and false forgeries, were not the repetition of them needelesse hauing shewed sufficient, or bootelesse seeinge those alleadged will not perswade you. (*E* 191)

Instead, Euphues presents Eubulus with the relativistic world of 'so many men so many mindes' (*E* 190), a world which anticipates a remark in John Keepers's *The Courtiers Academie* (1598): 'The maner of handling this controuersie pleaseth me well ... seeing euery one may reason to their owne minde.'[8]

The dichotomizing tendencies of euphuistic prose invite us to draw the commonplace Renaissance comparison between Eubulus' pedagogy and Euphues' courtliness.[9] Eubulus and Euphues not only fail to persuade each other because age and youth cannot live together. They fail because their two discursive strategies prove unassimilable. Eubulus' pedagogic tirade counts for nothing in the ornamental indeterminacy of Euphues' discourse, a style which exemplifies that 'exercise of the wyt' which Edmund Tilney saw as typical of the courtly debate.[10] And while we might be tempted to set the scales against Euphues, and to see him as a prodigal who eventually learns from the cautionary tale that is his life, we can equally interpret him as a courtier *par excellence*. A character in one of Barnaby Rich's tales, for example, pays tribute to Lyly's Euphues as a figure who could 'Court it with the best, and Scholler it with the most, in whom I know not whether I should more commende his maners or his learnyng, the one is so exquisite, the other so generall'.[11]

Euphues' rhetorical style belongs precisely to the 'ragionamenti' Bembo spoke about, or the 'bolder talking of this and that' which had aroused Ascham's suspicion. His answer to Eubulus resists conclusion and instead spirals off in a dazzling display of wit – a style which John Hoskins suggested was particularly apt and 'prettie to play wth amonge gentlewomen' even if entirely inappropriate for the likes of Eubulus.[12] For, as Sidney observes, euphuism is less a logico-rhetorical system than a device for amplifying speech:

Now for similitudes in certain printed discourses, I think all herbarists, all stories of beasts, fowls, and fishes are rifled up, that they come in multitudes to wait upon any of our conceits; which certainly is as absurd a surfeit to the ears as is possible: *for the force of a similitude not being to prove anything to a contrary disputer, but only to explain to a willing hearer*; when that is done, the rest is a most tedious prattling.[13]

Euphuism provided a means to argue endlessly *in utramque partem*, and to postpone closure for the very pleasure of specious debate. As a style of speech, euphuism approximates closely to one of the courtly tropes that Castiglione lists as being 'verye merrye and pleasant' 'whan one contrarye clause is sett agaynst another', suggesting an unequivocally courtly model for Euphues' controversial rhetorical style.[14]

In his answer to Eubulus, Euphues does not produce any conclusion but only 'quandary' – a reaction to speechifying that is to become increasingly typical as the tale proceeds, and that was indeed wholly characteristic of courtly *dubii*.[15] In *The Aduentures of Master F.J.*, for example, Dame Pergo remarks that 'though in deede in questioning . . . every one is at free libertie to aunswere what they list: yet oft have I heard a question demaunded in such sorte, and uppon such sodayne, that it hath bene hardly answered without moving matter of contention'.[16] In the fifth of Henry Grantham's *Thirtene Most Plesant and Delectable Questions* (1566) – a debate between the sufferings of jealousy or unrequited love – the lovers 'abode in a long contention, and in the end parted without any diff[i]nition'. This 'contention' recalls the conclusion of the first day's dispute in *The Courtiers Academie*, when 'on a sodaine great murmuring did arise, one defending one parte, and others another'.[17] Nashe prefaces his *Anatomie of Absurditie* (1589) with an account of several gentlemen who 'mooue diuers Questions, as touching the seuerall qualities required in *Castalions* Courtier'. But the 'discourse thus continued, [until] at length they fell by a iarring gradation, to the particuler demonstrations of theyr generall assertions'.[18]

So Euphues' courtly style – first exemplified in his speech to Eubulus – resists conclusion and instead entertains his listeners with a dazzling display of wit. But, as Barnaby Rich was to point out, Euphues' ability to 'Court it with the best' was just as admirable, to a number of Lyly's first readers, as his ability to 'Scholler it with the most'. In other words, while an Ascham, or a Lodge, or a Greene might have denigrated Euphues' courtliness (in favour of Eubulus' sober counsel), other readers clearly perceived it to be exemplary, and to belong to that civilized tradition of fifteenth- and sixteenth-century court debates which upheld the 'ragionamenti' between the sexes as a cultured form of social play and as a forum for genuine, philosophical inquiry.

Lyly thus aligns himself with an unmistakably courtly tradition, in order to establish familiarity with his destined audience, and to prove his credentials as a writer of courtly fiction. Courtly debates modelled themselves on academic disputation, arguing questions of love and sexuality on both sides. But while academic disputation aspired to a single, unified conclusion, the objective of courtly debate was simply the rehearsal of contrary views. Castiglione's *Book of the Courtier* is a *locus classicus* for this kind of 'contentious' reasoning, and, at its best, courtly debate derived a serious, even philosophic justification from its cultivation of a quintessentially composite truth. Henry Wotton defends the courtly speakers in his *Courtlie Controuersie of Cupids Cautels* (1578) in the following fashion:

I will meruayle no more, though in our Rurall Colledge a question which seemeth so cleare, is so earnestly debated: wherein me thinke we shoulde commende our Nobilitie, whiche will not after the maner of proude Sophisters, answere rashly, to be thereby constrayned to gainsay their arguments, or be proued liers by the veritie ... But as true Phylosophers, they seeke all meanes to finde out the trueth.[19]

Likewise, in Guazzo's *La civile conversatione*, the 'commendable controversies' of the courtly debate prove to be the only means of arriving at the truth because 'while [the speakers] dispute by lively reasons, indevouring to get the upper hand ech of other, the perfect knowledge of things is come by, and therupon it is commonly saide that Disputation is the sifter out of the trueth'.[20] For Pietro Bembo, the speakers in *Gli Asolani* debate issues to and fro because they would not 'be satisfied with a brief inquiry when the truth for which they seek is fraught with doubt'.[21]

John Lyly's debt to this courtly tradition was explored many years ago by Violet Jeffery, and has been acknowledged by those critics who consider the status of his texts as courtly fiction.[22] Most concede that dialogues of love form the staple of Lyly's plays and that his technique of composing dialogue 'set his scenes of courtship apart from the dramatic tradition of the 1560s and 1570s'.[23] Lyly's prose narratives are similarly indebted to courtly debates. And, as they locate themselves in a specifically courtly tradition, Lyly's fictions explore the moral ambivalence of courtship which Pietro Bembo and Roger Ascham had earlier signalled in their accounts of 'courtly courtesies'.[24]

Lyly amplifies and complicates his notion of courtly discourse in *Euphues* when he goes on to present his readers with an episode explicating a fully fledged *questione d'amore*. Not long after Eubulus' departure, Euphues accompanies his new-found friend Philautus to a *convivium* at the house of Lucilla, the latter's mistress. Lucilla, Lyly tells us, is the paragon of 'a courtly crewe of gentlewomen' (*E* 199) and after the banquet she calls for 'some discourse, either concerning loue or learning' (*E* 201). Her proposition initiates a time-honoured courtly scenario which derived from the great tradition of the *questione d'amore* enshrined in the writings of Boccaccio, Ficino, Alberti, Bembo, Castiglione, Tasso, and a host of others. Countless fifteenth- and sixteenth-century debates invoke the same recreative and festive courtly grouping in which men and women proceed to analyse and anatomize the minutiae of love and sexuality. In this tradition, the questions examined make little attempt at novelty or originality but tend rather to reflect so many variations on a common theme. One member of the group – usually a woman – is elected 'queen' for the occasion, often crowned with a garland, and asked to arbitrate the disputes.[25]

Euphues' deference-ritual on being asked to begin is entirely in keeping with the conventions of the *questione d'amore*. He claims to overcome his professed inadequacy and reluctance out of obedience to Lucilla and a sense of duty to entertain the other ladies.[26] And, in opting to speak of love, Euphues also conforms to tradition, for, as Whetstone writes in his *Heptameron*, 'the name of *Loue* gaue a large occasion of discourse', and, as the Hermit warns Lavinello in *Gli Asolani*, 'you and your friends have put a real burden on your shoulders in engaging to speak of love and its condition, not only because a multitude of things can be said about it, but even more because everybody discusses it all the time'.[27]

The issue with which Euphues opens the debate is, he says, 'a question often disputed, but neuer determined' (*E* 201), and, like so many of the courtly disputations under consideration, it is open-ended. The question – whether wit or beauty is more attractive in either sex – is a common variation on a standard theme (and one that Lyly will pick up again in *Euphues and his England*, 57, 58, 70, 154). Not attempting to resolve the question he has raised, Euphues shifts about, introduces a *carpe diem* theme, and then abruptly changes the subject to discuss the constancy of women. Euphues tacitly manipulates the discussion by taking the position that women are inconstant, hinting that Lucilla's three-year-old attachment to Philautus should make her disagree. He then takes 'the contrary' by arguing his point that women in general (and Lucilla in particular) are fickle (*E* 203). Lucilla thwarts his efforts, however, by behaving unpredictably. Instead of opposing him by defending female constancy, Lucilla *agrees* with his proposition, so that, trapped by the rules of the debate and by his own manipulative rhetoric, Euphues is forced to 'take the contrary' and to defend women's fidelity himself. The debate characteristically ends, like Euphues' former speech to Eubulus, in a 'quandarie' (*E* 204).

The *querelle des femmes* was a ubiquitous subject in courtly debates, and, of all courtly topics, perhaps the most self-perpetuating. Guazzo in Guazzo's *Conversatione*, Mossenigo in Whetstone's *Heptameron*, Phylopolo in Fenton's *Monophylo*, Gherardo in Domenichi's *Dialoghi*, and Perottino in Bembo's *Gli Asolani* each take up a misogynistic position, not so much to abuse women, but, rather, to stimulate debate. In Tilney's *Flower of Friendshippe* (1568), for example, the gallant Pedro defends the rebarbative Gualter on the grounds that 'hee increaseth our sporte, and therefore we can not well want him', while in his *Morando: The Tritameron of Love* (1587), Greene writes, 'Had not *Siluestro & Peratio* fallen out about loue, we had neuer brought it in question whether it be good to loue or no.'[28] By playing a similar game of dispute and counter-dispute in *Euphues*, Lyly constructs through apparent contradictions a composite view of women that is wholly characteristic of this kind of courtly disputation.[29]

Euphues' discourse at Lucilla's feast, then, clearly bears all the hallmarks of a classic courtly *questione d'amore*. Moreover, when Lyly came to revise the text of *Euphues* for a second edition in 1579, he made significant alterations to the original text: changes which reveal a growing interest in those courtly modes of courtship and social intercourse that were available (and indispensable) to a writer seeking a courtly entrée. The most important of the revisions in *Euphues* is the insertion of a long passage – amounting to some seventy lines (fifty-seven in Bond's edition) – which further extends the *questione* begun at Lucilla's. In the original 1578 text, Philautus is spirited away by Ferardo in order to make the formal arrangements for his marriage to Lucilla. In the 1579 text, however, Lyly inserts a conversation between Euphues and Lucilla at this point in which the latter invites Euphues to end 'your former discourse', and in which he duly addresses himself to a 'farther conclusion' (*E* 216).

By making this change, Lyly substantially expands the *questione d'amore* already initiated by Lucilla, that earlier discussion 'being left vnperfect' at Euphues' premature departure (*E* 215). And, by extending the debate in this way, Lyly thus reinforces the open-endedness of the question, which, in true courtly fashion, remains unresolved. For although Euphues is invited to a further conclusion, nothing, of course, is concluded. Instead, he summons familiar and traditional arguments in praise of women, before being interrupted (in the time-honoured fashion) 'whilest hee was yet speakinge' (*E* 217).

This substantial addition to the original text of *Euphues* seems to reveal a growing preoccupation on Lyly's part with the highly ambivalent relation between licit and illicit sexuality (later to be demarcated so rigidly by Lodge and Greene). From a didactic standpoint, the extended debate provides Euphues and Lucilla with a further opportunity to flirt with each other, thereby demonstrating that their 'endless' discourse is simply a means to achieve an improper end (or at least to defer achieving a proper one). Such conduct manifestly conflicts with the teleological bias shared by humanist hermeneutics and legitimized sexuality: 'the end of well-doing and not of well-knowing only . . . the ending end of all earthly learning being virtuous action'.[30] Lyly's narrator leaves us in no doubt that virtuous action is very far from being the end Euphues and Lucilla have in mind, and, for one critic, the whole episode represents 'human nature devoid of humanist education: unrestrained, self-indulgent, foolish, and easily corruptible'.[31]

And yet, for all this, an open-ended *courtly* structure still predominates. For the 'end' that Euphues and Lucilla seek is (like the end of the debate) never achieved. Indeed, Lucilla herself could be seen to become an emblem of 'endlessness'. Defending her treacherous love for Euphues to her father, she, like Euphues, is also interrupted 'in the middle of hyr discourse' and we never hear its conclusion (*E* 231). Her passion for Euphues quickly gives way to another, even more unsuitable, and the narrator ends the tale refusing to recount what became of her:

> but what ende came of hir, seeing it is nothing incident to the history of *Euphues*, it were superfluous to insert it, and so incredible that all women would rather wonder at it then beleeue it, which euent beeing so straunge, I had rather leaue them in a muse what it should bee, then in a maze in telling what it was. (*E* 245).

Only in the correspondence between Euphues and Philautus that follows do we learn that she meets a miserable death.[32]

The narrator's postponed ending epitomizes the courtly mode of inconclusiveness and aims to leave its female readers less in a state of moral outrage ('maze') than in one of curiosity ('muse'). Lyly's readers are not invited to experience a horrified reaction to a cautionary tale but, rather, a version of what Sir Thomas Hoby calls 'the beholding and musing of the mind', the proper response to a courtly text.[33]

It was here that Lodge and Greene made their mistake. For like *Love's Labour's Lost*, *Euphues* 'doth not end like an old play'.[34] Courtship does not end in marriage. Closure is only apparent. At the end of *Euphues*, Lyly's narrative breaks up and splinters into a series of apparently unrelated letters and tracts. The misogyny of Euphues' 'cooling card' is balanced in true courtly fashion by his epistle to the 'graue Matrones', and, for the second time since the *questione d'amore*, dispraise combines with praise in the delineation of women in order that closure might be forestalled.

An open-ended, 'courtly' ending of this kind suggests, therefore, that *Euphues'* golden legacy is not to be found in *Rosalynde* at all. Lodge's story ends with a multiple wedding, and with the legend that 'concord is the sweetest conclusion'.[35] But there is no such optimistic 'conclusion' to *Euphues*. Lyly's romance ends not with a wedding but with a degree of disillusionment about marriage. A more fitting 'legacy' might instead be found in the closing song of *Love's Labour's Lost*, the refrain of which, 'Cuckoo, Cuckoo', is 'Unpleasing to a married ear'.[36]

The failure of Euphues' courtship testifies, in some degree, to what we know of Lyly's sense of rejection at the hands of Elizabeth, and of his failure to achieve the court position he aspired to. Ironically, the courtly mode of open-endedness and inconclusiveness which informs so much of the structure of *Euphues* allowed Lyly not only to pose as a writer of courtly fiction, but also to enact his own marginalization and frustration. Moreover, the courtly tropes that Lyly had experimented with so successfully in *Euphues* are massively expanded in the sequel that he published in 1580, *Euphues and his England. Euphues and his England* is a more self-advertisingly courtly text in its scope and orientation, a work best fitted to 'lye shut in a Ladyes casket, then open in a Schollers studie' (*EE* 9), as Lyly puts it. Lyly here adopts the trivializing pose beloved of court writers, claiming to present 'more shewe of pleasure, then ground of profit' (*EE* 10), 'a toy' or 'trash', like Sidney's 'trifle . . . triflingly handled', and Gascoigne's 'thriftlesse Historie'.[37] Lyly models his work, perhaps, on Wotton's *Courtlie Controuersie of Cupids Cautels* (1578), which had begun with the following disclaimer: 'though it be a trifle too friuolous to molest your discret view & sound iudgement, yet considring worldly wights must of necessitie be sometime wearied with weighty affaires; & that the Bee gathereth hony from whence the Spider picketh poyson, I haue presumed to present the same vnto your honor'. 'It seemeth a shame', he adds, 'vnto all Gentlemen and Gentlewomen, nurtured in the schole of curtesie, but principally vnto Courtiers, to be ignoraunt thereof.'[38]

By addressing *Euphues and his England* to women, Lyly might be seen to place the tale lowest on the conversational scale described by Guazzo in which princely counsel and discourse with strangers come highest but conversation with women 'lowest of all'.[39] On the other hand, as we have already seen, the female roles of story-teller and arbitrator are staples of courtly fiction, and it is the women readers' judgement of Lyly's 'diuers questions and quirkes of loue' (*EE* 8) that places *Euphues and his England* squarely within the courtly tradition of the *questioni d'amore*. And, as the subject of Lyly's tale comes under the scrutiny, examination, and critique of a female-dominated readership, so Lyly could be seen to enact (like Sidney in *The Lady of May*) his own proneness as the subject of a queen.

In the prefatory letter to his female readers, Lyly draws our attention to the setting of his *discorsi*:

These discourses I haue not clapt in a cluster, thinking with my selfe, that Ladies had rather be sprinckled with sweete water, then washed, so that I haue sowed them heere and there, lyke Strawberies, not in heapes, lyke Hoppes. (*EE* 8)

His discourses of love are indeed scattered like choice morsels throughout the text. Near the beginning of Fidus' inset romance narrative, Lyly interjects with a tripartite *questione* typical of courtly *dubii*: 'whether in loue *Vlysses* more preuailed with his wit, or *Paris* with his personage, or *Achilles* with his prowesse' (*EE* 57). Versions of this question reappear during the course of Fidus' narrative, first in Iffida's tale of the three marriageable daughters (one beautiful but foolish, one witty but wanton, and one ugly but virtuous) and again in Fidus' own question: an '*English* controuersie' between three male suitors, with looks, wit, and wealth respectively. Summing up his narrative, Fidus turns the whole into a new *questione*, 'whether was [Iffida] a lady of greater constancie towards *Thirsus*, or courtesie towards me?' (*EE* 79). Philautus, likewise, woos Camilla 'with questions' (*EE* 104), like those lovers who 'vse discourses of Loue, to kindle affection' (*EE* 121), and at the end of his abortive courtship, he and Euphues embark on a long debate on love, a debate in which the narrator interjects with a 'controuersie' of his own: 'whether there be in [women] an art to loue . . . or whether it breede in you as it doth in men: by sight, if one bee bewtifull, by hearing, if one be wittie, by desertes if one be curteous, by desire, if one be vertuous' (*EE* 154). *Euphues and his England* concludes with a typically courtly scenario: a *convivium* at the house of Flavia in which she asks for 'some questions to sharpen your wittes' (*EE* 161), and in which Surius proposes that they 'vse some discourse, aswell to renue old traditions, which haue bene heertofore vsed, as to encrease friendship' (*EE* 163). Issues that have been raised throughout the tale now reappear as formal *questioni d'amore*: How should a woman respond to a true lover? Should the social intercourse between men and women be allowed? Should a lover be silent and fickle or constant but indiscreet? Asked to arbitrate the three questions, Euphues replies, 'better it were in my opinion not to haue your reasons concluded, then to haue them confuted' (*EE* 180).

In *Euphues and his England*, the questions are not simply pretexts for discussion but integral elements of the narrative, giving it a framework and rationale, and providing Lyly with a unique position from which to explore the possibility of effecting distinctions between licit and illicit sexuality. The effect of centring *Euphues and his England* so clearly around courtly *questioni d'amore* is to stress (even more than in *Euphues*) the intrinsic open-endedness of 'courtly courtesies' or 'ragionamenti'. And the very rhetorical indeterminacy which arose from debating for debating's sake provides Lyly with an obvious parallel for the sexual ambivalence of the courtship-situation – its teasingly licensed eroticism, and the uncertainty of sexual roles.

In *Euphues and his England* Lyly therefore focuses on the rhetorical strategies of courtship, and explores the full rhetorical and sexual ambiguities of Bembo's 'ragionamenti' or Ascham's 'bolder talking of this and that'. The first main courtship-narrative of the tale, the love-story between Fidus and Iffida presents us with a model for the idealized civil conversation which, as Bembo had insisted against the judgement of Castiglione's more cynical courtiers, could exist between a man and a woman.

When Euphues and Philautus first arrive in England, they are entertained by Fidus, a stock Hermit-figure who, having long retired from court life, now regales them with the story of his youthful courtship of a courtly lady, Iffida. During the course of his wooing, Fidus says, he fell sick for love, and when his very life was in danger, Iffida came to see him and to revive him with her conversation: 'If to talke with me, or continually to be in thy company, may in any respect satisfie thy desire, assure thy selfe, I wil attend on thee, as dilygently as thy Nourse, and bee more carefull for thee, then thy Phisition' (*EE* 77). Fidus' story (and recovery) is set within a well-established courtly tradition of telling stories for 'restoratives'.[40] In *The Aduentures of Master F.J.*, for example, F.J.'s love-sickness is cured by the ladies' devising pastimes and questions of love: 'his frendly entertainment togither with the great curtesie of the gentlewomen was such, as might revive a man although he were half dead'.[41] More generally, of course, courtly *trattati* are frequently set during periods of physical and spiritual convalescence. Wotton's *Courtlie Controuersie*, for example, is (like the *Decameron*) set during the aftermath of a plague, Marguerite of Navarre's *Heptaméron* after a flood, Fenton's *Monophylo* after a siege, when men and women gather to 'restore their late wearie time in warre with euery honest pleasure'.[42] The dialogues in Guazzo's *La civile conversatione* take place between a physician Annibale and Guazzo's sick brother. They conclude with the latter's recovery, a demonstration of the power of conversation to restore. In the *New Arcadia*, Musidorus recovers his health through ministrations and 'daily discourses' with Kalender.[43]

In the same way, Lyly's Fidus, also stricken by love-melancholy, recovers as a direct response to Iffida's conversation. Iffida can never be his, it transpires, because she is already in love with another gentleman, Thirsus. But – like Bembo's ideal courtly lady – she is permitted to converse with him, and, indeed, she admits that her attraction to Fidus formerly made her 'by questions moue thee to talke, or by quarrels incense thee to choller, perceiuing in thee a wit aunswerable to my desire, which I thought throughly to whet by some discourse' (*EE* 76). The very purpose of her taunts and gambits, then, had been to make Fidus demonstrate his own wit in civil conversation, and so to gratify her 'desire'.

In other words, only by translating desire and its gratification into *discourse* can it be contained and socially sanctioned. Once the playful parameters of their relationship are established, Fidus and Iffida continue to enjoy each other's company: 'Euery euening she wold put forth either some pretie question, or vtter some mery conceit, to driue me from melancholy' (*EE* 78). So, by the end of Fidus' inset narrative, he and Iffida come to exemplify civil conversation in action, that social intercourse which is contained and allowable within the rules of courtly 'ragionamenti'.

Fidus might well have subscribed to Guazzo's dictum that 'my chiefe purpose is not to discourse of love, but of the conversation with women', for what he learned from Iffida was how to engage in 'familiar and secret talke' with her without compromising either party.[44] Fidus eventually learned (like so many of the Desire-figures in Elizabethan court pageants) to detach courtship from a language of sexual appropriation. He became, in other words, one of Bembo's 'rational' lovers, capable of enjoying female company, of exchanging jests, dalliance, conversation, and kisses, but without degenerating into 'sensual' desire or physical gratification: not an easy task in an over-eroticized court-setting which half licensed courtship (as 'l'amor razionale') and yet half condemned it (as 'l'amor sensuale') as well.

If Fidus and Iffida typify Bembo's ideal courtly lovers, however, then the other main pair in *Euphues and his England*, Philautus and Camilla, present a rather different picture. While the conversations between Fidus and Iffida come to exemplify Bembo's chaste 'ragionamenti', Philautus' discourse is laced, from the outset, with sexual innuendo and intrigue. His exchanges with Camilla approximate much more closely to Ascham's feared 'bolder talking of this and that', the rhetorical procedure between men and women that made for social and sexual indeterminacy, and which led (in most cases) to seduction and sex.

In the Camilla–Philautus story it appears at first sight as if Bembo's objective of cultured and civilized conversation between the sexes was not, in practice, very easy to achieve. For Philautus' own response to Fidus' tale is highly sexualized: '*Philautus* eytching to hear what he would say, desired him to goe forward'; he is 'burning as it were, in desire of this discourse', a discourse which eventually brings him 'abedde' (*EE* 49). He remains 'tyckled in euerye vaine with delyght' (*EE* 56), and is loth to countenance any *interruptus* in his satisfaction: 'But he so eger of an end, as one leaping ouer a stile before hee come to it, desired few parentheses or digressions or gloses, but the text, wher he him-self, was coting in the margant' (*EE* 51).

In his approaches to Camilla, moreover, Philautus tries to cloak sexual desire behind apparently innocuous *questioni d'amore* – 'I meane only with questions to trye your wit', he says disingenuously, 'which shall neither touch your honour to aunswere, nor my honestie to aske' (*EE* 104). Camilla, however, remains justifiably suspicious of Philautus' questions, for 'such questions in these assemblyes, moue suspition where there is no cause', she says, 'and therefore are not to be resolued least there be cause' (*EE* 104). When an opportunity arises for a fully fledged *questione d'amore* between them, she pre-empts the occasion, fearing to be compromised in her answers: passing a letter to Philautus in her Petrarch, she asks him to construe one of the sonnets, but arrests the discussion that is about to ensue, 'whether loue came at the sodeine viewe of beautie, or by long experience of vertue . . . as one not willing in yᵉ company of *Philautus* eyther to talke of loue, or thinke of loue' (*EE* 129). Camilla's ploy is (like Iffida's) to try to legitimize Philautus' discourse by turning it away from Ascham's immoral 'bolder talking' toward Bembo's chaste 'ragionamenti': 'And this Gentle-manne I desire you, all questions and other quarrelles set aparte, you thinke me as a friende, so farre forth as I can graunt with modestie, or you require with good manners, and as a friende I wishe you, that you blowe no more this fire of loue' (*EE* 106).

For Camilla (as, later, for Lodge and Greene) love-making can only be legitimized by marriage. Although she converses with Philautus, therefore, the man with whom she takes greatest 'delight in talkyng' is her future husband, Surius. Indeed, she 'desired nothing more than to be questioning with *Surius*' (*EE* 164). Frauncis, Philautus' future spouse, behaves likewise, taking 'no little pleasure to heare *Philautus* talke' (*EE* 179). And later, after he has transferred his amorous designs from Camilla to Frayncis, Philautus recognizes her as 'a wench euer-more giuen to such disporte' (*EE* 221).

Throughout *Euphues and his England*, then, Lyly focuses attention on the discursive strategies that exist between men and women, and, in the utterances of his various lovers, he identifies the two types of discourse we have distinguished already: on the one hand, Bembo's 'ragionamenti' (exemplified by Fidus and Iffida, who successfully subsume sexual desire beneath 'platonic' conversation), and, on the other, Ascham's 'bolder talking' (a potentially illicit procedure, exemplified by Philautus' flirtation with Camilla, which is only legitimate if the partners intend it to lead to marriage). And while the difference between licit and illicit love-making had enormous social ramifications, and was therefore highly sensitized at court, such a distinction was none the less, as we have seen, virtually impossible to determine in practice. Men and women could indulge in their 'familiar and secret talke', their kissing and touching, their joking and dallying, while the world outside continued to speculate on whether their intentions were honourable or not.

Towards the end of *Euphues and his England*, Lyly presents his readers with a debate between precisely these two rhetorical procedures for courtship at court: courting for courting's sake, or courting for the sake of marriage. The debate takes place between Euphues and Philautus, Euphues (now chastened by love) supporting Bembo's argument that civil conversation between the sexes is the only means of maintaining civilized decorum at court, and Philautus taking Ascham's line that 'courtly courtesies' can only be justified if they are going to lead to marriage.

For Euphues, then, 'the effect of loue is faith, not lust, delightfull conference, not detestable concupiscence'. All he desires, he says, is 'the company of hir in common conference that I best loued, to heare hir sober talke, hir wise aunsweres, to behold hir sharpe capacitie, and to bee perswaded of hir constancie' (*EE* 158). For Euphues the discursive practices of courtship – including 'discourses of loue' (*EE* 157) – are a civilizing phenomenon because they alone can restrain concupiscent desires, conversation acting as a surrogate for sexual passion.

For Philautus, on the other hand, 'the ende of fishing is catching, not anglyng: of birding, taking, not whistlyng: of loue, wedding, not wooing' (*EE* 159). He objects that the endless talk of Euphues' prognostication has no purpose and is therefore fruitless:

An idle loue is that, and fit for him that hath nothing but eares, that is satisfied to heare hir speak, not desirous to haue himselfe speede ... thou makest Loue nothing but a continual wooing, if thou barre it of the effect, and then is it infinite, or if thou allow it, and yet forbid it, a perpetuall warfare, and then is it intollerable. (*EE* 158–9)

For Philautus, the open-ended, inconclusive courtly debate is not an effective means of persuasion, and Euphues' 'continual wooing' is pointless and time-wasting precisely because it leads nowhere.

Superficially, it looks as though Lyly's narrator concurs with Philautus and that he adopts the Aschamite dictum that 'the ende of loue is the full fruition of the partie beloued' (*EE* 160). But – and this is where Lodge was to go wrong – *Philautus does not win Camilla.* Indeed, his statement that the end of love is wedding not wooing is, in context, extremely ironic; especially as he cannot even succeed in marrying Frauncis without the intervention of someone else.[45]

On inspection, then, the debate on courtship between Euphues and Philautus takes the form of just those open-ended, indeterminate courtly *dubii* which, as we have been arguing, form a central part of *Euphues and his England.* The debate remains undecided, in true courtly fashion, when the narrator leaves Euphues and Philautus still 'debating their question' (*EE* 160). And, following the courtly tradition of such *discorsi*, the debate peters out as indecisively as it began. Euphues admits at the beginning that he has already been 'disputing w^t my selfe' of his friend's situation, 'yet can I resolue my selfe in nothing that either may content mee, or quiet thee' (*EE* 155). The dispute ends likewise, with Euphues and Philautus being summoned to a banquet, and with the narrator interrupting and addressing the gentlewomen readers: 'But I will not craue herein your resolute aunswere, bicause betweene them it was not determined, but euery one as he lyketh, and then – !' (*EE* 161).

The fact that this debate on courtship (the key issue of *Euphues and his England*) should end so indecisively has, of course, a peculiar significance of its own. It places the text once and for all within a *courtly* aesthetic. Like *Euphues*, the tale's legacy seems to lie in the rhetorically courtly world of *Love's Labour's Lost* rather than in the prose continuations of euphuistic romance. For the obsessive verbalizing of Lyly's characters is a symptom of the powerlessness of their rhetoric to persuade, and a hint that the Elizabethan courtier might expend as much energy as he liked without ever getting very far.

As if to emphasize the inconclusiveness of courtship at court,

Lyly's narrator bows out at the end of *Euphues and his England* with a supremely courtly gesture. The narrative ends not with a conclusion but, rather, with another 'hard question among Ladies, whether *Philautus* were a better wooer, or a husband, whether *Euphues* were a better louer, or a scholler' (*EE* 228).

The *questioni d'amore* are presumably meant to begin all over again, to be endlessly debated outside the confines of the narrative by Lyly's courtly audience, while Lyly remains forever on the margins of court existence, and while his story continues to lie unread, 'shut in a Ladyes casket' (*EE* 9).

THE *ARCADIA*

Sidney's *Arcadia* – that 'notable dumbshow of Cupid's kingdom' – is a courtship-narrative *par excellence*.[46] Sidney devotes the whole of the *Old Arcadia* and a good part of the *New* to a study of the wooing of his princes and princesses. And, as John Carey notes, he 'handles scenes of courtship [in a way] quite new in English literature, more subtle than anything that had been tried before ... in his delicately complicated syntax he creates a linguistic equivalent of the subtlety, mitigating, by his play of pattern, the crude force of ordinary language: making language sensitized enough for the task'.[47] When Gabriel Harvey recommended the *Arcadia* to his readers, one of the things that he singled out for attention was Sidney's treatment of 'amorous Courting':

Will you needs have a written Pallace of Pleasure, or rather a printed Courte of Honour? Read the Countesse of Pembrookes Arcadia, a gallant Legendary, full of pleasurable accidents and proffitable discourses; for three things especially very notable – for amorous Courting (he was young in yeeres), for sage counselling (he was ripe in judgement), and for valorous fighting (his soveraine profession was Armes).[48]

For Harvey, the *Arcadia* seems first and foremost to have been a 'palace of pleasure', the commonplace architectural metaphor signalling its allegiance to the tradition of William Painter, George Pettie, and Geoffrey Fenton in their collections of somewhat risqué tales.[49] But Harvey also considered the *Arcadia* to be a 'court of honour': a place (like Alma's castle in book II of *The Faerie Queene*) in which amorous courting was purged of its potentially licentious connotations and, instead, approved as a model of courtly etiquette and behaviour.

Harvey responded as positively as he did to the *Arcadia*, perhaps, because it seemed to him manifestly to fulfil the two Horatian imperatives – to teach and to delight. As a 'court of honour', Sidney's text promotes virtuous and gentle discipline, exemplifying the literary and moral idealism of the *Apology*. As a 'palace of pleasure', the *Arcadia* is full of titillating stories which verge teasingly on the erotic, and, in true courtly fashion, it addresses itself specifically to women. Just as Lyly's prose fiction had elicited a dual response from his earliest readers (Lodge and Greene interpreting *Euphues* as 'prodigal' fiction, Barnaby Rich, as more indulgent, 'courtly' writing) so Sidney's *Arcadia* appeals to a similar dichotomy. Much of the *Arcadia* appears to denigrate 'amorous Courting' as idle, affected, lascivious, and immoral – and we shall see how Sidney's later editors pursued this strand of polemic and did their best to revise the erotic content and curtail the *frissons* of desire that Sidney had made so central to his story. At the same time, Sidney's narrator frequently assumes the role of a Boccaccian story-teller, indulging his characters and readers, and inviting us to wink at the sexual proclivities of his 'stage-play of love' (*OA* 54).

As in Lyly's fictions, the *Arcadia*'s impulses to teach and to delight pull in opposite directions. On the one hand, there are many occasions when Sidney's narrator appears as an Aschamite polemicist whose outraged moral sensitivity frequently associates 'courting' with lax or illicit aristocratic mores. Throughout the *Old* and the *New Arcadia*, Sidney appears casually to associate courtly behaviour with flattery or promiscuity. In the *Old Arcadia*, for example, we are invited to laugh at the affected 'courtlike carelessness' of Dametas (*OA* 30), a parody of fashionable court melancholy. Cleophila puts off the embarrassingly amorous Basilius by warning him that she (unlike some disreputable women of the court) is not to be won by his 'courtly vanities' (*OA* 178). When the disguised Musidorus tells Pamela his story in the *New Arcadia*, he recounts how his uncle Euarchus had succeeded to the throne at a time when law was so corrupted that 'the court of a prince [was] rather deemed as a privileged place of unbridled licentiousness' (*90* 160). And while Euarchus' good government had restored the court to moral and juridical excellence, its former licentiousness was considered as serious as political feuding and internal factionalism. Later, in recounting his own adventures to Philoclea, Pyrocles unthinkingly equates court behaviour with concupiscence, for he describes how

Pamphilus was both promiscuous and unfaithful in his dealings with women – and how he 'thus played the careless prince' (*90* 240).

Sidney's use of the verb 'to court' invariably makes the connection between courtliness and morally dubious behaviour. The over-eager Phalanthus is said to have 'courted' the vain Artesia, while their wooing is a mere courtship-of-convenience, and a symptom of the very worst abuses to which the Elizabethan courtship system could lend itself (*90* 91). The evil and witchlike queen, Cecropia, boasts how once she had been flattered, 'courted and followed, of all the ladies of this country' (*90* 318). And, as if to stress the suspect content of 'courting', Sidney loads the verb 'to court' with the utmost moral condemnation when, at the end of the *New Arcadia*, he describes how Anaxius and his brothers resolve to take Zelmane and the princesses by force:

And where . . . he and his brothers had courted their ladies (as whom they vouchsafed to have for their wives), he resolved now to dally no longer in delays, but to make violence his orator, since he found persuasions had gotten nothing but answers. (*90* 458)

Here all Ascham's worst fears about the incipient dangers of courtship, of the 'bolder talking of this and that', are realized. Impatient with the verbal banter of courtship – 'persuasions' and 'answers' – Anaxius decides to show the princesses that he means what he says, and to do so in the most brutal and violent way.

In the *Old Arcadia*, Sidney had progressively held up aristocratic sexual mores for attack, contrasting them with the amorous practices of the shepherds. The hymeneal poems of the Third Eclogues, for example, celebrate a wedding (between Lalus and Kala) that is patently the outcome of a patient and conventional courtship: 'with consent of both parents . . . their marriage day was appointed' (*OA* 244). Sidney's narrator archly contrasts the shepherds' normative courtship with that of the 'greater persons' (who are 'otherwise occupied' at the time), and, in particular, with Pyrocles and Philoclea, who had shockingly trangressed sexual and literary norms in the preceding scene by consummating their passion (*OA* 244–5). By the Fourth Eclogues, the shepherds have withdrawn themselves from the 'garboils' created by the increasingly chaotic desires of the courtiers – desires which, by contrast, seem to be silently reproved (*OA* 327).

The contrast between the sexual values of courtiers and shepherds became a staple of pastoral fiction. In Lodge's *Rosalynde*, Aliena insists that 'our countrey amours are not like your courtly fancies', and in book VI of *The Faerie Queene*, Pastorella is sooner won by 'Colin's carolings' than by the more courtly 'kind courtesies' of Sir Calidore.[50] So, in the *Old Arcadia*, while the aristocrats indulge in those rhetorical strategies which (as Ascham had warned) could teeter on the edge of erotic exchange, the shepherds woo in plain terms. In the First Eclogues, Lalus (the real shepherd) had told Dorus (the shepherd-prince) that 'plain speech oft than quaint phrase better framed is' (*OA* 58). And, in his courtship of Kala, Lalus unashamedly puts his rhetorical precepts into practice, for he had 'not with many painted words, nor false-hearted promises ... won the consent of his beloved Kala, but with true and simple making her know he loved her' (*OA* 244).

Nico's fabliau of the jealous husband who was cuckolded by a 'courtly shepherd' (which forms a part of the epithalamic poems of the Third Eclogues), serves to bifurcate aristocratic and pastoral mores even further (*OA* 251). For the courtship procedures of the 'courtly shepherd', which succeed in seducing a newly married wife, provide an arch commentary on the courtly courtesies of Musidorus/ Dorus – the quintessential 'courtly shepherd'. Just as the category of 'courtly shepherd' destabilizes the normal social and sexual stratifi- cations of the pastoral world, so Musidorus' desire for Pamela threatens, for a time, to destabilize the Arcadian kingdom itself.[51]

In his presentation of 'courtly courtesies', then, Sidney creates a climate of contrast, comparison, criticism, and critique which satir- izes aristocratic sexual mores more trenchantly than some of his readers have been, over the centuries, prepared to admit.[52] On the other hand, the *Arcadia* is clearly much more than a skit on courtly self-indulgence. Like Lyly's fictions, the *Arcadia* frequently problem- atizes a simple, polemical approach, and constantly brings ambi- valence and ambiguity to bear on what might otherwise be inter- preted (Lodge and Greene-style) as a straightforwardly didactic narrative. While Sidney's use of the verb 'to court', for example, or his contrast between the shepherds and the 'greater persons', might appear to draw up the battle-lines for a satirical reading worthy of a 'court of honour' (in Harvey's words), the rest of the *Arcadia* is a 'palace of pleasure' – a construction which allows for and contains titillating *frissons* of desire.

In a moment, I will consider Sidney's treatment of sex in the *Old*

Arcadia as a way of showing how he exploited the social and sexual ambivalence of the courtship-situation to the full. But first, a word about the political ambivalence of the Arcadian courtships. Sidney's narratives, although more 'private' in one sense, are more obviously 'political' than Lyly's fictions for the simple reason that his courtly lovers are not mere gentlemen and gentlewomen, but princes and princesses of the royal blood. When Basilius determines to 'grant his daughters in marriage to nobody' and to block their courtships, he fills the stock role of the prohibiting parent that is a given in most romance fiction (*OA* 11). But at the same time, of course, he conflicts with the most basic dynastic injunction that a ruler should establish an indisputable succession through the marriage of his children. In other words, Basilius' prohibition allows the princesses, Philoclea and Pamela, to indulge in courtships which – in order to be courtships in the traditional sense – must needs transgress paternalistic rule. But his prohibition also represents a perverse paternalism, the transgression of which paradoxically sanctions the princesses' courtships because, in allowing Pyrocles and Musidorus to woo them, they are in effect actualizing the dynastic marriages which Basilius should (in a proper state of mind) have granted if not arranged.

Like Shakespeare's Ferdinand and Miranda, then, the princes and princesses of the *Arcadia* are actively involved in securing the safe succession of their kingdoms by means of the most genealogically and geographically sound of marriages. In that sense, the courtships between Pyrocles and Philoclea, Musidorus and Pamela are highly proper (and a good deal more legitimate than any of Basilius' crazy schemes). Indeed, Basilius' downright failure to act as a responsible ruler and father in assuring the succession of his kingdom through the marriages of his daughters is one of the things which furnishes both Musidorus in the *Old Arcadia* and Amphialus in the *New* with a pretext for abducting the inheritrices of the Arcadian kingdom.[53]

The princes and princesses therefore find themselves forced by Basilius' perversity to conduct their courtships as if they were illicit, secret affairs, and to transform what might have been wholly legitimate, arranged alliances into illegitimate subterfuge and provisionality. Pamela's response to Musidorus' 'tale of me', for example, reveals the extent to which she feels pressurized by the ambiguous legitimacy/illegitimacy of their relationship: 'in the end she said, that *if* she had been the princess whom that disguised prince had virtuously loved, she *would have* requited his faith with faithful affection' (90 308, my italics). As Touchstone remarks, 'your If is the only peacemaker', and here Pamela and Musidorus conduct a kind of 'subjunctive' courtship in which obfuscation and obscurity are the only means of making sense of their problem.[54]

So the courtships of the *Arcadia* are not only teasingly ambivalent because they occur outside the legitimate bounds of marriage, or because they position men and women in a unique relation to each other and allow us to explore a delicate area of human sexuality. The courtships of the *Arcadia* are doubly ambivalent because they are both illegitimate (secret, illicit, sexual) and legitimate (eligible, dynastic). Adding another dimension to the social, rhetorical, and sexual ambivalence of Lyly's courtships in *Euphues* and *Euphues and his England*, therefore, Sidney addresses his text to one of the most sensitive political issues of his day: royal succession, and the legitimacy or illegitimacy of royal courtship.

Such an essentially political context for the courtships of the *Arcadia* thus gives Sidney's text an edge over Lyly's. While, like Lyly, Sidney explores the ambivalence of the courtship-situation by examining the dubious area that exists between a declaration of love and its formal legitimization by marriage, and, by focusing on the temporary 'lawlessness' that we have already seen to be one of the most compelling features of courtship fiction, he loads the issue of legitimization by making the peaceful succession of a kingdom depend upon it. Philautus' courting of Camilla in *Euphues and his England* might have raised eyebrows because the two partners were not legally affianced, but it did not risk a kingdom or a succession. One of the things that preoccupies Sidney in the *Arcadia*, on the other hand, is the crucial point at which sexual desire is legitimized: is the fact that Philoclea and Pyrocles 'passed promise of marriage' between them, for example, enough to exonerate their pre-marital sex (*OA* 122, 90 233)? At what point is the incipient lawlessness of courtship made lawful if not by marriage? In the words of Walter Davis, 'once love has been pledged, what kind of relation, what kind of life, are the lovers to forge for themselves?'[55]

These are precisely the unanswerable questions which come to a head in the great arraignment scene in the final book of the *Old Arcadia*, and they are made all the more problematic by the often baffling ambivalence with which the narrator surrounds his descriptions of sex.

Sex is to the fore in the often outspoken world of the *Old Arcadia*,

and there is little doubt that the passions and jealousies which
Sidney depicts approximate more closely to Bembo's 'l'amor sensuale' than to his 'l'amor razionale'. Pyrocles (himself enticingly
disguised as the Amazon Cleophila) imagines for himself/herself
'how happy she should be if she could obtain her desires' (*OA* 39, not
in *90*), while Musidorus/Dorus acknowledges that his 'love is full of
desire' (*OA* 41, not in *90*). Philoclea falls prey to 'strange unwonted
motions in herself . . . a burning affection . . . an unquiet desire' (*OA*
97) which quickly escalates into 'a mountain of burning desire' (*OA*
109. Cleophila/Pyrocles suffers 'a daily increase of her violent
desires' (*OA* 113), while the tormented Gynecia becomes a victim of
her own 'deadly desires' (*OA* 123).

This melting-pot of passions predictably gives rise to physical
displays of love. There is much kissing and touching in the *Old
Arcadia*, and the 'courtly courtesies' between the princes and princesses frequently transgress the bounds of unimpeachable decency
and honesty, as Ascham had warned that they would. As Dorus and
Cleophila, the princes kiss and fondle the princesses at a much earlier
stage in their courtships than they do in the more slowly paced *New
Arcadia*. As early as the lion and bear episode in book I, for example,
Philoclea (apparently ingenuously) 'fell so right upon the breast of
Cleophila, sitting by her, that their faces at unawares closed
together' (*OA* 47). Pamela faints in the same episode, and Dorus
'took the advantage to kiss and re-kiss her a hundred times' (*OA* 52).
Basilius slaveringly touches Cleophila, 'still holding her by the hand
and sometimes tickling it' (*OA* 213), the hand being, for the
Elizabethans, a highly erogenous zone.[56]

The *Old Arcadia* foregrounds such erotic but still relatively harm-
less physical displays of affection in its capacity – as a 'palace of
pleasure' – to entertain its readers with the sexually risqué. But at
certain sexually critical moments, Sidney's narrator (described by
one critic as the 'primary agent of our disequilibrium') suddenly and
inexplicably resigns his role as a teller of salacious tales and, instead,
backs off under a veil of masterly evasion.[57]

The two most celebrated occasions where this occurs are in the
description of Musidorus' rape attempt and in the consummation
scene between Pyrocles and Philoclea. In his account of the first,
Sidney's narrator appears incapable of describing the mutually
recognized love between Musidorus and Pamela except in terms of
oxymoron. He exploits the paradoxes of Petrarchan wooing in order

to account for Musidorus' 'burdenous bliss' (*OA* 173), and for the 'virtuous wantonness' in which he and Pamela engage (*OA* 200). Having eloped with her lover, Pamela falls asleep with her head in his lap. Overcome by the sexual temptation offered by her defence-lessness, Musidorus is on the point of raping her when he is forestalled by the untimely clowns. But instead of posing as either a morally outraged spectator (as we know he was capable of doing), or as an indulgent, Boccaccian story-teller (ditto), Sidney's narrator here shifts teasingly from one role to the other, one moment figuring Musidorus' interruption as a 'just punishment' for his sinfulness, and the next as an 'infortunate bar' which any lover would bitterly resent (*OA* 202). Musidorus himself (in this a prefiguration of the constantly vacillating Amphialus) is equally torn between self-loathing and sexual passion: 'enraged betwixt a repentant shame of his promise-breaking attempt and the tyrannical fire of lust' (*OA* 306). In such a state, Musidorus exemplifies the typically divided Arcadian mind, and rehearses our own divided response to his attempted rape.

Even greater ambivalence surrounds the sexual scene between Pyrocles and Philoclea, and the narrator's account of how Dametas discovers the sleeping lovers might be held up as a masterpiece of evasiveness and equivocation:

by the light of the lamp he [Dametas] might discern one abed with her, which he, although he took to be Pamela, yet thinking no surety enough in a matter touching his neck, he went hard to the bedside of these unfortunate lovers, who at that time, being not much before the break of day – whether it were they were so divinely surprised to bring their fault to so open punishment; or that the too high degree of their joys had overthrown the wakeful use of their senses; or that their souls, lifted up with extremity of love after mutual satisfaction, had left their bodies dearly joined to unite themselves together so much more freely as they were freer of that earthly prison; or whatsoever other cause may be imagined of it – but so it was that they were as then possessed with a mutual sleep, yet not forgetting with viny embracements to give any eye a perfect model of affection. (*OA* 272–3)

The sheer length of the sentence (197 words in all), the wealth of subordinate clauses ('which ... although ... yet ... who ... whether ... or ...'), the cluster of qualifying adverbial phrases ('by the light of the lamp ... at that time'), and the conditional tense ('might discern ... may be imagined'), not to mention the notorious unreliability of Dametas himself, all combine to create the supreme suggestiveness of the passage. We have seen how both Lyly and the devisers of court pageants frequently employed a rhetoric of antithesis and antimetabole in order to obfuscate the nature of courtship. In *The Lady of May*, Sidney himself had used the non-committal structures of euphuistic syntax and the debate-form in order to enact and to exploit the full ambiguity of the courtship-situation and to give Elizabeth no indication at all of his own leanings. In this passage from the *Old Arcadia* he goes even further, delightedly leading his readers by the nose and forcing them to acknowledge that 'courtly courtesies' are no more than signals of inner intention – signals that, like any sign, remain wittily open to interpretation.

I dwell on these equivocal passages because it is from them that the central tension of the arraignment scene in book v derives. Pyrocles seduces Philoclea – his 'sweet subject' – and he exploits her 'confessing her late fault' (i.e. her harshness to him) in order to 'make her now the sooner yield to penance' (*OA* 242). There is more than an element of clichéd male wish-fulfilment in the account of how Philoclea's 'weak resistance . . . did strive to be overcome', and, while the militaristic imagery of this sexual scene is highly conventional, yet, in context, there is something sinister in Pyrocles' corruption of the princess, especially when it is contrasted with the marriage of Lalus and Kala which immediately follows (*OA* 243).

Pyrocles and Philoclea are found 'in act of marriage without solemnity of marriage' (*OA* 290) and are therefore subject to the Arcadian law which dictates that such sexual indulgence be punished by death. But the crucial issue of the legitimacy or illegitimacy of their action – the main debate of the arraignment scene – is, as we have seen, dogged by conflicting layers of comment and critique. At one level, Pyrocles and Philoclea are entirely justified in what they do. As royal heirs, the young prince and princess are simply fulfilling their duty to secure the successions of Macedon and Arcadia, and their sexual consummation has been legitimized already by their private 'promise of marriage' (*OA* 122). Private betrothal of this kind, followed by sexual consummation, was still considered legally binding in Sidney's day, and was certainly a convention of chivalric literature. In the case of Musidorus and Pamela, there is little doubt that the prince intends to marry Pamela for he abducts her 'under vehement oath to offer no force unto her till he had invested her in the duchy of Thessalia', that is, until she had become his wife (*OA* 172). Pamela justifies their elopement on the grounds that 'I have yielded to be your wife' (*OA* 197), and she later insists that 'married I am', and that Musidorus is 'my husband by me worthily chosen' (*OA* 319, 397).

But Sidney does not leave it there. He problematizes the sexual intimacy of the princes and princesses with a whole series of moral questions which stubbornly refuse to go away. Pyrocles and Philoclea, for example (especially the latter), seem surprisingly uncertain about the legitimate or illegitimate status of their sexual intercourse. Philoclea speaks of 'our virtuous marriage, whereto our innocencies were the solemnities' (*OA* 304) and she later contends that she 'never deserved evil' or chastisement (*OA* 369). And yet her judge, Euarchus, considers that she is 'not altogether faultless' (*OA* 380) and consigns her to a vestal's life of perpetual chastity in punishment for her sin. Does this indicate that she really did stain her honour, and that her appeal to innocence merely serves to expose an even more culpable moral failure (i.e. the inability to recognize sex as sin)?

On the other hand, Pyrocles and Philoclea both seem only too aware of their compromised position because they both lie about what actually happened, speaking, when challenged, of an *attempt* rather than a successful consummation. This suggests that they know all too well that they have transgressed deeply entrenched injunctions against the violation of chastity. When Pyrocles is accused in the arraignment scene, he compounds his guilt by lying, and by denying at first that he and Philoclea had consummated their love: 'whatsoever hath been done hath been my violence, which notwithstanding could not prevail against her chastity' (*OA* 380). What sense does 'chastity' have here when we know that Philoclea yielded to him? And if Pyrocles means to refer to her 'married' chastity, we are thrown back on the thorny issue of whether the two were legally married or not.

Pyrocles appeals to Euarchus to give credence to his story on the grounds that, were he to tell a falsehood, he would naturally do so in order to save his own skin: 'if I would lie, I would lie for mine own behoof' (*OA* 380). But it could be argued that Pyrocles' unconscious and quite inappropriate pun ('lie') adds insult to injury, and that Sidney is thoroughly enjoying his protagonist's discomfiture.

Besides, even when Euarchus pronounces judgement, we remain uncertain about exactly what Pyrocles is being punished for. In the final analysis, he is punished neither for raping Philoclea, nor for lying about the truth or falsity of the rape, but simply for having

attempted it and for having been found in compromising circumstances (the euphemism 'offered violence to the lady Philoclea' (*OA*
405) evades the issue of actual rape). In the end, of course, neither
Pyrocles nor Philoclea, Musidorus nor Pamela, are punished at all,
and their formal marriages in the last pages of the *Old Arcadia* finally
secure the dynastic matches that they had been engineering, legitimately or otherwise, all along.

Transforming the relatively straightforward trial scene in Heliodorus' *Aethiopian History*, Sidney massively complicates the issues of
crime and punishment, justice and injustice, individual sexuality
and its constraint by law.[58] And he offers us at least three alternative
and mutually conflictual readings of the arraignment scene. For, at
one level, we are invited to wink at the faults of the princes and
princesses, to follow the narrator's 'courtly' indulgence, and to
consider sex as no more than the light-hearted stuff of comedy. At a
second level, we are invited to condemn the princes and princesses,
and to take the polemic line of Philanax and Euarchus (and, no
doubt, of Roger Ascham if he had been alive), which refused to
compromise on an issue so politically and socially sensitive. At a
third level, Kerxenus' solution of making the best of a bad situation
and patching up what had happened by sanctioning the dynastic
marriages between the parties takes a middle road between the
'comic' irresponsibility of the first reading, and the 'tragic', unswerv-
ing cruelty of the second. It is Kerxenus' solution, of course, that
finally wins the day.

Sidney's treatment of sex in the *Old Arcadia* therefore exploits the
ambiguities and ambivalences of the courtship-situation to the full.
By departing from Heliodorus in making sex the central issue of the
trial scene, Sidney confirms the impossibility of successfully interpreting and judging what can only ever be external signs of inner
intention – 'courtly courtesies'. Instead, he offers us a series of
differing responses destined to leave us, like Philanax, in 'a strange
medley betwixt pity and revenge, betwixt liking and abhorring' (*OA*
301), or, like Lyly's *Euphues*, in a 'muse' rather than a 'maze' (*E* 245).
In mischievously complicating an otherwise simple correlation
between crime and punishment, Sidney's narrator succeeds in
reminding us only of the ultimate uncertainty of our 'mortal
judgements' (*OA* 416).

The central ambivalence of courtship allowed writers, as we have
seen, to explore the relation of individual sexuality to law, of

amorous courting to marriage, of men to women, and, above all, of Elizabethan courtiers to their Queen. In the *Arcadia*, Sidney excels himself in projecting the central ambiguity of 'courtly courtesies' by making paradox, oxymoron, qualification, and equivocation accrue so radically around two critical sexual junctures: the attempted rape of Pamela, and the seduction of Philoclea. He thus extends that delicate and critical stage between a declaration of love and its formal legitimization by marriage in order, perhaps, to subsume under the courtships of his princes and princesses – so nearly cata-strophic and yet finally rewarded, so nearly illegitimate and yet sanctioned in the end – his own relation with that unpredictable and difficult person (both princess and judge), Queen Elizabeth.[59]

Between 1582 and 1584, Sidney substantially revised books I and II of the *Old Arcadia*, and wholly rewrote book III. The result was the text which William Ponsonby published in quarto in 1590. In 1593, a folio was published under the aegis of Sidney's sister, the Countess of Pembroke, in which books III–V of the *Old Arcadia* were tacked on to the end of the 1590 text, while a series of editorial interpolations were made to bring the *Old Arcadia* narrative into line with the nomencla-ture and narrative developments of the *New*. The two scenes which underwent the most substantial revision were precisely those pas-sages which, in the *Old Arcadia*, bristle with sexual innuendo, equivocation, and erotic suggestion – Musidorus' attempted rape of Pamela, and Pyrocles' seduction of Philoclea.

In the Preface to the 1593 *Arcadia*, Hugh Sanford declares that the Countess of Pembroke had personally supervised the editing of her brother's text, and that she had 'begun in correcting the faults, [and] ended in supplying the defects'.[60] Sanford's words led R. W. Zandvoort to suggest that the Countess of Pembroke had herself suppressed the two blatantly erotic scenes from Sidney's narrative, thus bowdlerizing her brother's original text.[61] More recent editorial opinion, on the other hand, argues that the major revisions to the *Old Arcadia* (which first appeared in print in the final books of the 1593 *Arcadia*) were Sidney's own.[62] There is no hard evidence on either side, and, given the immensely complex transition of the *Arcadia* from a manuscript culture and circulation to a public and printed one, it remains impossible to speculate on what Sidney 'intended'. But it is certainly true that the effect of the 1593 revisions is substantially to alter interpretations of the Arcadian courtships.

Just as Lyly's earliest readers had responded variously to the
sexual ambiguities of his fictions – Lodge and Greene silently 'legitimizing' them, Barnaby Rich indulging them – so the sexuality
presented in Sidney's *Arcadia* evoked alternative responses. In the
New Arcadia, as we shall see later on, Sidney took the ambivalence
and ambiguities of his courtships even further, and, by slowing down
the pace of the princes' sexual encounters, he transformed the *Old
Arcadia* text into one of the most sexually heightened accounts of
courtship in Renaissance romance. In this, Sidney was adopting and
magnifying the role of the indulgent, 'courtly' narrator, the entertainer of ladies and teller of 'trifles'. Books III–V of the 1593 *Arcadia*,
on the other hand, pull in the opposite direction, suppressing the
most egregious indications of illicit sexual behaviour, and silently
assimilating them into a legitimate, 'marital' matrix.

In the 1593 *Arcadia*, the sexual scenes are revised and quite
radically altered. Musidorus' attempted rape of Pamela, for example, is simply omitted in the 1593 version, and his mental agony –
'enraged betwixt a repentant shame of his promise-breaking attempt
and the tyrannical fire of lust' (*OA* 306) – is utterly transformed into
the innocuous and innocent anger he feels at the unruly entry of the
clowns: 'enraged betwixt the doubt he had what these men would go
about and the spite he conceived against their ill-pleasing presence'
(*93* 753). In the same way, Pyrocles' seducing of Philoclea – the crux
of the *Old Arcadia* narrative, as we have seen – is subject to a whole
series of minor editorial changes which cumulate to transform their
scene of sexual passion into a quite different one of 'chaste embracements' (*93* 690).

So whereas the *Old Arcadia* text describes the excited Pyrocles
entering Philoclea's bedroom 'rapt from himself with the excessive
forefeeling of his near coming contentment' (*OA* 228), the later text
deflatingly adds 'as he assured himself' (*93* 680). The 1593 reading
makes a subtle but radical change in order to account for Pyrocles'
anticipated pleasure:

for so far were his thoughts passed through all perils that already he
conceived himself safely arrived with his lady at the stately palace of Pella,
among the exceeding joys of his father and infinite congratulations of his
friends, giving order for the royal entertaining of Philoclea and for
sumptuous shows and triumphs against their marriage. (*93* 680–1)

Whether the 'palace of Pella' is an authorial or an editorial
interpolation, it provides a wholly new interpretation of Pyrocles'

intention, and, in effect, does to the *Old Arcadia* text what Lodge and Greene had attempted to do to Lyly: i.e. it silently assimilates dubious sexual encounters into an incontestably legitimized, married framework.[63]

In the same way, while the Pyrocles of the *Old Arcadia* is so dazed by the sight of Philoclea that he is in danger of forgetting to enjoy the 'great fruit of his love' (*OA* 231), in the 1593 text he forgets, rather, 'the enterprise undertaken for his love' (*93* 683), their planned elopement and future marriage. In the *Old Arcadia*, Pyrocles looks forward to 'perfecting the mutual love' between them (*OA* 234), but in the 1593 version, he simply informs Philoclea of his plans for their 'departure' (*93* 686). From this point the two texts diverge widely. In the *Old Arcadia*, Pyrocles recovers from his faint, carries Philoclea to the bed, and makes love to her. In the 1593 *Arcadia*, he faints, revives, carries her to her bed, and then engages her in conversation. And their discourse is not the eroticized 'luf-talkyng' of *Sir Gawain and the Green Knight*, but plans and decisions about their imminent get-away.

The effect of the 1593 emendations is to smooth out the very sexual ambiguities around which the *Old Arcadia* had so teasingly and importantly centred. And the pastoral marriage between Lalus and Kala, which follows archly and ironically on from the sexual indulgence of Sidney's lovers, becomes, in the 1593 text, quite different. For, in the *Old Arcadia*, the shepherds' wedding represents the outcome of a patient, normative courtship, and patently contrasts with the desires of the aristocrats, who were 'otherwise occupied', as Sidney suggestively writes (*OA* 245). But if Pyrocles and Philoclea have simply engaged in innocent conversation and sleep (as in the 1593 version) then the marriage of Lalus and Kala becomes a reflection and simulacrum of their aristocratic honour, and not a pointed contrast to it.

The overall effect of the 1593 alterations to books III–V of the *Old Arcadia* is therefore to iron out the passages of ambivalence, innuendo, and equivocation, and generally to sanitize the earlier version. When Dametas discovers Pyrocles and Philoclea the next morning, for example, he does not find the prince 'abed with her' (*OA* 272) but only (far more innocently) 'on the bed by her' (*93* 722). When Pyrocles realizes that the Arcadian laws punish those 'found in act of marriage without solemnity of marriage' (*OA* 290), the 1593 reading discreetly adds, 'as Dametas reported of them'

(*93* 737); while Philoclea's anguished cry to her lover – 'will you leave me . . . not only dishonoured as unchaste with you' (*OA* 299) – becomes 'not only dishonoured, as supposed unchaste with you' (*93* 746).

So one result of the 1593 emendations is to smooth out the oxymoron, paradox, and sexual ambivalence that had characterized the *Old Arcadia*. The discrepancy between the princes' aristocratic code of honour and their actual sexual practice in the *Old Arcadia* thus gives way, in the 1593 text, to a portrait of unstained virtue that is (on the surface) more consistent with the higher, heroic strain of the *New Arcadia*.

One major consequence of the 1593 interpolations is the effect they have on the culminating episode of the *Old Arcadia*: the trial scene. For, as we have seen, in the *Old Arcadia* Sidney had foregrounded the sexual ambivalence of the princes' amorous court-ing in order to demonstrate the teasing uncertainty of their situation, which is equally legitimate and illegitimate. When, in the *Old Arcadia*, Pyrocles claims not to have seduced Philoclea, he further complicates what is already a critical issue by demonstrating how difficult it is to judge inner intention on the evidence of mere externalities. But what is a fiction in the *Old Arcadia* – that Pyrocles did not rape Philoclea – is, of course, fact in the 1593 *Arcadia*. In the *Old Arcadia*, Pyrocles pretends that Philoclea repulsed him with her 'inviolate chastity', and that he 'could not prevail against her chastity' (*OA* 380). But in the 1593 version there is no need for him to pretend or lie because that is exactly what happened: when he defends himself by saying that he 'never intended against her chastity' (*93* 811), he is telling the truth.

So while, in the *Old Arcadia*, the questions of legitimacy or illegitimacy, sex or sin, innocence or guilt, are impossibly confused and tangled, in the 1593 *Arcadia*, Pyrocles does not violate Philoclea, is wrongly accused, and, is therefore, in the end, justly saved. In other words, courtship in the *Old Arcadia* is fraught, hazardous, and beset by moral, social, and narrative problems. But, in the 1593 *Arcadia*, the courtships of the princes and princesses are wholly honourable, just, and legitimate. Admittedly at the expense of much of the tension, irony, and satire of the *Old Arcadia*, the 1593 text exonerates Pyrocles, and re-establishes the correlation between crime and punishment, between law and transgression.

What is so odd, however, is that books I and II of the *New Arcadia*

(1590) pull in the opposite direction from the general sanitizing of the 1593 text. While the 1593 ending assimilates and absorbs the *Arcadia* narrative into a more moralistic framework, legitimizing the otherwise dubious and uncertain courtships of Sidney's protagonists, books I and II expand and explore issues of sexual depravity and political anarchy with an incisiveness and scepticism that is normally associated with Jacobean tragedy. Indeed, books I and II go beyond the already chaotic scenes of the *Old Arcadia* in that they radically destabilize the ubiquitous 'Arcadian laws' which, in the earlier narrative, had formed a stable juridical backdrop against which the sexual liberties of the princes and princesses could (however harshly) be judged. In the *New Arcadia*, on the other hand, the relation between law and precedent is far more problematic, for the text abounds with figures who constantly reinterpret laws and invent new ones, simply in order to accommodate their incestuous or perverted desires. The blind king of Paphlagonia, for example, privileges his concubine over his lawful wife and thus bastardizes his legitimate heir (*90* 181); Pamphilus marries one woman when he is still formally betrothed to another (*90* 260); Basilius thinks to 'legitimize' his hoped-for adultery with Zelmane on the pretext that he will marry her in the future (*90* 296–7); Antiphilus makes 'an unlawful law of having more wives than one', while his legitimate wife, the wretched Erona, is reduced to suing to Artaxia on his behalf, 'content for the public good to be a second wife' (*90* 299–300).[64] As a result, the *New Arcadia* focuses far more insistently and cynically than the *Old* on the most important and public mechanism for regulating sexual behaviour: marriage.

As Jon Lawry notes, while in the *Old Arcadia* 'marriage and other reintegrative unions had resolved the work ... In the *New*, marriage within a vastly enlarged idea and implication, is placed "in the beginning".'[65] For the *New Arcadia* opens with Strephon and Klaius mourning the departure of the quasi-divine Urania – the Muse of heavenly love, but also (in Catullus) the mother of the marriage-god, Hymen.[66] The pointed absence of any benign deity to bless and legitimize human marriage suggests that the perverted and evil relationship between Antiphilus and Artaxia – in which 'Hymen had not there his saffron-coloured coat' (*90* 301) – becomes the norm for the fallen and depraved world of human sexuality which Sidney portrays in his text. In place of Urania or Hymen, we have, instead, the witchlike Cecropia, whose name alludes ironically to Cecrops, the legendary king of Athens, and founder of the institution of monogamy. Cecropia's own marriage to Basilius' brother was evidently a dynastic match designed to continue the patrilinear line in the light of Basilius' 'bachelorly intention' (*90* 317). But, her plans for Amphialus thwarted by Basilius' late marriage to Gynecia and production of heirs, Cecropia becomes an icon of perverted dynastic ambition, and never more so than when she encourages her son to take Philoclea by force, urging him with examples of legendary heroes who had been born of rape.

Sidney's use of marriage-imagery in the *New Arcadia* betokens a deep cynicism which is fully justified in the case of Cecropia's wicked intentions. The imprisoned and tortured Pamela, for example, continues, against all odds, to take care of her appearance, 'as if it had been her marriage time to affliction, she rather seemed to remember her own worthiness than the unworthiness of her husband' (*90* 355); and Cecropia's mock execution of the princess 'divorces the fair marriage of the head and body' (*90* 426). Traumatized by the feigned death of Philoclea, Pyrocles cries out at a similar separation: 'O cruel divorce of the sweetest marriage that ever was in nature! Philoclea is dead!' (*90* 433).

Marriage is normatively the outcome of courtship – the public recognition and social sanction of a sexual relationship. Marriage also gives an indication that a courtship has reached fruition, and that the strategies of persuasion and manipulation have succeeded in winning over the object of desire, as Lalus succeeds in winning over his beloved Kala in the *Old Arcadia* (he significantly fails to do so in the *New Arcadia*). Where marriage is denied, or fraught with difficulty, then the strategies of persuasion may be deemed to have failed, and the courtship to have culminated in nothing but loss and humiliation. A number of scholars have recently argued that, in the inconclusive ending of *Astrophil and Stella*, Sidney figures the public and notorious failure of his 'courtship' as a courtier of Queen Elizabeth.[67] Without making any crude allegorical equivalence, I suggest that Sidney's portraits of marriage in the *New Arcadia* betoken a similar attempt to come to terms with the frustrations, hopes, and disappointments of his political 'courtship' with the Queen.

As the first courtship in the *New Arcadia*, the story of Argalus and Parthenia sets a tone for the rest of the book, and for the portraits of marriage that follow. For, although Argalus and Parthenia are later held up as models of matrimonial contentment, their initial conflict against parental injunction has dire and irremediable consequences. Argalus first sees Parthenia only shortly before her arranged marriage to Demagoras, but 'before her word could tie her to a Demagoras, her heart hath vowed her to Argalus' (*90* 28).[68] Typifying romance convention, the love between Argalus and Parthenia flourishes in a context of prohibition and secrecy. And yet their passion gives rise to serious civil war and deadly internecine strife. For the marriages of Argalus and Clitophon are both deferred (in the latter's case indefinitely) by the civil war against Demagoras which Parthenia's change of heart occasions. And the catastrophic social disintegration, which is both created and epitomized by this civil war, is figured in the strongest possible terms in the combats between father and son (Kalender and Clitophon), and cousin against cousin or friend against friend (Pyrocles and Musidorus).

In other words, Argalus and Parthenia's love upsets the decorum of an unpleasant but none the less legitimate dynastic match (Parthenia and Demagoras) with nearly disastrous consequences. And although Sidney appears to load the scales against Demagoras by burlesquing him and by making Argalus and Parthenia icons of nuptial harmony, he does not let us forget that the price for their happy marriage has been a high one. Indeed, their love approximates to that 'passionate love' which Robert Burton was to describe in *The Anatomy of Melancholy*: 'It subverts kingdoms, overthrows cities, towns, families; mars, corrupts, and makes a massacre of men; thunder and lightning, wars, fires, plagues, have not done that mischief to mankind, as this burning lust, this brutish passion.'[69]

Without denying the virtue of their mutual love, or the emblematic nature of its presentation, it is important not to bracket Argalus and Parthenia off as 'ideals of marriage' while forgetting the trouble they have in getting married, and, indeed, in remaining so.[70]

Argalus and Parthenia embody the ideals of conjugal happiness and companionship most movingly when they are found together – 'he reading in a book the stories of Hercules, she by him as to hear him read ... a happy couple, he joying in her, she joying in herself (but in herself because she enjoyed him); both increasing their riches by giving to each other' (*90* 371–2). Yet (for all Tasso's words that 'love and friendship are subjects entirely suitable for the heroic poem'), the mixture of epic and romance which appears to be so happily combined in the married couple's reading matter in effect proves both sinister and dangerous.⁷¹ For it is at precisely this moment of domestic stasis and stillness that the epic erupts unexpectedly into the romance as Basilius' messenger enters to summon Argalus – fatally, as it turns out – to war.

The epic thus brutalizes and destroys the fragile peacefulness that existed between Argalus and Parthenia, and, indeed, becomes an ironic version of their married bliss. For when the departing Argalus kisses his wife, she faints and does not revive before he has gone. The frustrated kiss emblematizes the inconclusiveness and tragic foreshortening of their marriage, just as Argalus' wrestling with Amphialus – their 'unlovely embracements' – become a horrible parody of the marriage-bed (*90* 376). Argalus' love for Parthenia comes to a poignant close when, wounded and dying, he kisses her for the last time: 'his last breath was delivered into her mouth' (*90* 378).

The marriage between Argalus and Parthenia, therefore, is only made possible by violent war and bloodshed, and it is precisely such violence which brings the marriage to a fruitless and untimely end. For, like her husband (and like the *New Arcadia* itself, of course) Parthenia also dies in mid-sentence, her broken words a symbol of a broken marriage which does not even have any hopeful offspring to continue the family line or to testify to the parents' great love. If their marriage represents the outcome of a 'successful' courtship, then the subsequent history of Argalus and Parthenia hardly bodes well for the courtier who hoped to succeed in courting Elizabeth, suggesting that Sidney figured in the two lovers his own resignation and despair at ever getting Elizabeth to heed him.

The relationship between Plangus and Erona, another courtship that is central to the *New Arcadia*, takes us beyond Argalus and Parthenia as a monument to emotional failure, and to the social and political disaster that follows inexorably on from misalliance. Erona's name suggests that she is 'possessed by eros', but also (from Latin *errare*) that she has gone astray. Plangus – first found in 'most wailful lamentation' (*OA* 67) – becomes an emblem of the complaint-form, but also (from Greek *planus*), perhaps, as much of a 'wanderer' as his erring mistress. For both he and Erona are sexual aberrants and emotional misfits. Plangus begins as the lover of the 'man-crazy' Andromana in what is a purely sexual relationship: 'so possessed he his desire without any interruption' (*90* 216). As for Erona, she refuses an arranged and dynastic match in order to indulge a disastrous passion for the aptly named Antiphilus: a character who, soon tiring of Erona, institutes a law of polygamy to enable him to marry Artaxia.

As a tale of emotional disaster, frustrated desire, and political catastrophe, the Plangus–Erona narrative also serves as an ironic commentary on the chaotic desires of the duke, duchess, princes, and princesses of Arcadia. In the *Old Arcadia*, the Plangus and Erona story had comprised a short, self-contained narrative, a cautionary tale illustrating the emblem of Anteros – 'A horned head, cloven foot, and thousand eyes' (*OA* 65) – in Dicus' poem. But in the *New Arcadia*, the story proliferates and splinters into a series of strung-out episodic tales which are narrated 'by pieces' by Basilius and his daughters (*90* 306).[72] The fragmented narration of the story in the *New Arcadia* figures the social and political disintegration that is so enmeshed in the tale itself, and also, of course, the deferrals, interruptions, and disruptions that are created by the passions and jealousies of Basilius, Gynecia, and the others. For Philoclea begins to narrate the story in her bower (the traditional locale for courtly *ragionamenti*) but is interrupted when Basilius declares to Pyrocles/ Zelmane that he intends to 'enjoy' her (*90* 226). Basilius' interruption of the story not only disrupts Philoclea and Pyrocles' courting: it also reflects the social and political disintegration which his own immoral (and unwittingly homosexual) passion threatens to bring about. And when Basilius later takes over the task of continuing the Plangus–Erona story, he unashamedly treats the narrative as a blanket for and an illustration of his own desires, and concludes by asking Zelmane to consider 'the strange power of love' and therefore 'to do the more right to the unfortunate historian', that is, himself (*90* 307).

In the *New Arcadia*, broken speech is almost invariably a symptom of frustrated desire. Pyrocles' words are 'interrupted continually with sighs which served as a burthen to each sentence, and the tenor of his speech (though of his wonted phrase) not knit together to one constant end' (*90* 51–2). Philoclea guesses correctly that her sister is in love when she remarks that 'the constantness of your wit was not wont to bring forth such disjointed speeches. You love!' (*90* 151), while Musidorus complains of his love-writing that 'never words more slowly married together' (*90* 310).

This kind of rhetorical fragmentariness is epitomized in Amphialus, the man so torn by love as to be virtually incapable of completing his sentences: 'somewhat before half the sentence were ended . . . he would break it off, and a pretty while after end it' (*90* 328). He would 'exercise his eloquence when she could not hear him', but in the presence of his beloved Philoclea he would be 'dumb-stricken' (*90* 239). The song which he delivers to Philoclea recounting his first falling in love with her is the same poem that is performed, in the *Old Arcadia*, by that melancholy icon of failed courtship, Philisides, hinting, perhaps, that Amphialus himself is similarly doomed to fail. As it is, Philoclea gives ear only to 'some pieces' of his already fragmentary utterances (*90* 333), creating an equivalence between Amphialus' love-speeches with the Plangus–Erona story that had, as Basilius said, been told 'by pieces' (*90* 306).

Amphialus' rhetorical frustration exemplifies the thwarted court-ships of the *Arcadia*, for, as we have seen, 'courting' took its definition from those rhetorical procedures – *questioni d'amore, ragionamenti*, the 'bolder talking of this and that' – that were practised at court. When those rhetorical practices are cut short, then amorous courting is necessarily curtailed and the Elizabethan courtier finds himself silenced, as Sidney had written in a different context: 'my only service is speech and that is stopped'.[73] When, on the other hand, lovers do succeed in speaking to each other, their linguistic facility mirrors, conceals, and substitutes for their sexual desire.

When Pyrocles uses the ruse of story-telling in order to inform Philoclea of his real identity and to declare his love for her, for example, it is only a matter of minutes before they had 'passed promise of marriage' between them (*90* 233). Continuing his delighted narrative, Pyrocles constantly interrupts his story-telling by attempting to kiss Philoclea, his 'narrating' tongue threatening to convert to a 'kissing' tongue at any moment. Indeed, kissing itself becomes an alternative kind of story, 'another discourse' (*90* 258). Pyrocles would willingly delay his story-telling in order to use his tongue to more enjoyable effect, and hints to Philoclea that they are wasting valuable time: 'So you think I can think so precious leisure as this well spent in talking?' (*90* 276). Pamela, meanwhile, engages Musidorus with the same delicate interplay of conversation and innuendo by 'entertaining his discourses' (*90* 308).

In Bembo's defence of love at the end of *The Book of the Courtier*, the kiss between two acknowledged lovers represents the apotheosis of chaste desire for the very reason that the mouth is the channel for words as well as kisses: 'for this doe all chaste lovers covet a kisse, as a coupling of soules together'.[74] It is such a kiss – 'and but a kiss' –

which Philoclea allows Pyrocles (*90* 439). As I have already suggested, however, it is dangerously difficult to differentiate between a kiss bestowed in such 'platonic' innocence, and an ordinary, sexual kiss. As a gesture, an external symbol of inner intention, the kiss itself remains tantalizingly open to interpretation.

In the *Arcadia*, Sidney exploits to the full the 'hidden agenda' of kissing. Both Philoclea and Pamela, for example, are described as paradigms of the sacrosanct aristocratic, virgin, 'classic' body (in Bakhtin's sense), the orifices of which are firmly closed and discreetly hidden.[75] When Pamela falls asleep with her head in Musidorus' lap, the prince apostrophizes her enclosed body – 'Lock up, fair lids, the treasures of my heart' (*OA* 200) – and gazes on 'the roses of her lips', now closed, but 'whose separating was wont to be accompanied with most wise speeches'. Pamela's closed lips 'drew his sight to mark how prettily they lay one over the other, uniting their divided beauties, and through them the eye of his fancy delivered to his memory the lying (as in ambush) under her lips of those armed ranks, all armed in most pure white, and keeping the most precise order of military discipline' (*OA* 201). Musidorus' blason alludes to the commonplace image of the locked mouth, its teeth like armed guards, and alerts us to Pamela's perilous defencelessness against his own attempted sexual 'ambush'. In an identical image, Philoclea is likewise praised for exemplifying the decorously closed orifices of the virgin body:

> But who those ruddy lips can miss,
> Which blessed still themselves do kiss?
> Rubies, cherries, and roses new,
> In worth, in taste, in perfect hue,
> Which never part but that they show
> Of precious pearl the double row,
> The second sweetly-fenced ward
> Her heav'nly-dewed tongue to guard,
> Whence never word in vain did flow.   (*OA* 239; *90* 192)

For George Puttenham, Sidney is here drawing a resemblance between Philoclea's mouth and 'some naturall thing of excellent perfection', and the image of the princesses' locked tongues is related not only to their discretion but also to their truthfulness.[76] Philoclea first rejects Pyrocles' 'falsified tongue' (*OA* 205), for example, and, in the *New Arcadia*, retains the 'true simplicity of my word' (*90* 232). Pamela similarly rejects wanton conversation and never utters more than 'chaste plainness' (*90* 308).

As versions of the 'classic' body – virgin, impenetrable, enclosed, sacrosanct – Pamela and Philoclea are simulacra of that most public of virgin bodies: Elizabeth I.[77] The princesses take care to circumscribe their tongues, those organs of 'courtly courtesies', speaking and kissing. But the princes respond by celebrating the sexual function of those tongues, most notably in that 'highly titillating lyric' 'What tongue can her perfections tell'.[78] In the *Old Arcadia*, the poem coincides with the consummation of Pyrocles and Philoclea's love, and distracts our attention from the sexual scene with a highly eroticized blason. In the *New Arcadia*, the blason is performed at the bathing scene, long before Philoclea's 'promise of marriage' to Pyrocles, but, as a surrogate for Pyrocles' desperate and as yet unfulfilled sexual desire, it is equally if not more erotic.

The opening lines of the poem – 'What tongue can her perfections tell / In whose each part all pens may dwell' (*90* 190) – create an obscene correspondence between Pyrocles' tongue and his pen (that archetypal phallic image), both of which desire metaphorically to be inserted into Philoclea's 'each part'. The poem's use of the pathetic fallacy hints at a connection between the 'upper streams' and 'nether' of the River Ladon and Philoclea's own naked body (*90* 189–90). And the very repetitiveness that exists within individual lines – 'smallest small', 'more white than whitest', 'back unto her back' (*90* 194) – creates a kind of rhetorical oscillatoriness which, like the 'see-saw' of Sterne's 'désobligeant' in *A Sentimental Journey*, mimics the sexual act itself.

The teasingly rhetorical movement back and forth, moreover, is also reflected in a witty interplay of allusion that exists within the poem. For, in Ovid's *Metamorphoses*, the River Ladon is the place where the fleeing Syrinx escapes Pan's clutches by being transformed into reeds. The reeds in turn become Pan's pipes, and his playing upon Syrinx's body thus becomes converted instead into pastoral poetry. So, in Sidney's poem, while Philoclea's tongue (like everything else) remains locked within her virgin body, as untouched as Syrinx, Pyrocles continues to play upon her body by performing, like Pan, a pastoral blason. The poem not only acts as a surrogate or alternative to sex, but Sidney's allusions to Ovid and back again also serve to compound the already obscene movement of the poem.[79]

In the 1590 *New Arcadia*, therefore, Sidney pushed the moral ambivalence of the *Old Arcadia* even further by heightening the eroticism of his 'amorous courtings' and by problematizing the already ambiguous relation between legitimacy and illegitimacy with his wealth of inset stories concerning incestuous, adulterous, and perverted desire. In the final two and a half books of the 1593 text, on the other hand, the potentially anarchic courtships of the *New Arcadia* are radically toned down, thus converting the desires of Pyrocles and Philoclea, Musidorus and Pamela into semi-legitimate relationships, which contrast sharply with the catastrophic courtships of Basilius, Gynecia, Plangus, Erona, Artaxia, Helen, Amphialus, Artesia, Phalanthus, and the rest.

So, like Lyly's fictions, Sidney's *Arcadia* as it was published in 1593 (and in all subsequent editions until this century) pulls in opposite directions. On the one hand we have a text (books I–III) in which courtships are largely corrupt, depraved, or perverse; in which even those courtships which conclude in happy marriage are subsequently wrecked; and in which the honourable loves of the princes and princesses are compromised by their sexual desires, making judgement of their actions virtually impossible. On the other hand, we have a text (books III–V) in which the princes' proper intentions are upheld; in which we know that Pyrocles and Musidorus are innocent of the sexual crimes of which they are accused; and in which the eventual alliances they make with the princesses are wholly legitimate, and not dogged by the uncertainty of exactly what went on between them before.

Was Sidney figuring in the ambivalent courtships of his narrative – some disastrous, some, eventually, successful – the highly complex position of the Elizabethan subject at court: one whose own personal relation with the monarch had publicly and notoriously failed? The textual uncertainty which surrounds the *New Arcadia* makes it impossible to say what Sidney 'intended', of course. But not one of the Arcadian courtships is simple or straightforward. And that, if nothing else, was equally true of Sidney's relation with the Queen.

It is fascinating to see how the two impulses – alternately, the heightening and the restraining of courtship's moral ambivalence – are equally evident in the later reception of Sidney's text. In 1725, for example, Mrs Stanley 'translated' the *Arcadia* for modern readers, her aim being (as she notes in the Preface) to make Sidney's text 'consistent with good Manners and Morality'.[80] At certain moments where Sidney's text is deliberately vague, therefore, Mrs Stanley elaborates and amplifies in order to remove any hint of doubt about the lovers' intentions. That key moment in the *Arcadia* when Pyrocles and Philoclea 'passed the promise of marriage', for example – the justification for their pre-nuptial love-making, and the source of so much of the ambiguity of the trial scene – becomes in Mrs Stanley's version something far more clearly stated: they 'pass'd a solemn Promise of marrying each other as soon as e'er they cou'd beguile the crafty Spies, who with more than Argus' Watchfulness attended them' (194).

Mrs Stanley is here bringing the *Arcadia* into line with 'good Manners and Morality', but there are other occasions when she veers in the opposite direction, allowing her lovers (at times) even greater sexual liberties than Sidney himself. At the beginning of book III, for example, Musidorus attempts to kiss Pamela, but she 'as if she had been ready to drink a wine of excellent taste and colour which suddenly she perceived had poison in it, so did she put him away from her' (*90* 309; *93* 436). In Mrs Stanley's version, however, 'the frighted Fair was so astonish'd at his presumptive Rashness, that for some Time, without Resistance, she permitted him to hold her' (262). Mrs Stanley thus modifies the uncompromising frigidity of Sidney's Pamela (who makes no allowances for the dangerous space between a declaration of love and its legitimate enjoyment) presenting her readers with a more titillating (and perhaps more realistic) version of the scene.

Mrs Stanley effects a similar change in her account of the attempted rape of Pamela after her abduction by Musidorus. In the *Old Arcadia* (which Mrs Stanley would not have read, of course), Musidorus' treacherous attempt on the sleeping Pamela is the result of his kissing her, so that 'now his promise began to have but a fainting force' (*OA* 201). The 1593 text, on the other hand, drops this scene of attempted rape altogether, so that what is interrupted by the noisy clowns is not Musidorus' treacherous attempt but his wholly innocent rapture on gazing at the face of the sleeping princess. Mrs Stanley, in turn, expands the coy silence of the 1593 text by infusing the scene with eroticism again, for she makes Musidorus kiss Pamela 'a thousand times'. Indeed, Mrs Stanley succeeds in both heightening and restraining the erotic elements of the episode when she congratulates Musidorus on his honesty. For although he kisses Pamela, he refrains from raping her and therefore displays the more admirable a restraint: 'so different ... from our modern Lovers, who even before Possession, if once they think themselves secure of Conquest, despise the Giver and contemn the Gift' (412-13). By holding Musidorus up (for all his kissing) as a model of sexual restraint, Mrs Stanley's winking aside none the less hints at what a contemporary lover would have done or would have attempted to do in the same circumstances, and therefore allows her readers the same titillating *frisson* that had existed in Sidney's original version of events.

In both heightening and curtailing the erotic ambivalence of courtship, therefore, Mrs Stanley's text mediates a seamless transition from Sidney's *Arcadia* to a tale which, although very different, clearly signals in its title a debt to Sidney's romance – that most famous courtship-narrative of all, Samuel Richardson's *Pamela* (1740).

CHAPTER 5

'Of Court it seemes, men Courtesie doe call': the Amoretti, Epithalamion, *and* The Faerie Queene, *book* VI

In *Euphues* and the *Arcadia* Lyly and Sidney had exploited the social, sexual, and political ambiguities of courtship, partly in order to portray the games of love between men and women, and partly as a response to (and a conscious or unconscious reflection of) their own self-positioning before a woman whom they had each had to court: Queen Elizabeth. And, as we have seen, both writers envisaged courtship as a complex nexus of relations – some successful and others thwarted – in ways that invite us to see traces of their own frustrations and desires.

The prose fictions of Lyly and Sidney pull in opposite directions as they attempt to combine the two conflicting impulses of an Elizabethan would-be courtier: crudely, the need to sue for favour, on the one hand, and the temptation to complain of neglect, on the other. The present chapter considers a similar opposition in two texts by Spenser which also take courtship as their underlying theme: the *Amoretti and Epithalamion* (1595), and book VI of *The Faerie Queene* (1596).

On 25 February 1591, a few months after the publication of the first part of *The Faerie Queene* in 1590, Spenser was awarded a royal pension of £50 per annum for life, a distinction which made him (Thomas Churchyard apart) the only poet to be rewarded by the Crown during Elizabeth's reign.[1] Spenser therefore had good reason to allude to the Queen's 'honour and large richesse', her 'rich bountie and deare cherishment'.[2] None the less, for all his tokens of gratitude, Spenser's contemporaries continued to lament the poet's poverty, and to complain (on his behalf) of what they evidently perceived to be a want of proper recognition and respect for him, and, by extension, for poetry itself.

In 1593, for example, George Peele singled Spenser out as the first of many contemporary poets to fall victim to 'Courts disdaine, the enemie to Arte', and he expresses the hope that Elizabeth (as 'Augusta') will mend the situation, and 'restore / The wrongs that learning beares of covetousnes'.[3] In May 1602, a few years after Spenser's death, John Manningham noted in his diary that,

When hir Majestie had given order that Spenser should have reward for his poems, but Spenser could have nothing, he presented hir with these verses:

> It pleased your Grace upon a tyme
> To graunt me reason for my ryme,
> But from that tyme untill this season
> I heard of neither ryme nor reason.[4]

While we cannot know if Spenser actually wrote these lines, they are certainly consistent with the feelings of frustration in being a hanger-on at court that he was frequently to touch on in his poems.[5] And, more importantly, they show that Spenser was thought by his contemporaries to have been badly done by. In the *Conversations with William Drummond*, Ben Jonson is reported as saying of Spenser that he died miserably 'for lake of bread', and that he refused a last-minute proffer of money from the Earl of Essex on the grounds that it had come too late.[6]

Jonson may be guilty of sensationalism here, and the account of Spenser's last-ditch stand has the same colourful overtones as a report of Jonson's own pained response to tardy royal favour.[7] And yet – while it would obviously be a mistake to take Spenser's words describing 'What hell it is ... To haue thy asking, yet waite manie yeeres' as evidence that Lord Burghley had in fact failed to pay the pension which the poet had been awarded – it was despairing comments such as this which fuelled speculation that Spenser's disenchantment with the patronage system did indeed derive from some sense of personal disappointment.[8]

In other words, we are left with an image of Spenser as a man who was indisputably honoured with a royal pension, and yet as one whose writing seemed to express pain at the crude evaluation of poetry which the patronage system inevitably entailed. Whether Spenser found himself in the curious position of having to thank Elizabeth for her token of esteem, while being piqued at its price, can only be a matter for surmise. But, as we shall see, his portrayals of courtship express the same conflicting impulses toward gratitude and toward grievance that we saw in Lyly and Sidney. For, as I go on to suggest, Spenser's account of a purely 'private' courtship in the

Amoretti and Epithalamion is shot through with allusions to the court and to Queen Elizabeth, inviting an obvious parallel between the wooing of his beloved and his difficult 'courtship' of the sovereign. And, in book VI of *The Faerie Queene*, Spenser makes his Legend of Courtesy the site for a sustained meditation on the relations between a poet and his patron, one which manages to celebrate the patronage system while simultaneously and subtly reviling it.

THE POLITICS OF SPENSER'S *AMORETTI*

Elizabeth Boyle – the Irish gentlewoman whom Spenser married in June 1594, a few months before entering his sonnet-sequence and marriage-poem in the Stationers' Register – has traditionally been identified as the addressee of the *Amoretti* and *Epithalamion* – the volume which William Ponsonby published in 1595.[9] Most critics consequently interpret the sonnet-sequence as the celebration of a private courtship – a personalized outpouring of neo-platonic idealism that is to be clearly differentiated from the fraught, difficult, degenerate world of the court, and from the poet's 'public' role as a writer of epic and eulogizer of England's sovereign, Queen Elizabeth. For one recent critic, echoing many of his predecessors, the sonnets 'contain an extended, complex, and sustained framework of metaphors and analogies presenting the experience of the poet's love for his lady in the much larger context of Christian belief and cosmic time'.[10]

So far so good. But Spenser departs from convention in many ways. To take the most immediately striking example, he distances himself from the literalizing and fictionalizing of the beloved's name that was normal practice in contemporary Elizabethan sonnet-sequences. After all, Spenser's *Amoretti* are not addressed to a Stella or a Delia, to a Phillis, Diana, or Pandora. Rather, they are addressed to a woman who calls herself Elizabeth. Indeed, in *Amoretti* 73–5 – a group of sonnets which treat of his beloved's name – the poet vows (like Sir Henry Lee in 1590) to sing a 'Vivat Eliza' for his mistress: 'to sing your name and prayses ouer all' (*Am* 73). And, like Ralegh in *The Ocean's Love to Cynthia*, Spenser's lover scratches the name of his beloved in the sand (*Am* 75) as an emblem of the fleetingness of love. Both Spenser's phraseology and his imagery are thus embedded in other, well-known poems, works that were directed explicitly toward that unavoidable object of public devotion – Elizabeth Tudor. Moreover, *Amoretti* 74 celebrates the poet's personal trinity of loves, for his mother, beloved, and sovereign all share same name: Elizabeth. Genetrix, mistress, and monarch were all, of course, roles fashioned by the Queen herself, and by those poets, artists, and courtiers who were actively engaged in the production of her 'cult'.

Naturally, I am not seeking to propose that Queen Elizabeth is the addressee of the *Amoretti and Epithalamion*, or that she in any way displaces Elizabeth Boyle from her privileged place as Spenser's bride. But I am suggesting that, however connected with the circumstances of his own life, Spenser's invocation of a mistress called Elizabeth is inescapably a symptom of the phenomenon described by Peter Stallybrass and Ann Jones whereby 'the supposedly "private" sphere of love can be imagined only through its similarities and dissimilarities to the public world of the court . . . In England, indeed, idealizations of a virtuous private love found one possible resolution in a rededication to that supreme object of public devotion, "fayre Elisa, Queene of shepheardes all"'.[11]

Spenser's *Amoretti* are unique among sonnet-sequences of the period in that they conclude with a marriage-poem – the *Epithalamion*.[12] Other English sonnet-sequences of the 1580s and 1590s tend to portray a courtship which is essentially – even architecturally – structured so as to create a sense of stasis and unresolvable predicament.[13] But Spenser's sonnets uniquely trace a narrative and temporal development from the lover's initial refusal through to his final acceptance and marriage. More significantly, the *Epithalamion* replaces the long, Ovidian narrative-poem with which some other sequences end. Samuel Daniel's *Delia* (1592), for instance, concludes with the 'Complaint of Rosamund', a dramatic monologue spoken by the dejected victim of male lust. Thomas Lodge's *Phillis* (1593) ends with a similar poem, the 'Complaint of Elstred', as does Richard Barnfield's *Affectionate Shepherd* (1594), which concludes with 'The Complaint of Chastitie' and 'Helens Rape', while his *Cynthia* (1595) rounds off with the 'Legend of Cassandra'. It was the same tradition that may have prompted Thomas Thorpe to publish 'A Lover's Complaint' as the end-piece to Shakespeare's *Sonnets* in 1609.[14]

Complaint-poems are conventionally interpreted as testaments to sexual weakness, emotional failure, and to the fragility and instability of human affection. And it was common for sonnet-sequences in

Spenser's day to portray a love-relation 'whereof', as George Puttenham wrote, 'there is no assurance, but loose and fickle affection
occasioned for the most part by sodaine sights and acquaintance of
no long triall or experience, nor vpon any other good ground
wherein any suretie may be conceiued'. By contrast, Puttenham
approvingly holds up the 'Epithalamie' or wedding hymn as a
socially (and therefore artistically) legitimized form. For 'honorable
matrimonie', he says, is 'a loue by al lawes allowed, not mutable nor
encombred with such vaine cares and passions, as that other loue'.[15]

Spenser's *Epithalamion* is therefore all the more unusual in that it
concludes a sonnet-sequence with the celebration of nuptials, fec-
undity, and closure. Indeed, as the formerly abject male poet comes
to assert social and sexual mastery over his cruel mistress, I suggest
that an element of male wish-fulfilment enters Spenser's poem, as he
celebrates his own husbandly domination over a woman called
Elizabeth. After all, we should remember that, in the Letter to
Ralegh, Spenser had written that the Queen 'beareth two persons',
and that he saw her as 'a most vertuous and beautifull Lady' as well
as 'a most royall Queene or Empresse'. In the *Amoretti*, as in the later
parts of *The Faerie Queene*, he appears to experiment with both
personae, his mistress – suggestively called Elizabeth – alternately
taking on the roles of 'Tyrannesse' (*Am* 10) and submissive bride.

Spenser may thus be seen to reverse and refashion the highly
complex relation that exists between a monarch and subject. As
Louis A. Montrose has recently suggested, Elizabeth's male subjects
occasionally indulged in psycho-sexual fantasies of dominating their
female sovereign. In January 1597, for example, the diarist Simon
Forman recalled a dream he had had about Elizabeth:

She had a long, white smock, very clean and fair, and it trailed in the dirt
and her coat behind. I took her coat and did carry it up a good way, and
then it hung too low before. I told her she should do me a favour to let me
wait on her, and she said I should. Then said I, 'I mean to wait *upon* you
and not under you, that I might make this belly a little bigger to carry up
this smock and coats out of the dirt.'[16]

In the *Amoretti and Epithalamion*, Spenser clearly signals a reversal
of the sexual roles normally associated with the Petrarchan sonnet-
sequence, rather as Forman obscenely substitutes 'upon' for 'under'
in order to describe his fantasy relationship with the Queen. For, at
the beginning of the *Amoretti*, Spenser's Elizabeth is a 'souerayne
beauty' whose 'titles dew' cannot be enumerated (*Am* 3); she is a

terrifying 'Tyrannesse' (*Am* 10) possessed of 'awfull maiesty' (*Am* 13), who raises him from baseness, and yet holds him captive, silencing and censoring his utterance: 'you stop my toung' (*Am* 8).

But, after sixty-two sonnets, the traditional Petrarchan scenario radically and irretrievably alters, leading some critics to suggest that the *Amoretti* constitute two distinct sonnet-sequences, which Spenser then merged (with varying degrees of success).[17] For the proud fair relents, allows the poet a rapturous kiss, and agrees to be his bride. The mistress's formulaic and entirely conventional intransigence, therefore, suddenly and inexplicably melts away, her tigerish jibes giving way to 'the message of her gentle spright' (*Am* 81).

Henceforth, the images of power and subjection which have structured the self-positioning of the poet and his mistress are changed around, for it is no longer the male poet who suffers in captivity but, rather, his beloved. So while, in *Amoretti* 23, the poet had described himself as trapped in his mistress's Penelope-like web – a commonplace image of female conniving – he reverses the image in sonnet 71:

> Right so your selfe were caught in cunning snare
> of a deare foe, and thralled to his loue:
> in whose streight bands ye now captiued are
> so firmely, that ye neuer may remoue.   (*Am* 71)

In acknowledging the poet as her suitor, therefore, the lady ritually loses her 'liberty', although the poet-husband assures her that 'the gentle birde feeles no captiuity / within her cage, but singes and feeds her fill' (*Am* 65). And while Elizabeth had formerly lorded it over those 'humbled harts' whom Cupid had brought 'captiues vnto thee' (*Am* 10), she is now metamorphosed into the 'gentle deare' who willingly approaches her former hunter and allows herself to be seized:

> So after long pursuit and vaine assay,
> when I all weary had the chace forsooke,
> the gentle deare returnd the selfe-same way,
> thinking to quench her thirst at the next brooke.
> There she beholding me with mylder looke,
> sought not to fly, but fearelesse still did bide:
> till I in hand her yet halfe trembling tooke,
> and with her owne goodwill hir fyrmely tyde.
> Strange thing me seemd to see a beast so wyld,
> so goodly wonne with her owne will beguyld.   (*Am* 67)

Spenser's sonnet here subtly reverses the Actaeon myth. In legend, Actaeon spies the naked Diana while he is hunting game in the forest. As a punishment, Diana transforms him into the object of his own sexualized quest – the deer – so that, in being torn apart by his own hounds, Actaeon thus suffers the fate that his own lusts threatened to inflict on the goddess.[18] In *Amoretti* 5, Spenser's mistress is described as 'thretning rash eies which gaze on her so wide', precisely as Diana scorns Actaeon's voyeurism. In *Amoretti* 67, on the other hand, the 'panting hounds' are 'beguiled of their pray', until the deer approaches its captor apparently of her own accord. The virgin's threatening eyes have lost their power, and Spenser–Actaeon is not only allowed to gaze his fill, but to indulge his sexual fantasy.[19]

Such reversals and revisions of myth and convention are typical of the *Amoretti*. Here, the capture of the deer alters the Petrarchan commonplace that was epitomized in English in Wyatt's lyric 'They Fle From Me', for the willingness of the beast to be taken captive betokens the sexual mastery of her captor. The deer's submission, moreover, figures the trembling compliance of the bride in the *Epithalamion*, and, also, of Amoret in *The Faerie Queene*. Amoret is abducted from the Temple of Venus by Scudamore, upon whose shield ('escu d'amour') stood '*Cupid* with his killing bow / And cruell shafts emblazond' (*FQ* IV. x. 55). The thrusting masculinity of the shield quells the 'terror' of Amoret and her female companions, and leads her away like a docile deer – 'Like warie Hynd'. Like the *Amoretti* poet, Amoret associates marriage with capture, imprisonment, and constraint. For, having captured Amoret, Scudamore refuses to grant her the liberty that she begs from him: 'but yet for nought, / That euer she to me could say or doe, / Could she her wished freedome fro me wooe' (IV. x. 57). As her husband, he remains in a position to grant or to refuse her 'freedome'.

Strategies of dominance and manipulation are, of course, a given in any Petrarchan scenario, for the male poet traditionally fashions, speaks for, berates, accuses, abuses, and sometimes even kills that creature of his own devising – the 'cruel fair'. But Spenser goes even further in acting out the 'hidden' dominance of his courtly maker when, in the *Epithalamion*, he allows the poet to do the unthinkable in claiming the mistress as his bride. For it was a Renaissance commonplace that the institution of marriage reined dangerous sexual appetites, and restricted and normalized human sexuality in order

'Our foolish lusts in honest rules to stay', as Geron says in the Third Eclogues of the *Old Arcadia*.[20] Spenser's *Epithalamion* therefore celebrates a moment of social and sexual appropriation in which the female body is passive, available, exposed to view, and noticeably silent, thus transforming the stereotypical Solomonic or Petrarchan blason into an anticipation of sexual dominance that verges on the cannibalistic:

> Her cheekes lyke apples which the sun hath rudded,
> Her lips lyke cherryes charming men to byte,
> Her brest like to a bowle of creame vncrudded,
> Her paps lyke lyllies budded,
> Her snowie necke lyke to a marble towre,
> And all her body like a pallace fayre,
> Ascending vppe with many a stately stayre,
> To honors seat and chastities sweet bowre.   (lines 173–80)

Spenser's palace-metaphor figures in the poet's penetrative, upward movement a clear anticipation of sexual pleasure. It is almost as if that archetypal virgin body – the Castle of Alma, home of 'a virgin Queene most bright' (*FQ* II. xi. 2) – is here being stormed and taken over. Alexander Dunlop has recently suggested that the *Epithalamion* can be read as a 'demonstration of mastery', a 'ritual of subordination', and, in George Puttenham's account of the epithalamic genre, the form is argued to have been designed to ritualize (even institutionalize) aggressive physical mastery over the female body.[21] Puttenham describes how

the tunes of the songs were very loude and shrill, to the intent there might no noise be hard out of the bed chamber by the skreeking and outcry of the young damosell feeling the first forces of her stiffe and rigorous young man, she being as all virgins tender and weake, and vnexpert in those maner of affaires.[22]

The girl's screams are thus drowned out by the singing and revelry of the wedding guests, and by the 'casting of pottes full of nuttes round about the chamber'. The most violent and brutal aspect of the wedding ceremony is therefore acknowledged (the girl was to be inspected the following morning for signs of having been 'maimed by any accident nocturnall') but ritually suppressed, as the woman's utterance is edited out of the proceedings, and obliterated by the general rowdiness which is designed precisely to block out the pain and fear of defloration.[23] In *The Faerie Queene*, the figure of Amoret typifies this female fear, for, abducted during her own 'bridale feast' (*FQ* IV. i. 3), and taken prisoner in Busirane's castle, Amoret is there entertained by the 'rude confused rout' of Cupid's masque (III. xii. 25), a crude and horrible parody of the wedding feast and its celebrations.

In the *Amoretti and Epithalamion*, then, Spenser thus enacts a major shift in roles when he, as the formerly abject male suitor, assumes a position of authority and power over Elizabeth. Moreover, given the subtle game of power that lies embedded and encoded in the courtship scenario, it is all the more difficult to separate off the object of the *Amoretti* from that dominating object of public devotion – England's Elisa. For although Spenser's poems are not necessarily addressed directly to the Queen, they allow both writer and reader to override convention, and to seize, appropriate, penetrate, master, and dominate a woman who calls herself Elizabeth.

For all this, however, the simple domination of Elizabeth that we seem to see rehearsed in the *Amoretti and Epithalamion* in fact belies a more complex interplay of identities and roles than may at first have been supposed. Louis A. Montrose has brilliantly argued that, in the April eclogue of *The Shepheardes Calender*, Colin 'produces' Elisa while he himself is absent, thus 'gesturing toward the controlling power of the writing subject over the representation he has made'.[24] But what Montrose neglects to say, of course, is that Colin continues to remain under subjection of another kind. For, while Colin is not obviously repressed by Elisa herself, he is thoroughly disabled by the mysterious Rosalind, a woman who, in effect, cuts out his tongue and renders him fatally silent. So the poet is not exercising his own self-mastery over Elisa quite as straightforwardly as Montrose suggests. For, although Colin is empowered to produce Elizabethan iconography to order, he is still subject to devastating constraint. And for all his translation of Elisa into the subject of his own artistic fashioning, Colin remains under the subjection of another woman – Rosalind.

In his *Life of Sidney*, Fulke Greville includes a fascinating passage which sums up just the kind of subjection to which men like Sidney and Spenser might fall victim under Elizabeth I:

So that although [Sidney] found a sweet stream of sovereign humours in that well-tempered lady to run against him, yet found he safety in herself, even against that selfness which appeared to threaten him in her; for this happily born and bred princess was not (subject-like) apt to construe things reverently done in the worst sense, but rather – with the spirit of anointed greatness, as created to reign equally over frail and strong – more desirous to find ways to fashion her people than colours or causes to punish them.[25]

It is an extraordinary passage. Greville's syntax is overloaded with his conflicting imperatives – equally to praise the Queen and a man who found himself in opposition to her. Greville finds himself caught up in a complicated nexus of identities when he attempts to describe the nature of Sidney's relation with Elizabeth: for Sidney bows to a version of Elizabeth ('self') in which he can find safety, although another 'self' of hers appears to threaten him. And Elizabeth – explicitly 'not subject-like' – here resists being 'produced' or fashioned by her subject, and instead 'fashions' him (together with the rest of her people). According to Greville's account, Sidney was in no position to object to Elizabeth's own fashioning of a role for himself – one that must have seemed to him bitterly humble and apologetic.

In the April eclogue, Spenser's Colin remains under subjection in a similar way. For he is entirely absent from the poem (and, as such, is noisily mourned by his fellow shepherds). The erasure of Colin from the scene testifies more powerfully than anything else to the subject's ultimate subordination to a superior female force. And, in the same way, having triumphantly (and wholly unconventionally) asserted power and authority over his mistress, the poet-husband of the *Amoretti and Epithalamion* continues (perversely) to find himself constrained under images of female power.

In *Amoretti* 73, for example, the poet complains of being 'captyued here in care' – 'here' being an unspecified location, since it is uncertain precisely what constrains him. Unwilling to be bound by anything other than his mistress's 'golden hayre', the poet escapes 'his prison' and flies to her, where he promptly becomes her prisoner: 'Doe you him take, and in your bosome bright, / gently encage, that he may be your thrall.' And, from this position of captivity, he suggests that 'perhaps he there may learne with rare delight, / to sing your name and prayses ouer all': which name, we discover for the first time in the following sonnet, is Elizabeth.

Amoretti 73 consciously mirrors sonnet 37, a poem in which the poet finds himself helplessly entangled in the 'golden snare' of his lady's hair. Her 'guilefull net, / in which if euer ye entrapped are, / out of her bands ye by no meanes shall get' (*Am* 37), hints strongly at the 'subtile web' with which Acrasia ensnares her victims in the Bower of Bliss (*FQ* ii. xii. 77), and makes it all the more paradoxical

that – even after the mistress has apparently submitted to his superior power – the male poet should continue to find himself her victim
and her prisoner.

Amoretti 80 presents us with a dense interplay of identities in which
Spenser's mistress, wife, and queen – all Elizabeths – are apparently
differentiated, but in fact confusedly entangled. The poet seems to
address the Queen:

> After so long a race as I haue run
> through Faery land, which those six books compile,
> giue leaue to rest me being halfe fordonne,
> and gather to my selfe new breath awhile.
> Then as a steed refreshed after toyle,
> out of my prison I will breake anew:
> and stoutly will that second worke assoyle,
> with strong endeuour and attention dew.
> Till then giue leaue to me in pleasant mew,
> to sport my muse and sing my loues sweet praise:
> the contemplation of whose heauenly hew,
> my spirit to an higher pitch will rayse.
> But let her prayses yet be low and meane,
> fit for the handmayd of the Faery Queene.

At first sight, the sonnet signals an unmistakable difference
between the public and private spheres. As on Mount Acidale,
Spenser here presents two distinct objects of devotion – handmaid
(Elizabeth Boyle) and queen (Elizabeth Tudor) – as well as two
distinct poems, the *Amoretti* and *The Faerie Queene*. Spenser's images
of imprisonment in the sonnet are none the less deeply perplexing.
For it seems, at first glance, as if the 'prison' of which he complains is
the onerous task of completing *The Faerie Queene* according to the
ambitious plan sketched out originally in the Letter to Ralegh. But,
on inspection, the 'prison' turns out to be wherever the poet remains
when he is *not* composing his epic. The release he begs for from one
Elizabeth is, paradoxically, an extension of his prison term under
another Elizabeth. For he asks to be allowed to remain stabled, 'in
pleasant mew, / to sport my muse', and only after will he bound
back, refreshed and reinvigorated, into Faery land. In other words,
the Elizabeth whom he has just mastered – the Elizabeth who only a
few sonnets earlier had replaced her dismissive attitude for a
submissive one – strangely continues to keep him in thrall. The poet
himself becomes a victim of that pleasant prison which he has
already urged his mistress to enter of her own accord – 'so sweet your

prison' (*Am* 71) – while another Elizabeth (the Queen) offers him the possibility of liberty and escape.

The images of captivity and subjection therefore contradict and interweave with each other as the poet confusingly shifts from a position of abject humiliation to that of a prison warder, while still remaining an (apparently willing) captive to Elizabeth.

Persisting images of constraint and imprisonment in the *Amoretti* suggest, therefore, that the poet-husband's triumphant conquest over a recalcitrant female in the *Epithalamion* is, at best, incomplete. For the social and sexual mastery which he celebrates in the concluding sonnets of the *Amoretti* and in the wedding hymn continue to be in doubt. The suggestion would seem to be that, although he has mastered the body of one Elizabeth, the 'vertuous and beautifull Lady', the poet still continues to suffer under the authority and power of another Elizabeth, just as Colin remains silenced by the cruel Rosalind.

Spenser's subjection in the *Amoretti* and the *Epithalamion* is made all the clearer by a group of untitled poems which lie between the sonnets and the marriage hymn. These apparently slight poems have traditionally been called 'anacreontics' after the Greek poet Anacreon, imitations of whose amorous and convivial poems were popularized in the Renaissance lyric.[26] Barnabe Barnes includes a 'Carmen Anacreontium' among the closing poems of his *Parthenophil and Parthenope* (1593), for example, while a concluding ode of John Soowthern's sonnet-sequence *Pandora* (1584) apostrophizes Anacreon as follows: 'Heere holde my Anacreon quaffe, / When we are droonke, we haue no sorrowe', while another adds 'But like the olde poet Annacron, / It pleases mee well to be Biberon. / And thus in a Sellor to quaffe, / So that some Wench be by to lauffe.'[27] Spenser explicitly refers to Anacreon, 'that sweete *Teian* Poet', in his *Hymne of Heavenly Beautie* (line 219), and his positioning of the anacreontics after the *Amoretti* sonnets signals an allegiance to the convention – evident in Daniel's *Delia*, Lodge's *Phillis*, and Shakespeare's *Sonnets* – which traditionally ended sonnet-sequences with such poems.

Anacreontic poems habitually express resignation and loss, as the mature and chastened poet turns aside from the madness of love to more stable sources of pleasure. Normally coming at the end of sonnet-sequences in which a courtship has faded out inconclusively, anacreontics stand as testaments to emotional instability and fragility, deferral and postponement. In the *Amoretti*, true to form,

Spenser's anacreontic poems present a speaker who has grown old, who acknowledges the failure of his courtship, and who is resigned to the role of unmitigated suffering that had been explored in earlier sonnets. Here, the poet remains stung with Cupid's shaft: 'So now I languish till he please, / my pining anguish to appease.' There is no sense of triumph or anticipation here, and the poems therefore sit strangely between the eager *Amoretti* and the triumphant *Epithalamion*.

Spenser's anacreontic poems are usually regarded as an embarrassing irrelevance which seriously disrupts the momentum of the narrative sequence, otherwise moving inexorably from courtship to marriage. In the words of one critic, there is only one solution to offer for the anacreontics: 'ignore them'.[28] But I suggest that these apparently slight poems are absolutely central to Spenser's design. For they allow him, in effect, to provide two 'alternative' endings to the *Amoretti*. On the one hand, Spenser's sonnet-sequence deviates from the norm by concluding with the union of the lovers and the celebration of their marriage: the monumental *Epithalamion* represents the reassertion of male dominance and power over the female. But, on the other hand, the sonnets also end (conventionally) with anacreontics, poems which testify to the poet's unchanged state as a resigned and suffering victim of love.

In other words, Spenser's courtship of Elizabeth could be seen to end both in failure and in success, both in domination and in submission, both in sexual appropriation and in age and resignation. Indeed, the *Amoretti* and *Epithalamion* seem to me to be designedly ambiguous, and to hint strongly that, in tracing two alternative outcomes for his courtship, Spenser explores – as Sidney did in his poetic fictions – the multiple responses of the Elizabethan subject to the persona and ideology of their monarch. Themes of submission, humiliation, and frustration go hand in hand with triumph, acceptance, and reward. There is no need to ignore the anacreontics because they disrupt the transition from courtship to marriage, or because their placing seems to be the result of careless or casual publication. On the contrary, Spenser's *Amoretti* and *Epithalamion* quite deliberately pull in opposite directions – toward failure and success – and are thus typical of the courtship-scenario, as depicted so frequently in the literature of the Elizabethan period.

The two 'endings' of the *Amoretti*, moreover, reflect the two alternative fates that meet their namesake, Amoret, in *The Faerie*

Queene. For the *Amoretti* were entered into the Stationers' Register in 1594 and published in 1595, at a time when only the first half of *The Faerie Queene* (1590) was in circulation. The reference in *Amoretti* 80 to 'those six books' of 'Faery land', would therefore have been the first indication to Spenser's reading public (other than the programmatic Letter to Ralegh) that the text which they had was incomplete, and that there were another three books to follow. In other words, the *Amoretti* first signal a hiatus between two halves of *The Faerie Queene*, a hiatus which, when bridged by the publication of the six-book *Faerie Queene* in 1596, radically revises the former ending of the Amoret story.

In the 1590 text, Scudamore and Amoret are reunited at the end of a fraught and difficult courtship, and the eventual consummation of their love is presented as a moment of stillness and closure:

> Had ye them seene, ye would haue surely thought,
> That they had beene that faire *Hermaphrodite* . . .
> So seemd those two, as growne together quite.
>
> (1590 *FQ* III. xii. 45)

In the 1596 revisions to book III, on the other hand, this sexual consummation is delayed even further, for, at the moment when the two lovers are supposed to be reunited, Scudamore has mysteriously disappeared.[29]

Amoret and the *Amoretti* are therefore alike in more than just name. For Amoret's alternative fates figure the two endings of the *Amoretti* courtship: on the one hand, marriage, and, on the other, 'endless' deferral. The marriage of Amoret and Scudamore in the 1590 text of *The Faerie Queene* restores the same sexual and social hierarchies as the *Epithalamion*, reasserting male power over female. But, in the 1596 text, Scudamore's courtship is further prolonged, and the satisfactions of his desire further delayed, suggesting that, like the anacreontic poems which intervene so strangely at the end of the *Amoretti* sonnets, the male poet has been less than successful in overcoming Cupid's smart, and that he continues to remain in love's thrall.

The *Epithalamion* is in itself a highly complex poem. In his account of the epithalamic genre, Puttenham acknowledges that, as a form which celebrates male pleasure and female pain, the wedding hymn invites a register of paradox and oxymoron. The bride who endures the 'terrible approches' of her husband, for example, is dubbed 'the laughing lamenting spouse', her mixed response to her first sexual encounter setting the tone for the generic uncertainty characteristic of the form.[30] After all, Spenser's bride submits to her husband with an oxymoronic 'proud humility' (line 306), while many critics have felt that joyous themes of marriage and sexual consummation in Spenser's *Epithalamion* are in some degree undercut by more ominous, even sinister undertones.[31] The sonorous echo refrain of the *Epithalamion*, for example, is particularly haunting. The fact that the poet-husband repeats variations of 'The woods shall to me answer and my Eccho ring' throughout his wedding hymn hints that he is still within the metaphorical forest of the Petrarchan love-chase. Echo – which seems here to represent self-generated monologue – is conventionally associated with failed courtship, as in Philisides' last poem in the *New Arcadia* eclogues, and in countless lyrics and romances. In the ode that intervenes between the end of Daniel's *Delia* and the 'Complaint of Rosamund' that follows, for example, Daniel invokes 'Eccho daughter of the ayre, / Babbling gheste of Rocks and Hills, / Knowes the name of my fearce Fayre, / And soundes the accents of my ills.'[32] Shakespeare's *A Lover's Complaint* opens with echo – 'From off a hill whose concave womb reworded / A plaintful story from a sist'ring vale' (lines 1–2) – and weaves the Echo and Narcissus story into the narrative of failure and rejection. Shakespeare also includes a comic *reductio ad absurdum* of the echo motif in his *Venus and Adonis*, published in 1593. Venus makes 'verbal repetition of her moans' (line 831) when she fails to urge the cold boy Adonis to love: ' "Ay me!" she cries, and twenty times, "Woe, woe!" / And twenty echoes twenty times cry so ... Her heavy anthem still concludes in woe, / And still the quire of echoes answer so' (lines 833–40).[33]

The ambivalence of the *Amoretti* and *Epithalamion* therefore seems to enact Spenser's sense of the complexity of his position as a poet on the margins of Elizabeth I's court. For ambivalence allows him to scrutinize from every angle the power politics that lie embedded in the courtship situation. As a social transaction, courtship involves a carefully graduated series of economies – strategies that include giving (and being seen to give), accepting, and giving in return. In the courtship of the *Amoretti*, Spenser therefore experiments with alternative roles: with humiliation, failure, loss, together with acceptance, reward, and triumph – all of them aspects of his position as an 'Elizabethan subject'. He is at one and the same time a triumphant and self-congratulatory 'producer' of Elizabeth (just as Colin fashions Elisa), and a prisoner in her thrall, a lover resigned to loss, failure, and humiliation (as Colin is 'erased' from the April eclogue by Rosalind).

On the one hand, Spenser repeatedly praises the 'maker' of his mistress for fashioning so perfect an example of human beauty: 'When I behold that beauties wonderment . . . I honor and admire the makers art' (*Am* 24). 'Maker' is here an English transliteration of the Greek *poietes*, for, in effect, Spenser is congratulating himself on the literary construct called Elizabeth whom he, the poet, has fashioned. Yet, on the other hand, Spenser remains the subject of a monarch who, in Greville's words, was 'desirous to find ways to fashion her people'. Spenser therefore rehearses his continued subjection to a female power, together with his own 'making' by a mistress who 'bids me play my part' (*Am* 18), but who sometimes fails to recognize or to applaud his attempt.

COURT, COURTESY, AND COURTSHIP IN BOOK VI OF
THE FAERIE QUEENE

In 1593 George Peele published his *Honour of the Garter*, a poem which laments the fate of poetry in a patronless world, and which gives moving testimony to what the author saw as Spenser's plight:

> Augustus long agoe hath left the world:
> And liberall Sidney, famous for the love
> He bare to learning and to Chivalrie;
> And vertuous Walsingham are fled to heaven.
> Why thether speede not Hobbin and his pheres?
> Great Hobbinall on whom our shepheards gaze.[34]

Peele demonstrates his sympathy for Spenser's position by packing *The Honour of the Garter* with Spenserian allusions, most notably to Spenser's own complaint-poems on a similar subject *The Teares of the Muses* and *The Ruines of Time* (1591). Moreover, by styling him as 'Hobbinall', Peele consciously employs the very image of patronage which Spenser had used in the two *Shepheardes Calender* eclogues (April and June) where Hobbinol appears – the image of the three Graces. For Peele resigns himself to the lack of interest in and support for impecunious poets, and hints that the Graces themselves are the only patrons left to poets in a world that is bereft of rewards:

And you the Muses, and the Graces three,
You I invoke from Heaven and Helicon.
For other Patrons have poore Poets none,
But Muses and the Graces to implore.

(Prologue, lines 31–4)

Peele reduces the Graces to an emblem of the relation between a poet and his patron, and, with a subsumed pun on Garter/gratia, hints that the Garter knights newly created that year should step into the breach. For the encircling emblem of the garter in itself figures the entwined and interlinked arms of the Graces, which 'with golden chaynes / They lincked were' (lines 67–8).

As in the April and June eclogues of *The Shepheardes Calender*, then, the three Graces are here associated closely with images of patronage.[35] In April, two of the Graces look forward to face the viewer while the third looks away, her back to the viewer, 'noting double thanke to be due to us for the benefit, we have done', as E.K. would have it, an emblem that most critics have identified with gratitude, eulogy, and reward. For the central figure amidst the Graces, of course, is unmistakably Queen Elizabeth, just as, in *The Teares of the Muses*, Spenser had praised the Queen 'That with rich bountie and deare cherishment, / Supports the praise of noble Poesie' (lines 573–4) as the patroness of 'all heavenly graces' (line 578). Like Spenser, Peele also harks back longingly to a time when monarchs exemplified the generosity of the Graces, 'when learning was in price, / And Poesie with Princes gracious' (Epilogue, lines 3–4).

A problem immediately presents itself, however, because, as we have already seen, Spenser's emblem of gracious patronage in the April eclogue is severely compromised by the conspicuous absence of Colin Clout – the supposed recipient and beneficiary of that 'double thanke' which E.K. glosses. Similarly, in the June eclogue, Hobbinol urges Colin to renounce his sorrow and return to a world of 'many Graces' (line 25) – again glossed by E.K. as an emblem of 'charites' – but Colin chooses to remain in a world marked by absence and denial. In other words, the April and June eclogues suggest that the traffic between the poet ('vnder whose person the Author selfe is shadowed') and images of return, thanks, gratitude, and reciprocity are, to say the least, made problematic.

For, as in *The Teares of the Muses*, the encircling dance of the three Graces – representing an unbroken flow of giving and thanksgiving – is broken off, suspended, and despoiled. In the complaint-poem, the Grace, Thalia, mourns how 'all is gone' –

Where be the sweete delights of learnings treasure ...
In which I late was wont to raine as Queene,
And maske in mirth with Graces well beseeme?   (lines 175–81)

In the same way, Peele uses an image of dispersal and departure as he urges contemporary poets to desert the unrewarded and unrewarding cause of poetry:

Why goe not all into th'Elisian fieldes,
And leave this Center, barren of repast.   (Prologue, lines 64–5)

Peele's sensitivity to the tensions and ambiguities inherent in Spenser's images of thanks, moreover, neatly anticipates the wholesale elaboration of the theme which was to appear in book VI of *The Faerie Queene*. Spenser's Legend of Courtesy parables the social arts of giving, receiving, and requiting at every level, and never more so than in its central image of the Graces: 'Those three to men all gifts of grace do graunt', 'These three on men all gracious gifts bestow' (VI. x. 15, 23). And yet, as in Peele's poem, and as in *The Teares of the Muses*, the dance of the Graces is characterized by its fragility, for their encircling choreography is irretrievably destroyed when Sir Calidore stumbles in on the scene and causes the fleeting dancers to disperse.

The vision of the Graces in book VI therefore amplifies the complex nexus of relations that exists between poet and patron, and suggests that the ties of gratitude and reward (constituted by their acts of giving and receiving) are habitually problematized. Queen Elizabeth – standing at the centre of the Graces in the April eclogue, and the sole patroness of poets in *The Teares of the Muses* – is, after all, strikingly absent from Spenser's image of thanks in book VI, a dereliction by the poet that seems particularly pointed in a book which draws attention to its own status as a gift in the name of its hero – Calidore, the 'beautiful gift' (from the Greek *kalon doron*).

It is worth pausing for a moment to consider more fully some of the complexities inherent in Spenser's presentation of patronage in the Legend of Courtesy. For the image of the Graces – so often called upon to encapsulate and characterize the whole of book VI – is the site of a well-known textual crux which, though frequently edited away, neatly demonstrates Spenser's subtlety in tracing so sensitive a subject. Most modern editions of *The Faerie Queene* present Calidore's vision of the three Graces as follows:

That two of them still froward seem'd to bee,
But one still towards shew'd her selfe afore;
That good should from vs goe, then come in greater store.

(VI. x. 24)

It is generally argued that Spenser here reverses the traditional positioning of the Graces (in which one faces away and two forward, as they do in the April eclogue) in order to suggest that the giver gets less back than he originally gave, and that he therefore receives only half his due.[36] This reading depends upon interpreting 'then' as a conjunction ('than') rather than an adverb (so as to read: 'good should rather go from us than come in greater store'), transforming the assembled Graces from an icon of 'double thanke' into one of self-sacrifice, the giver expecting to get considerably less than he gave.

The keyword here is 'froward', an elision of 'fromward', which is the word used both by E.K. and by other English Renaissance commentators to describe the backward-looking maidens.[37] But, while 'froward' is the reading that appears in the 1611 *Faerie Queene*, the first two editions of book VI (1596 and 1609) read 'forward', radically altering the perceived positioning of the Graces:

That two of them still forward seem'd to bee,
But one still towards shew'd her selfe afore;
That good should from vs goe, then come in greater store.

(VI. x. 24)

This earlier version of the lines suggests that the Graces keep the traditional positions of their counterparts in the April eclogue (in which one faces away and two towards the giver), thus indicating what E.K. called the 'double thanke to be due to us'. So, instead of becoming an image of self-sacrifice as above, the 1596 Graces retain their traditional status as figures of courteous reciprocity, a diametrically opposite reading which hangs tenuously on the ambiguous 'then' (here, an adverb rather than a conjunction, as to read 'good should from us go, and then come in greater store').[38]

Moreover, fully exploiting all the possibilities of 'functional ambiguity', Spenser's text also allows for a third potential reading, in which the three Graces *each* face outward with their backs to one another. Thus, two of the maidens face 'forward' (as the 1596 and 1609 editions have it), while the third 'still towards shew'd her selfe afore', that is, has her back to the viewer, but still faces toward some other viewer because she is looking outward.[39] This third reading – which retains the original 'forward', makes sense of 'afore', and interprets 'then' as an adverb – therefore suggests that the viewer is to expect not only 'double thanke' but a threefold reward for his pains, for each one of the Graces, when she comes round, looks out promisingly to him.

Throughout this study I have attempted to suggest that the kind of ambivalence and multi-layering of differing interpretations that we see here is absolutely typical of Renaissance courtly texts. For Spenser's 'forward' seems almost calculatedly unstable – inviting the editors of the 1611 *Faerie Queene* to change it to 'froward' – and thus giving rise to a manifest ambiguity which seems designed, perhaps, to rehearse a series of different scenarios: first to insinuate to Elizabeth a sense of pique at her faint reward, second to thank her for the gift she has already made, and third to hint that she has even more to give.

To take any one of these readings by itself, however, would be excessively crude, and would fail to do justice to the masterly ambiguity of Spenser's text. For, in addition, the vision of the Graces in book vi depends for its interpretation upon whether the person who views them is identified as the 'giver' or the 'receiver' in the cycle of gift-exchange which they represent. For, if Colin Clout (the 'giver'), for example, sees one of the Graces show her back to him while two come forward, then he seems to be hoping for a 'double thanke'. But if Elizabeth (the 'receiver') pictures the Graces in the same formation then – the suggestion is – she is getting back twice what she has given. And these 'subjective' interpretations are, in turn, each affected by who the 'giver' and 'receiver' are taken to be, and also by the way in which the Graces are taken to stand – both issues which, as we have already seen, are fraught with uncertainty.

The wholesale complexity of Spenser's image of patronage and reward is therefore compounded by the very reciprocity of the thanks which is figured in the Graces' dance. For, in a perfect gift-exchange, the giver, the receiver, and the giver-in-return should each be indistinguishable from the other in an endless cycle of courteous transactions – what Nohrnberg calls 'mysterious reciprocities of deference and demeanor'.[40]

Moreover, the ambivalence that manifestly surrounds interpretations of Spenser's three Graces is further exacerbated by the deep uncertainty that surrounds the figure who stands in their midst: 'Who can aread, what creature mote she bee?' (vi. x. 25). There is a general tendency in book vi to telescope inwards, to search out the midpoint of the Legend's concentric circles: thus, for C. S. Lewis, 'the shepherds' country and Mount Acidale in the midst of it are the core of the Book, and the key to Spenser's whole conception of Courtesy'.[41] In the celebrated case of the 'fourth grace', Spenser's text is indeed curiously insistent on the centrality of this mysterious female figure, inviting us to focus our gaze on her privileged position at the centre. For she is said to stand 'in the midst of them', 'in the middest of those same three', 'Amidst a ring' (VI. x. 12), 'she that in the midst of them did stand' (VI. x. 14), 'That in the midst was placed parauaunt' (VI. x. 15), 'that fourth Mayd, which there amidst them traced' (VI. x. 25).

So great an emphasis is placed on the positioning of this female figure 'in the middest', in fact, that commentators tend to forget another very important person who is also said to stand 'in the midst' (VI. x. 10) – the piping shepherd, Colin Clout. Most critics suggest that Colin in fact stands on the margins of the dance, and that Calidore's first glimpse of the shepherd 'in the midst' is then revised and corrected as he gets closer and sees that the central figure within the spiralling circles is actually a woman. Yet, if Colin does indeed stand at some point outside the whirling circles of the dance, then he necessarily disrupts the harmonious concentricity of the scene in which he is explicitly said to participate. Instead, it is tempting to infer that Calidore was right all along, and that *both* Colin and the female figure stand at the centre of the Graces' dance – both singer and sung, lover and beloved, thanker and thanked, poet and theme.[42]

In which case, Spenser adds yet another layer of complexity and ambiguity to what is already a manifestly polyvalent image. For, if Colin Clout positions himself at the centre of an icon of 'charites', is Spenser suggesting that he can expect no reward but his own? Or is he hinting that he deserves (or has received) a superlatively great reward? Such questions are unanswerable, of course, because, as we have seen, an already complex and multiple reading of the Graces' dance simply threatens to proliferate into a tangled knot of conflicting interpretations. My point is that the passage is so presented as to generate such a multiplicity, and that the textual uncertainty surrounding Spenser's 'forward/froward' is quite deliberately designed to figure the ineffably complex nexus of relations that existed at court.

As for Lyly and Sidney, therefore, courtship provides Spenser with an obvious model with which to characterize the relations between poet and monarch. In a sense, of course, it could be argued that the whole of *The Faerie Queene* is predicated upon a courtship – Arthur's quest for the Faerie Queene, Gloriana. But what Spenser does above all in book VI is to draw attention to the status of his poem as an *act* of courtship, a 'beautiful gift' like its main protagonist, Calidore.[43] And, just as the *Amoretti* and *Epithalamion* do, book VI of *The Faerie Queene* rehearses a series of different outcomes – success as well as failure, thanks as well as bitter resignation.

Book VI draws attention to its main theme of thanks, reward, patronage, and gratitude by opening with an image of the reciprocal exchange of gifts between the poet and his monarch, Queen Elizabeth:

> Then pardon me, most dreaded Soueraine,
> That from your selfe I doe this vertue bring,
> And to your selfe doe it returne againe.
> So from the Ocean all riuers spring,
> And tribute back repay as to their King.   (VI. Pro. 7)

As we have already seen, Spenser's lines here implicate their addressee by obliging her to respond to the poet's public act of gift-giving with some token of reciprocal generosity – an active 'courtesy', which, as long as her response is delayed, creates unfulfilled tensions of debt and owing between them.[44] Both the poet (the recipient of a pension in 1591) and the Queen (the recipient of the poem) are beneficiaries of gifts; and both, equally, are givers. Their acts of courteous return are necessarily, therefore, presented as mutually constitutive and unending – the poet is to return poetry to the Queen in token of his thanks for her recognition; the Queen is to reward the poet for his continued gift to her of a highly eulogistic and nationalistic epic, and so on. But, as Bourdieu has argued, it is in the very nature of gift-exchange to conceal its structure – its laws of debt and obligation – behind a strategic veil, whereby both giver and recipient each reserve and delay their return gestures, thus creating ties of suspense, uncertainty, ambivalence, and, of course, power between them. And such stratagems of delay, procrastination, and prevarication provide the very dynamics of courtship – in both senses of the word (both amorous play and courtly etiquette) – two meanings which Spenser effectively collapses into one in his Legend of Courtesy.

The courteous cycle of giving and requiting in book VI of *The Faerie Queene* is from the outset, therefore, temporarily arrested, stayed, and suspended (as the poet awaits Elizabeth's response) just as the purely ritualized, pre-regulated, mechanical 'laws' of reciprocity are temporarily arrested by the illusion of reversibility embedded in any act of gift-exchange.

One of the ways in which Spenser's text enacts the 'structural ambivalence' of such courteous behaviour is, as I have suggested, by revealing the fragility of the Graces' circular dance – apt to break up and disperse at any moment. Moreover, the pattern of the courteous cycle that is arrested or in some way despoiled repeats itself time and time again throughout book VI. For the Legend of Courtesy is full of images of circles which are systematically broken.[45] The remaining section of this chapter therefore considers how, throughout book VI, motifs of return, cycle, and circularity conflict with themes of fragmentation, division, and disruption – how frequently the enclosed world of a bower or a ring is irrevocably interrupted; how images of return (the return of words to meanings, of children to parents, of Calidore to the court) conflict with a relentless centrifugal movement away from the centre; how those ties or bands which should tie things up, contain and circumscribe them, so often prove ineffective and brittle; and, finally, how the cyclic structure of the poem as a whole (veering toward closure as it attempts to return to its pastoral origins) is flawed by the open-endedness created by the Blatant Beast, as it eludes its chain and escapes, leaving the circle incomplete.

The contradictory images of circularity, cycle, reciprocity, and return, on the one hand, and fragmentation, division, disruption, and deviation, on the other, suggest that book VI (like the *Amoretti* and *Epithalamion*) provides us with two 'alternative' endings: one celebrating return, success, and closure; the other marking loss and the poet's final resignation at his own sense of marginality and subjectivity. And the two contrasting impulses – alternately toward continuity and discontinuity – are at odds throughout the book, creating a highly restless, oppositional, and conflictual text.[46]

The cycle of reciprocity creates subtle ties or bonds between individuals, whereby, as we now say, we are 'bound to do something', in the sense of having an obligation imposed upon us by becoming indebted to another person. Now, 'to be bound to do something' in this modern, figurative sense was a relatively new meaning of the verb 'to bind' in Spenser's day (*OED*, s.v. 'bind', 17).

Spenser therefore represents this figurative, social 'binding' in book
VI with a constant imagery of physical fettering or tying up. Thus the
three Graces are described as patrons of those 'friendly offices that
bynde' (VI. x. 23). Spenser figures the binding ties of obligation as
'bands of ciuilitie' (VI. i. 26) which are closely related, of course, to
'bands of loue' (VI. iii. 15). And he characteristically draws attention
to the Graces as representing these 'bands of ciuilitie' by means of a
pun: the fourth Grace is described as 'the beauty of this goodly band'
(VI. x. 14), that is, of the encircling garland (or band) of dancers, and
of the troupe (or band) as a whole.

Binding is therefore a central motif in book VI of *The Faerie Queene*,
and, as in each of the preceding books, the key image moves from
relative simplicity to profound complexity. Calidore's first encounter
thus involves a relatively straightforward restoration of courteous
bonds. For his first adversaries, Briana and Crudor, 'breake bands of
ciuilitie' when, instead of hospitably welcoming the Squire to their
castle, they tie him up by 'hand and foot vnto a tree' (VI. i. 11).
Calidore releases the Squire, and, in breaking those fetters, ironically
forces Briana and Crudor to abide by the bands of civility. Briana
therefore acknowledges herself to be 'bound for that accord', and
'her selfe bound to him for euermore' (VI. i. 45–6), while Crudor does
the same, 'Byndyng himselfe most firmely to obay' (VI. i. 44).

As we have seen, however, it is in the nature of any social
exchange to introduce an element of doubt, and as book VI pro-
gresses, Spenser's images of the 'bands' of civility indeed become
increasingly ambivalent. We have already seen how ambiguous the
images of imprisonment and subjection were in the *Amoretti*. So, in
book VI, Spenser's images of courteous binding become ever more
convoluted. Thus Calepine, for example, begs Matilda to divulge
the cause of her sorrow 'if need doe not you bynd' (VI. iv. 28), and
she does so. Arthur and Timias are both perplexed by Serena's
companion, the Salvage Man, and have difficulty in interpreting her
situation: 'whether free with him she now were, or in band' (VI. v.
27).

As book VI moves forward, images of civility's 'bonds' grow ever
more restrictive, cumbrous, tyrannical, unjust, and even hateful.
The Hermit, for instance, perceives civility to consist of bridling and
constraining the passions, and he advises Timias and Serena to
'Your eies, your eares, your tongue, your talk restraine' (VI. vi. 7),
and to 'restraine your will, / Subdue desire, and bridle loose delight'

(VI. vi. 14). And yet the Hermit seems himself to be strangely trapped by his own principles of constraint, for 'small was his house, and like a little cage' (VI. v. 38), 'His Hermitage, / In which he liu'd alone, like carelesse bird in cage' (VI. vi. 4). As we saw in the *Amoretti*, the image of the golden cage which is gleefully enjoyed by its prisoner is a highly fraught one.

In the figure of Mirabella – a *reductio ad absurdum* of the 'cruel fair' of sonneteering convention – Spenser shows how easy it is to parody the 'bands of loue' (VI. iii. 15). For Mirabella converts them into 'yron chaines' (VI. viii. 1), and cruelly captures her lovers 'in bands' (VI. vii. 33) while she, ironically, remains the 'Ladie of her libertie' (VI. vii. 31). Punished for her behaviour by Disdain, Mirabella falls victim to the very 'chaines' which she imposed on others, in the form of 'hempen raines' (VI. vii. 44). Meanwhile, Timias is similarly subjected: 'heauy hand the Carle vpon him layde / And bound him fast' (VI. vii. 48); 'Led in a rope which both his hands did bynd' (VI. vii. 49); 'with an hempen cord / He like a dog was led in captiue case' (VI. viii. 5), even though he is 'vnworthy of your wretched bands' (VI. viii. 7). Sir Enias, likewise, is 'bound, and thrald without delay' (VI. viii. 11), 'They downe him hold, and fast with cords do bynde' (VI. viii. 12).

Spenser's images of binding grow progressively more negative throughout book VI. Thus Serena is tied up by the cannibals, to be released (only just in time) by Calepine (VI. viii. 50). Pastorella, captured by the brigands, is 'led / Into captiuity' (VI. x. arg), where she suffers 'in bondage strong' (VI. xi. 2), until the time when 'Fortune would her captiue bonds vnbynde' (VI. xi. 8). She is then sold to merchants as a 'bondslaue' (VI. xi. 10), and is subsequently 'in wretched thraldome bound' (VI. xi. 24). Pastorella thus relives the unhappy experience of her mother, Claribell, who had been imprisoned by a cruel father, seeking her 'in wedlocke to have bound' against her will (VI. xii. 4), and who, with her lover, Bellamour, also endured cruel 'bands' (VI. xii. 10).

But perhaps the most serious of Spenser's revisions of the 'bands of ciuilitie' occurs in Sir Calidore. For he is unequivocally 'bound by vow' to obey the Faerie Queene and pursue the Blatant Beast (VI. ii. 37). And yet he breaks this binding oath in order to bind himself to 'Another quest, another game in vew', his love for Pastorella (VI. x. 2). Spenser dwells on the equivalence of the two quests, both of which Calidore has to 'follow' (VI. x. 1), and both of which result in

similarly incurable wounds (VI. x. 31). And it is specifically in order
to evade the 'painted show' of courts, set 'T'entrap vnwary fooles'
(VI. x. 3), that Calidore finds himself being ensnared by other means:
'He was vnwares surprisd in subtile bands / Of the blynd boy' (VI. ix.
11), 'now entrapt of loue' (VI. x. 1).

The images of captivity which here surround the descriptions of
Calidore's love serve to revise the 'Goodly golden chaine, wherewith
yfere / The vertues linked are in louely wize' which Spenser defines
in book I (ix. 1), and which forms the central image of concord or
friendship in book IV. For in book VI love is not presented straightforwardly as a courteous exchange (or courtship), but is dogged by
images of restriction and imprisonment, leaving us in some doubt
about the possible benefits of being 'bound' either by love or by
civility.

Spenser relates the theme of binding to those acts of ritual
disarming, divestment, and unloosening which fill book VI, for, in
each case, an act of untying is associated with freedom from an
unwelcome encumbrance. Thus, when Calepine is found resting,
'His warlike armes he had from him vndight' (VI. iii. 20). He is
similarly unarmed when he encounters the bear: 'Well then him
chaunst his heauy armes to want, / Whose burden mote empeach his
needfull speed, / And hinder him from libertie to pant' (VI. iv. 19).
For once a Spenserian knight is glad to be rid of his armour, for it
enables him to run away without hindrance, rather as the Salvage
Man removes the borrowed armour which he has been wearing –
'And streight his cumbrous armes aside did lay' (VI. v. 10). The
Hermit has permanently disarmed himself, 'hanging vp his armes
and warlike spoyle, / From all this worlds incombraunce did himselfe
assoyle' (VI. v. 37), while Arthur rests, 'Hauing his armes and
warlike things vndight' (VI. vii. 19). Likewise, Melibee and his wife
entreat Calidore to put off his knightly accoutrements, and to
'disattyre' (VI. ix. 17), while Calidore voluntarily disarms for Pastorella, 'doffing his bright armes' (VI. ix. 36).

Any form of restriction or bond in book VI thus proves to be as
ineffectual as it is unwelcome, and never more so than in the
culminating episode in which the elusive Blatant Beast is finally
captured. 'Calidore doth the Blatant beast / subdew, and bynd in
bands', the argument to the twelfth canto tells us confidently, the
Beast's talkative tongue being finally muzzled in a chain 'Of surest
yron, made with many a lincke' (VI. xii. 34). There is a curious

insistence on the binding of the Beast in 'a greate long chaine' (VI. xii. 34) – it is 'fast bound in yron chaine' and caught in 'bondage strong' (VI. xii. 35, 37); it chafes under 'those / Straunge bands', and submits to Calidore's 'powre' (VI. xii. 36) – which renders the final outcome all the more bathetic and ironic. For the Blatant Beast, of course, escapes, 'broke his yron chaine', and gets away, seriously compromising Sir Calidore's achievement – 'the maystring might / Of doughty Calidore' (VI. xii. 38). Moreover, the escaped Beast is more of a menace than before, for it 'Ne euer could by any more be brought / Into like bands', and no future knight 'could euer bring him into band' (VI. xii. 39).

Like so many of the agents of binding or enclosing in book VI – clothes, arms, fetters, cages, bonds, bowers, and chains – the muzzle of the Blatant Beast breaks, powerfully suggesting that the 'bands of ciuilitie' and 'bands of loue', emblematized by the three Graces, may also be irrevocably damaged or destroyed. And the sense that circles are rarely (if ever) left intact infuses with pessimism Spenser's portrayal of courteous gift-exchange. For his initial act of 'returne' at the opening of book VI – 'from your selfe I doe this virtue bring, / And to your selfe doe it returne again' (VI. Pro. 7) – requires a counter-gesture of return from Queen Elizabeth. Yet it is precisely cyclic gestures of return that Spenser problematizes throughout book VI.

Take, for example, the structural cycle that is marked by Calidore's departure from and return to the Faerie court. That the knight *does* eventually go back to the Faerie Queene is, of course, a positive image – an act of return that has been successfully charted, plotted, and concluded, rather as the poet-husband finally secures the love of his mistress in the *Epithalamion*. And yet Calidore's return is marred by his much-commented-on truancy, and by the relentlessly centrifugal movement which takes him away from the place where he belongs:

> Him first from court he to the citties coursed,
> And from the citties to the townes him prest,
> And from the townes into the countrie forsed,
> And from the country back to priuate farmes he scorsed.
> From thence into the open fields he fled.   (VI. ix. 3–4)

Moreover, Calidore's return to the court is not only problematized by a digressive and dilatory impulse, but also by the curious ambivalence that surrounds his intentions. As he says to Melibee:

Giue leaue awhyle, good father, in this shore
To rest my barcke, which hath bene beaten late
With stormes of fortune and tempestuous fate,
In seas of troubles and of toylesome paine,
That whether quite from them for to retrate
I shall resolue, or backe to turne againe,
I may here with your selfe some small repose obtaine.

(VI. ix. 31)

Calidore's equivocal 'whether' is not resolved until the final canto of book VI when he finally leaves Pastorella to pursue his quest and to return to the Faerie court. The crucial issue of whether Calidore intends his idyll to be temporary or permanent is therefore left tantalizingly open-ended, and, as we shall see, book VI is full of such equivocations, such 'whethers'. At the beginning of canto x, for example, the narrator tells us with assurance that Calidore – reprehensibly 'Vnmyndfull' of his binding vow to Gloriana – becomes 'entrapt' of a love that has overtones of the Blatant Beast, so that 'certes mote he greatly blamed be'. And yet the narrator then goes on to excuse Calidore for abandoning his quest on the grounds that his unique and privileged sight of the Graces justified his dereliction. Spenser's narrator is being as equivocal as Sidney's in the *Old Arcadia* here, carefully balancing the conflicting demands of a binding vow on the one hand and the snares of love on the other, or of the imperatives of the court and the temptations of the country.[47] The use of rhetorical questions serves to compound the ambivalence:

For what hath all that goodly glorious gaze
Like to one sight, which Calidore did vew? ...
Saue onely Gloriana's heauenly hew
To which what can compare?

(VI. x. 4)

Does Calidore's vision compare with the beauty of the Faerie Queene or not? Is his privileged glance worth it? The rhetorical questions, of course, are left unanswered, as is the mystery surrounding the escape of the Blatant Beast: 'whether wicked fate so framed, / Or fault of men, he broke his yron chaine' (VI. xii. 38). Again, we are left in doubt about whether Calidore's quest is complete or not, and about whether he succeeds or fails in closing the circle which the Beast's iron chain and the return to the Faerie court both represent.

The equivocation which infuses Sir Calidore's intentions and motivation is related to the mystery which habitually surrounds figures' origins in book VI. While, to give an obvious example, the motif of children being returned to their parents recurs (as in the return of Aladine to Aldus, or Pastorella to Claribell and Bellamour), a nagging suspicion remains that they are not always necessarily being returned to the place from which they came. As Tristram declares guardedly to Sir Calidore, origins are best kept concealed: 'May be / Sir knight, that by discouering my estate, / Harme may arise vnweeting vnto me' (VI. ii. 27). Thus, while the bear-baby is reassuringly returned to its nominal father (Sir Bruin) we do not know where it came from. Similarly, the poet fails to divulge the origins of the Salvage Man although he promises to do so 'when time shall be to tell the same' (VI. v. 2). Confusing and contradictory genealogies are most noticeable, however, with regard to the two central emblems of book VI – the Graces and the Blatant Beast. In book VI, the Graces are the daughters of 'sky-ruling Ioue' and 'faire Euronyme' (VI. x. 22), but, in an earlier manifestation, they are specifically the children of Venus (II. viii. 6). And, at VI. i. 8, the Blatant Beast is said to be the offspring of Cerberus and Chimaera, but, according to the Hermit, it was also born of Echidna and Typhaeon (VI. vi. 9).[48] The relation between parents and children is therefore shown to be a site for uncertainty and confusion, as a critical amnesia creeps in between generations and consequently fudges identity.

The motif of cycle which Spenser problematizes in Calidore's return to court and in the return of children to their parents reappears, most significantly, in the apparent impulse to return words to their meanings. At the beginning of the first canto of book VI, Spenser marks an act of etymological return when he seeks to restore the 'true' meaning of courtesy by looking for it at the court:

> Of Court it seemes, men Courtesie doe call,
> For that it there most vseth to abound.   (VI. i. 1)

Spenser's oft-quoted lines draw on the ancient and much-debated controversy between aristocratic privilege and meritocratic virtue: an issue that had been a matter of speculation and debate for many centuries. And, initially at least, Spenser's words imply an underlying principle of continuity and contiguity whereby 'courtesy' is literally (as well as philologically) derived from the 'court'. The impulse to return words to their 'true' meanings (deriving ultimately from Plato's *Cratylus*) serves here to bolster the aristocratic fiction that the court was indeed the defining referent of courteous conduct, as Dante suggested, in the *Convivio*, that 'cortesia' originally derived from 'corte'.[49] Likewise, Spenser's contemporary, Simon Robson, wrote of 'This Court, the which of Curtesie takes name', and, later, George Herbert was to suggest that 'Courtesie grows in court.'[50]

As most commentators go on to point out, however, Spenser loads the word 'seemes' in order to hint at a radical fissure between the two elements – court and courtesy, word and meaning. For, instead of a principle of etymological continuity, it is argued, he gives us one of discontinuity, whereby the court is the last place where true courtesy might be found. In other words, an initial humanistic optimism that the return of words to their etymological source will establish their 'true' meaning gives way instead to a profound scepticism. And again, Spenser was in good company. For the derivation of 'cortezia' had been a constant theme in the troubadour lyric, in which it was argued, on the whole, that 'cortezia' was not the behavioural embellishment of a man already courtly, nor an additional virtue serving to round off the nearly perfect courtier, but a virtue possessed by some individuals irrespective of their rank. Indeed, in the egalitarian atmosphere of 'fin' amors', 'cortezia' was frequently denied to loutish aristocrats, for love was the great social leveller, allowing the basest man who loves with true love to be courteous.[51] 'E cortesia es d'amar', writes Marcabru; 'greu er cortes / Hom qui d'amor se desesper', writes Cercamon; and 'greu er pros ni cortes / qui ab amor no·s sap tener', Pierre d'Auvergne.[52] For Guillaume IX:

> Per son joy pot malautz sanar,
> E per sa ira sas morir
> E savis hom enfolezir
> E belhs hom sa beautat mudar
> E·l plus cortes vilanejar
> E totz vilas encortezir.[53]

That courtesy was not exclusively a court virtue was therefore a commonplace. Thus Richard Lanham describes a badly prepared and ill-served banquet at the 1575 Kenilworth entertainment, which was 'disorderly wasted & coorsly consumed, more courtly methought then curteously'.[54] In his account of Elizabeth's progress to East Anglia in 1578, Thomas Churchyard describes with agreeable surprise the good behaviour of the common people 'albeit it seemeth strange, that people nurtured farre from Courte, shoulde vse muche courtesie'.[55] In Webster's White Devil, Flamineo describes how he 'visited the Court, whence I return'd / More courteous, more letcherous by farre'.[56] And in Robert Greene's pastoral romance

Menaphon, the protagonist woos the heroine Samela 'with such courtesie, that shee finding such content in the cotage, began to despise the honors of the Court'.[57]

So the philological circle which returns 'courtesy' to the 'court' is broken, or at least redefined, rather as Stefano Guazzo defines his key term 'civility' in *La civile conversatione* (one of Spenser's chief source-books for book VI of *The Faerie Queene*):

GUAZZO: What meane you by that woord, ciuile?
ANNIBALE: If you meane to know my meaning of it, I must first aske if you know any citizen which liueth vnciuilly?
GUAZZO: Yes mary doe I, more then one.
ANNIBALE: Now let me aske you on the contrarie, if you know any man of the countrey which liueth ciuilly.
GUAZZO: Yea very many.
ANNIBALE: You see then, that we giue a large sense and signification to this woorde (ciuile) for that we would haue vnderstoode, that to liue ciuilly, is not sayde in respecte of the citie, but of the qualities of the minde.[58]

Guazzo's interlocutor here overtly critiques the obvious 'etymological' sense of 'civility' (as deriving from the 'civitas') on the grounds that civility is to be found outside the city and incivility within it. Experience thus overgoes the limits of etymological convention, for true civility is less to be found in the city than in 'the qualities of the minde', just as Spenser's courtesy is as likely to be found 'deepe within the mynd' as at court (VI. Pro. 5).

As Guazzo says, 'we giue a large sense and signification to this woorde'. In the same way, the 'large sense' or instability of the keyword of book VI generates a multiplicity of meanings, for lying behind Spenser's 'Courtesie' (both in book VI and in *The Faerie Queene* as a whole) is a wealth of reference and association which derives from the rich semantic field of the word in the Middle Ages. 'Courtesy' is thought by philologists to have shifted from a highly specific sense – the virtue exemplified by a man of the court or a chevalier – to accrue what J. W. Nicholls calls 'a complete band of ethical and moral meanings'.[59] At root, therefore, courtesy was essentially a knightly virtue.[60] Thus Sir Lancelot is noted for his great courtesy, and Malory calls him 'the curtest knyght that ever bare shelde'. In *Sir Gawain and the Green Knight* (which explores the rich polysemy of the word 'cortaysye' in Middle English) it is specifically its reputation for courtesy that brings the green interloper to Arthur's court.[61] Spenser draws on this earliest sense of 'courtesy', therefore, when he writes of the exemplary Calidore: 'What vertue is so fitting for a knight . . . As Curtesie' (VI. ii. 1).

But courtesy was not solely the virtue belonging to a knight, for the semantic parameters of the word expanded massively throughout the twelfth century, to become infused with profound Christian signification. In *The Parson's Tale*, for example, Christ is described as 'the curteis Lord'.[62] The Incarnation is considered a 'greate cortaysie' in the *Ayenbite of Inwyt*, and, in the *Cursor Mundi*, not only do Christ's miracles manifest 'curtasi', but even the punitive vengeance on the Tower of Babel is called a 'curtais wrak' since it was undertaken to reform the wrongdoers.[63] Christ personifies courtesy in *Purity* – 'Alle called on þat Cortayse and claymed his grace' – while, in *Pearl*, the Virgin Mary is dubbed the 'Quen of cortasye'.[64] Harking back to this sense, Spenser clusters 'courtesy' around the House of Holiness, which (structurally parallel with the Acidalian vision in book VI) is described as a 'court' where Redcrosse and Una are entertained with 'courteous glee', 'rare courtesie', 'court' sies', and 'court' sies seeming meet' (I. x. 6, 7, 11, 15, 32).

At the other end of the spectrum, 'courtesy' also comprised what W. O. Evans calls a 'purely conventional reference to acquired patterns – the right thing to do'. Such simple etiquette is exemplified by the model table-manners of *Sir Degaré*, who

> coupe of curteisie:
> He set a chaier bifore þe leuedie,
> And þerin himselue set,
> And tok a knif and carf his met,

or of Chaucer's Squire, who 'Curteis . . . was, lowely and servysable, / And carf biforn his fader at the table'.[65] For Spenser the word 'courtesy' could likewise refer simply to etiquette, as in the 'courteous conge' (II. xi. 17, III. i. 1) or 'courteous leaue' (VI. ii. 38) which make for graceful departure. As a form of purely external behaviour, moreover, this kind of courtesy was frequently feigned, as in the 'dissembling curtesie' of the courtiers in *Colin Clouts Come Home Againe* (line 700), the 'idle curtesie' of Genius in the Bower of Bliss (II. xii. 49), or the 'curtesies' of the 'courting fooles' of whom the Hermit complains in book VI (v. 38).

The use of 'courtesy' as a term in the art of love was, in turn, a further specialization of the word. Thus the young princess in *Havelok the Dane*, for example, 'covþe of curteysye / Don, and speken of loue-drurye', rather as Spenser's Priscilla and Aladine, enjoying their 'franke loues', are said to indulge in 'louely courtesyes' (VI. ii. 16).[66] The amorous sense of 'courtesy' easily lent itself to sexual innuendo, as in the Lady's highly ambiguous 'cortaysye' to Gawain in *Sir Gawain and the Green Knight*. In the fourteenth-century lyric *The Bird with Four Feathers*, the 'craft of curteseye' is associated unequivocally with lust.[67] We have already seen how Gascoigne perverts the meaning of 'courtesy' in *The Adventures of Master F.J.*, while one of the women in Lyly's *Sapho and Phao* remarks that 'Me thinks lyking, a curtesie, a smile, a beck, and such like, are the very Quintessence of loue.'[68]

Spenser's apparently bland articulation of an etymological commonplace – 'Of Court it seemes, men Courtesie doe call' – is therefore nothing of the sort. It inaugurates a mode that opens up the possibility of endless debate, for the word 'courtesy' covered a field of different meanings ranging from divine grace to sex. At the most basic level, the instability of the keyword of book VI thus creates a justifiable suspicion about the relation between word and thing, and about the function and use of etymology. Moreover, Spenser's register of equivocation lies behind the well-worn debate between nature and nurture which book VI also rehearses. For the semantic imprecision embedded in the relation of 'courtesy' to the 'court' is reflected in the confusing shifts Spenser's narrator makes between identifying meritocratic and aristocratic virtue.

At the beginning of canto ii, for example, we are assured that some individuals are possessed of natural grace, which others, 'Though they enforce themselues, cannot attaine', although the lesser, 'enforced' virtue is also to be praised. But when the following stanza begins 'That well in courteous Calidore appeares' the ambiguity of Spenser's 'That' leaves us wondering whether Calidore's courtesy is the natural or the studied kind, or both (VI. ii. 1–2). Indeed, Calidore's courtesy is here like Blandina's flattery, which 'Whether such grace were giuen her by kynd ... Or learn'd the art to please, I doe not fynd' (VI. vi. 43). In each case, the source of a figure's courtesy (be it genuine or false) remains, even for the narrator, a matter of speculation.

At the beginning of canto iii, the narrator declares that 'The gentle minde by gentle deeds is knowne' (VI. iii. 1), that is, that courtesy remains the privilege of a gentleman – a doctrine which 'well may be in Calidore descryde' (VI. iii. 2). In the following canto, however, Calepine assures Matilda that nurture and upbringing are known to make 'braue and noble knights' of those 'whose lignage is vnknowne' (VI. iv. 36). The Salvage Man represents just such a noble creature of unknown origin. And, while in canto iii the poet had declared that seldom 'one in basenesse set / Doth noble courage shew, with curteous manner met' (VI. iii. 1), the Salvage Man does exactly that, his apparently 'gentle blood' manifesting itself through his ungentle exterior. As one critic writes, Spenser thus maintains 'the aristocratic fiction at the expense of a great deal of irony'.[69]

Spenser's play with semantic discontinuity – suggesting that the court is not always (and is certainly not necessarily) the source of courtesy – is related, therefore, to the overall themes of equivocation, subversion, and fragmentation which are explored throughout book VI. For the failure to return words to their 'original' meanings corresponds to the problems that surround the return of children to their parents, and the delayed return of Sir Calidore to the Faerie court. And, while returns *are* made – Calidore does go back to Gloriana, children do return to their parents, and some courtiers are courteous – yet in every case these restorative gestures are made problematic. Spenser's text thus hints that those acts of courteous return which mark the ideal traffic of gifts between a patron and a poet (and which the encircling dance of the Graces represents) are similarly fragile and prone to delay.

So it comes as no surprise, then, to find that the overarching cyclic movement which book VI appears to gesture toward in *The Faerie Queene* as a whole is, like all the other circles and cycles in the Legend of Courtesy, similarly flawed.[70] Commentators have repeatedly pointed out that the narrator's noticeable change of tone in the Proem to book VI argues for a return to the pastoral mode which the poet had formally relinquished in the Proem to book I, thus reversing 'the development of civilization, which the development of Virgil's poetic canon was alleged to have recapitulated', as Nohrnberg writes.[71] As the poet returns home again (like Colin Clout in another poem), he appears to come full circle, and to go back to the point from which he began in a movement that A. Leigh DeNeef has described as 'comfortably closural'.[72]

At the beginning of book VI, this veering toward closure is identified strongly with both Sir Calidore and the narrative voice,

each of whom finds himself guideless, alone, and bemused, and each
of whom considers the pastoral world a suitable escape from his
'tedious' and 'weary trauell' (vi. Pro. 1; i. 10). Yet the 'comfortably
closural' movement exemplified here is seriously disrupted by the
fragmentation of Spenser's poetic voice which occurs in canto x. For
there – at the very heart of the pastoral retreat which both Calidore
and Colin ('the Author selfe') have sought out for themselves –
Spenser's two personae fail to recognize each other. Apparently
unsure who this creature of his own devising is, Colin addresses
Calidore as 'shepheard, whatsoeuer thou bee' (vi. x. 21). And
Calidore, in turn, ironically becomes the 'author' of his own author's
loss when he destroys the Acidalian vision (vi. x. 29).

    In other words, the return movement – associated up to this point
with both 'the Author selfe' (Colin Clout) and the knight of his
creating (Sir Calidore) – here breaks up as a third voice intervenes to
berate each of them for their parallel acts of truancy. It is this third
voice that announces itself in the rhetorical questions of canto x:
'Who now does follow the foule *Blatant Beast*?', 'Saue onely *Glorianaes*
heauenly hew / To which what can compare?', 'who knowes not
Colin Clout?' While both Colin and Calidore are truant poets,
idolizing private loves instead of following royal behests (to fulfil a
quest, to compose a national epic), this third voice separates itself
from each of them:

> Now turne againe my teme thou iolly swayne,
> Backe to the furrow which I lately left;
> I lately left a furrow, one or twayne
> Vnplough'd, the which my coulter hath not cleft.   (vi. ix. 1)

On every other occasion when Spenser employs the familiar
georgic image the motif serves to stress the poet's exhaustion.[73] But
here the furrow signifies a revival of strength that is markedly
different from the enervated and holiday moods of Calidore and
Colin, and which hints that the third voice approximates most
closely to the portrait of an ideal courtier in *Mother Hubberds Tale*.
When 'this Courtly Gentleman with toyle / Himselfe hath wearied',
Spenser writes, he entertains himself with music, and 'with Loues,
and Ladies gentle sports' (lines 753–4, 757), rather as Calidore
indulges himself in his own pastoral retreat. But, in addition, the
virtuous courtier also obeys the summons to the epic genre as he 'His
minde vnto the Muses he withdrawes',

With whom he close confers with wise discourse,
Of Natures workes, of heauens continuall course,
Of forreine lands, of people different,
Of kingdomes change, of diuers gouernment,
Of dreadfull battailes of renowmed Knights.   (lines 763–7)

Book VI of *The Faerie Queene* thus seems to contain at least three
distinct and separable poetic personae, some of whom trace a
backward return movement, and some of whom do not. For while
Calidore eventually returns to the court and its discursive economies, and while Colin reverts to the pastoral 'Oaten reeds' left
behind at the Proem to book I, the third voice remains as the epic
poet who carries on forward, through to the twelfth canto and
beyond.

We can see, then, that the very structure of *The Faerie Queene* as a
whole can be held to embody the sense of uncertainty about gestures
of return which forms the underlying theme of Spenser's Legend of
Courtesy. For, just as the 'goodly band' of the Graces (VI. x. 14)
proves to be frighteningly fragile, so the bounds of Spenser's
narrative are incapable of containing that monster of detraction, the
Blatant Beast. In his *Discorso intorno al comporre dei romanzi* (1554),
Giraldi Cinthio describes the principle of order in the romance form
as being like a continuous thread or chain – 'deue in queste digres-
sioni esser molto aueduto il Poeta in trattarle di modo, che una
dipenda dall'altra, et siano bene aggiunte con le parti della materia,
che si ha preso a dire con continuo filo et continua catena'.[74] So,
when the Blatant Beast bursts its 'greate long chaine' (VI. xii. 34) at
the end of book VI and roars out of the poem into the poet's own
world, it threatens to shatter the structural circularity of the poem,
and to destabilize the fragile bonds of gratitude and debt upon
which Spenser was forced to depend:

Ne may this homely verse, of many meanest,
Hope to escape his venemous despite,
More then my former writs, all were they clearest
From blamefull blot, and free from all that wite,
With which some wicked tongues did it backebite,
And bring into a mighty Peres displeasure,
That neuer so deserued to endite.
Therefore do you my rimes keep better measure,
And seeke to please, that now is counted wisemens threasure.
                                                    (VI. xii. 41)

Book VI of *The Faerie Queene* therefore centres round those models of reciprocity and cycle which Spenser sets up in the opening stanzas of the Proem when he takes the virtue of courtesy from Elizabeth and 'to your selfe doe it returne againe' (VI. Pro. 7). The proper response to this very public act of 'returne' is, of course, another return. But until the royal gesture has been satisfactorily made, poet and patron remain locked in a strategic game of wait-and-see. And it is just such a game – with its conflicting demands for gratitude and gripes, thanks and pique, outspokenness and subtlety – that Spenser operates at every level of his poem.

Epilogue

Faced with the problem of concluding a book which has tried to set out the values and virtues of open-endedness, I would like to close by looking briefly at *King Lear*, a text which, in its orientation toward a style of court and kingship very different from Elizabeth's, appears to meditate long and hard on the strategies of courtship at court.

At the end of the play, Edgar (or Albany in the Quarto text) looks out over a corpse-strewn stage and admonishes us to 'Speak what we feel, not what we ought to say' (v. iii. 325). At one level, these words carry all the resonance of a lesson learned, fulfilling an emotional desire to see vindicated and restored those truth-tellers who have been penalized at every turn throughout the play. But at another more ironic level the final, caption-like statement strikes a discordant note. For it is spoken over the ruins of a family and a court that has been devastated precisely by individuals speaking what they feel. In failing to subordinate what she felt to what the circumstances required her to say, Cordelia's well-intentioned tactlessness in the opening scene constitutes a grievous sin against courtesy – a skill of which her sisters, for all the 'glib and oily art' of their hypocrisy, at least maintain an outward semblance (i. i. 224). In book vi of *The Faerie Queene*, Sir Calidore's automatic use of white lies, half-truths, approximations, and euphemisms is shown to be the essence of courtesy. Cordelia's catastrophic lack of *savoir-faire*, by contrast, reveals her baleful ignorance of such judicious and prudent courtship.

The first scene of *King Lear* dramatizes the dangers of plain speaking in the most striking way, powerfully suggesting that the truth must be preserved for the proper time and place. As Bacon was to write in his essay 'Of Truth' (1625):

Doth any man doubt, that if there were taken out of men's minds vain opinions, flattering hopes, false valuations, imaginations as one would, and the like, but it would leave the minds of a number of men poor shrunken things, full of melancholy and indisposition, and unpleasing to themselves?[1]

What Bacon is concerned about here is courtesy, the myriad graces and adjustments that are necessary to maintain a tactful and dignified appearance of social and political decorum. Cordelia's lack of courtesy at the beginning of *King Lear* in turn inaugurates a series of monstrous crimes as outrageous as anything that we find in book VI of *The Faerie Queene*: a king and father stripped of his retainers, mocked, abused, and left out in the cold (on a night when a dog would have fared better); a courteous host horribly abused when his guests take over his house and put out his eyes.

These egregious crimes against courtesy belong, I suggest, with those perpetrated by the villains, cannibals, and brigands in Spenser's Legend of Courtesy. They also cast a critical light on Cordelia's own lack of diplomacy – her inability to recognize the proper occasions for speaking 'what we feel, not what we ought to say'. For it is not that truth-telling is intrinsically wrong: as Kent tells Lear, 'To plainness honour's bound, / When majesty falls to folly' (I. i. 148–9). But, as parables about the virtues of 'functional ambiguity', both Shakespeare's play and Spenser's Legend suggest that there are times when circumspection and a judicious economy with the truth serve better than downright honesty. Bluntness can be deceptive, for the disguised Kent presents himself to Lear as being 'no less than I seem' when he is at his most dissembling (I. iv. 12). And, as Cornwall warns,

> These kind of knaves I know, which in this plainness
> Harbour more craft and more corrupter ends
> Than twenty silly-ducking observants
> That stretch their duties nicely. (II. ii. 101–4)

To reduce such texts to 'parables', on the other hand, makes for an interpretational crudity that inevitably conflicts with the complexity and ambivalence which it has been the aim of this book to explore. *King Lear* is, in one sense, the paradigmatic courtly text. For the subtle and contradictory devices of royal representation that had to be set against the exigencies of a court performance (the Quarto text) are further distorted, submerged, and simplified in the later,

Folio version, creating a text that is, in Annabel Patterson's phrase, 'deeply ambiguated'.[2] Seeing *King Lear* as a play which is concerned, at every level, with the power and propriety of *in*direction at court thus attempts to avoid schematizing the play, while making a virtue of its complexity and contradictoriness.

To return to Bacon:

> truth is a naked and open day-light, that doth not shew the masks and mummeries and triumphs of the world, half so stately and daintily as candle-lights. Truth may perhaps come to the price of a pearl, that sheweth best by day; but it will not rise to the price of a diamond or carbuncle, that sheweth best in varied lights.[3]

Bacon's haunting, candle-lit world resonates with Spenser's description of the imprisoned Pastorella in book vi of *The Faerie Queene*:

> The sight of whom, though now decayd and mard,
> And eke but hardly seene by candle-light,
> Yet like a Diamond of rich regard,
> In doubtfull shadow of the darkesome night,
> With starrie beames about her shining bright,
> These marchants fixed eyes did so amaze,
> That what through wonder, and what through delight,
> A while on her they greedily did gaze,
> And did her greatly like, and did her greatly praize.
>
> (*FQ* vi. xi. 13)

Like Bacon's diamond, Pastorella also shows best by candle-light. Indeed, the cave in which she lies trapped is illuminated solely by 'candlelight, which delt / A doubtfull sense of things', a semi-darkness which takes us back to the 'dreadfull doubts' of Error's den in the first canto of book i, lit dimly only by 'A little glooming light' (*FQ* i. i. 12–13).

Bacon and Spenser thus return us to the sense of 'doubtfulness' with which this book began. For, as we have seen, the structural and semantic ambivalence of courtship as a mode of language and gesture led to the cultivation of confusion, unintelligibility, and conflicting signals in Renaissance courtly texts. Sincerity and deception cannot be disentangled from each other. It is no accident, then, that when Lear brings out the dead Cordelia in his arms at the end of the play, Shakespeare gives us a horrible parody of the old adage that 'Truth is the daughter of Time'. The emblem books illustrate the motto with an old man leading his daughter, a young and beautiful maiden, from a cave. But at the end of *King Lear* Truth is not only dead; she is carried in the arms of a man whose very name hints at 'liar'.

Shakespeare's play therefore seems to leave us in the candle-lit cave of Spenser's Pastorella and Bacon's Truth: a truth which, while she has to be courted, is most often found in dark and flickering places, carefully hidden in obscurity. Like so many of the texts we have been looking at, *King Lear* thus meditates upon the virtues of indirection and ambivalence which courtship – in all senses of the word – characteristically defines.

Notes

PROLOGUE

1. The manuscript (British Museum, Royal MS 18 A xlviii) is transcribed in *The Complete Works of George Gascoigne*, ed. J. W. Cunliffe, 2 vols. (Cambridge: Cambridge University Press, 1907–10), ii. 473–510, this quotation p. 476. (Unless otherwise indicated, arabic numerals refer to page numbers throughout.)
2. From a printed version of the Tale of Hemetes, *The Queenes Majesties Entertainment at Woodstocke* (1585), collated with Gascoigne's manuscript by Cunliffe, this quotation p. 581.
3. George Gascoigne, *A Hundreth Sundrie Flowers* (1573), ed. C. T. Prouty (Columbia: University of Missouri Press, 1942), all page references are to this edition.

1 THE RHETORIC OF COURTSHIP: AN INTRODUCTION

1. See, in particular, Arthur Marotti, ' "Love Is Not Love": Elizabethan Sonnet Sequences and the Social Order', *Journal of English Literary History* 49 (1982), 396–428; Louis Adrian Montrose, 'Celebration and Insinuation: Sir Philip Sidney and the Motives of Elizabethan Courtship', *Renaissance Drama* 8 (1977), 3–35; Maureen Quilligan, 'Sidney and his Queen', in Heather Dubrow and Richard Strier, eds., *The Historical Renaissance: New Essays on Tudor and Stuart Culture and Literature* (Chicago: University of Chicago Press, 1988); Leonard Tennenhouse, 'Sir Walter Ralegh and the Literature of Clientage', in Guy Fitch Lytle and Stephen Orgel, eds., *Patronage in the Renaissance* (Princeton, NJ: Princeton University Press, 1981); Peter Stallybrass and Ann Rosalind Jones, 'The Politics of *Astrophil and Stella*', *Studies in English Literature* 24 (1984), 53–68. See also, Daniel Javitch, *Poetry and Courtliness in Renaissance England* (Princeton, NJ: Princeton University Press, 1978).
2. Marc Bloch, *Feudal Society*, trans. L. A. Manyon (London: Routledge and Kegan Paul, 1961).

3. D. A. L. Morgan, 'The House of Policy: The Political Role of the Late Plantagenet Household, 1422–1485', in David Starkey, ed., *The English Court from the Wars of the Roses to the Civil War* (London: Longman, 1987), 67–8.

4. Edmund Spenser, *The Ruines of Time* (1591), lines 200–2. All references to Spenser are to the Variorum edition, ed. Edwin Greenlaw *et al.*, 8 vols. (Baltimore: Johns Hopkins University Press, 1932–8). John Donne, *Satire I*, lines 23–4, in *John Donne: The Satires, Epigrams and Verse Letters*, ed. W. Milgate (Oxford: Clarendon Press, 1967), 3.

5. Stephen Ullmann, *The Principles of Semantics*, 2nd edn (Oxford: Blackwell, 1957), 223.

6. Spenser, *Mother Hubberds Tale* (1591), lines 793, 784.

7. Spenser, *The Faerie Queene* (1596), III. x. 6.

8. Dante Alighieri: 'La mente innamorata, che donnea / con la mia donna sempre, di ridure / ad essa li occhi più che mai ardea', *La Divina Commedia*, Paradiso, xxvii. 88–90, ed. Natalino Sapegno (Milan: Ricciardi, 1957), 1116 ('My loving mind, which never ceased to woo my lady as her lover, longed still more ardently to meet her eyes'). Contrast *The Romaunt of the Rose*, lines 1291–4: 'Les queroles ia remenoit; / Car tuit li plusor s'en aloient / O lor amies ombroier / Soz ces arbres, por donoier' ('They were already ceasing their carols, for most of them were disappearing to make love to their mistresses under the shade of the trees'), in Guillaume de Lorris and Jean de Meun, *The Romaunt of the Rose*, ed. Ronald Sutherland (Oxford: Blackwell, 1968), 27.

9. See Norbert Elias, *The Civilizing Process*, trans. Edmund Jephcott, 2 vols. (Oxford: Blackwell, 1982), and *The Court Society*, trans. Edmund Jephcott (Oxford: Blackwell, 1983).

10. Elias, *The Court Society*, 243.

11. Emile Durkheim, *The Rules of Sociological Method* (New York: Free Press, 1965); see also Steven Lukes, *Emile Durkheim: His Life and Work* (London: Allen Lane, 1973).

12. Pierre Bourdieu, *Outline of a Theory of Practice*, trans. Richard Nice (Cambridge: Cambridge University Press, 1977), 5. For another account of transactional gift-exchange, see David Parkin, 'Exchanging Words', in Bruce Kapferer, ed., *Transaction and Meaning: Directions in the Anthropology of Exchange and Symbolic Behaviour* (Philadelphia: Institute for the Study of Human Issues, 1976).

13. Bourdieu, *Outline of a Theory of Practice*, 9, Bourdieu's italics.

14. Spenser, *The Faerie Queene*, VI. Pro. 7.

15. John Donne, *Satire 4*, in *The Satires, Epigrams and Verse Letters*, ed. Milgate, 16.

16. John Lyly, *Euphues and his England* (1580), in *The Complete Works of John Lyly*, ed. R. Warwick Bond, 3 vols. (Oxford: Clarendon Press, 1902), ii. 181.

17. Robert Greene, *Mamillia*, part 2 (1583), in *The Life and Complete Works in Prose and Verse of Robert Greene*, ed. A. B. Grosart, 15 vols. (London: private publication, 1881–6), ii. 180.

18. See e.g. David Starkey and Christopher Coleman, eds., *Revolution Reassessed: Revisions in the History of Tudor Government and Administration* (Oxford: Clarendon Press, 1986); David Starkey, ed., *The English Court from the Wars of the Roses to the Civil War* (London: Longman, 1987); Lawrence Stone, *An Open Elite? England 1540–1880* (Oxford: Clarendon Press, 1984); and Kevin Sharpe, *Criticism and Compliment: The Politics of Literature in the England of Charles I* (Cambridge: Cambridge University Press, 1987).

19. For a brief guide to the historiography of this vast subject, see Roger Boase, *The Origin and Meaning of Courtly Love: A Critical Study of European Scholarship* (Manchester: Manchester University Press, 1977); F. X. Newman, ed., *The Meaning of Courtly Love* (Albany: State University of New York Press, 1968); Nathaniel B. Smith and Joseph T. Snow, eds., *The Expansion and Transformations of Courtly Literature* (Athens: University of Georgia Press, 1980); and Glyn S. Burgess, ed., *Court and Poet* (Liverpool: Cairns, 1981).

20. For a critique of the phrases 'courtly love' and 'amour courtois', see A. J. Denomy, 'Courtly Love and Courtliness', *Speculum* 28 (1953), 44–63; Jean Frappier, 'Vues sur les conceptions courtoises dans les littératures d'oc et d'oïl au XIIe siècle', *Cahiers de Civilisation Médiévale* 2 (1959), 135–56; and Moshé Lazar, *Amour courtois et 'fin'amors' dans la littérature de XIIe siècle* (Paris: Klincksieck, 1964).

21. Gaston Paris, 'Lancelot de Lac: II. Le Conte de la charrette', *Romania* 12 (1883), 459–534. 'One wonders why nobody has brought into the discussion the English word "to court" for "to make love" or "to woo",' remarks F. L. Utley, 'Must we Abandon the Concept of Courtly Love?', *Medievalia et Humanistica* NS 3 (1972), 299–324 (323).

22. E. T. Donaldson, 'The Myth of Courtly Love', in *Speaking of Chaucer* (London: Athlone Press, 1970), 154; Newman, ed. *The Meaning of Courtly Love*, x; D. W. Robertson, 'The Concept of Courtly Love as an Impediment to the Understanding of Medieval Texts', ibid. 1; T. Silverstein, 'Guenevere, or the Uses of Courtly Love', ibid. 87.

23. Georges Duby, *Mâle Moyen Age* (Paris: Flammarion, 1988), 75.

24. Peter Dronke, for example, argues that the court–love connection has been grossly over-exaggerated, *Medieval Latin and the Rise of European Love-Lyric*, 2 vols. (Oxford: Clarendon Press, 1965–6).

25. See e.g. Violet Paget (Vernon Lee), *Euphorion: Being Studies of the Antique and the Mediaeval in the Renaissance*, 2 vols. (London: Unwin, 1884); W. T. H. Jackson, *The Literature of the Middle Ages* (New York: Columbia University Press, 1960); Friedrich Heer, *The Medieval World: Europe 1100–1350*, trans. Janet Sondheimer (London: Weidenfeld and Nicolson, 1962); and Elizabeth Salter, 'Courts and Courtly

Love', in David Daiches and Anthony Thorlby, eds., *Literature and Western Civilization: The Medieval World* (London: Aldus, 1973).

26. See e.g. Marc Bloch, *Feudal Society*; and Georges Duby, *The Knight, the Lady, and the Priest: The Making of Modern Marriage in Medieval France*, trans. Barbara Bray (Harmondsworth: Penguin, 1983).

27. See Eric Köhler, *Ideal und Wirklichkeit in der höfischen Epik* (Tübingen: Niemeyer, 1956), *Trobadorlyrik und höfischen Roman* (Berlin: Rütten and Leoning, 1962), and 'Observations historiques et sociologiques sur la poésie des troubadours', *Cahiers de Civilisation Médiévale* 7 (1964), 27–51; Herbert Moller, 'The Social Causation of the Courtly Love Complex', *Comparative Studies in Society and History* 1 (1958–9), 137–63, and 'The Meaning of Courtly Love', *Journal of American Fiction* 73 (1960), 39–52; and Maurice Valency, *In Praise of Love: An Introduction to the Love-Poetry of the Renaissance* (New York: Macmillan, 1958).

28. See Duby, *The Knight, the Lady, and the Priest*, ch. 11.

29. For discussions of this ideology, see Denis de Rougemont, *Love in the Western World*, trans. Montgomery Belgion (Princeton, NJ: Princeton University Press, 1983); Philippe Ariès and André Béjin, *Western Sexuality: Practice and Precept in Past and Present Times* (Oxford: Blackwell, 1985), and Jean-Louis Flandrin, *Le Sexe et l'Occident* (Paris: Editions de Seuil, 1981).

30. Marc Bloch, *Feudal Society*; see also Georges Duby, ed., *A History of Private Life*, ii: *Revelations of the Medieval World* (Cambridge, Mass.: Harvard University Press, 1988); R. Howard Bloch, *Medieval French Literature and Law* (Berkeley and Los Angeles: University of California Press, 1977), and *Etymologies and Genealogies: A Literary Anthropology of the French Middle Ages* (Chicago: University of Chicago Press, 1983).

31. R. Howard Bloch, *Etymologies and Genealogies*, 69.

32. Duby, *The Knight, the Lady, and the Priest*, 18–19.

33. It is surprising that Foucault only addresses the question of courtship directly when discussing the relatively marginal subject of Hellenistic homosexual practice, *The History of Sexuality*, trans. Robert Hurley, 4 vols. (Harmondsworth: Penguin, 1981–), ii.

34. Johan Huizinga, *Homo Ludens: A Study of the Play Element in Culture*, trans. R. F. C. Hull (London: Routledge and Kegan Paul, 1949), 11.

35. For some important anthropological and literary studies of carnival and game, see Mikhail Bakhtin, *Rabelais and his World*, trans. Helen Iswolsky (Cambridge, Mass.: MIT Press, 1968); Huizinga, *Homo Ludens*; Clifford Geertz, *The Interpretation of Culture* (London: Hutchinson, 1975); Natalie Zemon Davis, *Society and Culture in Early Modern France* (London: Duckworth, 1975); and Leah Marcus, *The Politics of Mirth: Jonson, Herrick, Milton, Marvell, and the Defense of Old Holiday Pastimes* (Chicago: University of Chicago Press, 1986).

36. William Congreve, *The Old Bachelor* (1693), v. i. 388, in *The Complete*

Plays of William Congreve, ed. Herbert Davis (Chicago: University of Chicago Press, 1967), 107.

37. See Ferdinand de Saussure, *Course in General Linguistics*, ed. Charles Bally and Albert Sechehaye, trans. Roy Harris (London: Duckworth, 1983), 98.

38. Ullmann, *The Principles of Semantics*, 171.

39. Jacques Derrida, *Of Grammatology* (Baltimore: Johns Hopkins University Press, 1976).

40. See Roland Barthes, *Criticism and Truth*, trans. Katrine Pilcher Keuneman (London: Athlone Press, 1987), part 2.

41. Michel de Montaigne, 'Of Vanity', in *The Complete Works of Montaigne*, ed. Donald M. Frame (London: Hamish Hamilton, 1957), 751, from the French: 'J'escris mon livre à peu d'hommes et à peu d'années ... Selon la variation continuelle qui a suivy [notre langage] jusques à cette heure, qui peut esperer que sa forme presente soit en usage, d'icy à cinquante ans? Il escoule tous les jours de nos mains', *Œuvres complètes*, ed. A. Thibaudet and M. Rat (Paris: Pléiade, 1962), 960–1.

42. See e.g. R. Howard Bloch, *Etymologies and Genealogies*; Thomas Greene, *The Light in Troy: Imitation and Discovery in Renaissance Poetry* (New Haven, Conn.: Yale University Press, 1982); and Terence Cave, *The Cornucopian Text: Problems of Writing in the French Renaissance* (Oxford: Oxford University Press, 1979).

43. Leonardo Bruni, *Vita di Messer Francesco Petrarca* (1436), quoted by Eugenio Garin, *Italian Humanism: Philosophy and Civil Life in the Renaissance*, trans. Peter Munz (Oxford: Blackwell, 1965), 18.

44. For studies on the relation of humanist philology and history, see Garin, *Italian Humanism*; Donald Kelley, *Foundations of Modern Historical Scholarship: Language, Law, and History in the French Renaissance* (New York: Columbia University Press, 1970); George Huppert, *The Idea of Perfect History: Historical Erudition and Historical Philosophy in Renaissance France* (Urbana: University of Illinois Press, 1970); Nancy Streuver, *The Language of History in the Renaissance* (Princeton, NJ: Princeton University Press, 1970); Thomas Greene, *The Light in Troy*; Richard Waswo, *Language and Meaning in the Renaissance* (Princeton, NJ: Princeton University Press, 1987); and Peter Burke, *The Renaissance Sense of the Past* (London: Edward Arnold, 1969).

45. Leo Spitzer, *Linguistics and Literary Theory: Essays in Stylistics* (Princeton, NJ: Princeton University Press, 1948), 25.

46. Thomas Greene, *The Light in Troy*; see also Waswo, *Language and Meaning*, 156: 'Puns celebrate the Protean fluidity of signifiers, exploiting as many different semantic dimensions – of sound, of multiple definition, of etymological association, of grammatical function, of social register – as individual ingenuity can deploy. The greatest literature of the Renaissance enacts the energies and the fears

produced by this new fluidity as it emerged from all the argument of the period about words.'

47. Spenser, *The Faerie Queene*, VI. i. 1; Antonio de Guevara, *Aviso de privados*, trans. 'F.B.', 'The Larum of the Court', Houghton Library MS Eng 517, fol. 12ᵛ, by permission of the Houghton Library.

48. Huizinga, *Homo Ludens*, 5–6.

2 THE SEMANTICS OF COURTSHIP

1. I am grateful to the editors of the *Journal of Medieval and Renaissance Studies* for permission to reproduce here a modified version of my article ' "Of Court it Seemes": A Semantic Analysis of Courtship and to Court', 20 (1990), 21–57.

2. 'I sent them to France to court it in Paris. Charlemagne took great joy in them, and all were dubbed knights', anon., *La Chanson des Quatre Fils Aymon d'après le manuscrit de Vallière*, ed. Ferdinand Castets (Montpellier: Coulet, 1909), 380–1.

3. 'Sir William, go and graze your horse, and stable him comfortably. Then come back to the court to eat. You come and court it too modestly; haven't you got a sergeant or a squire to serve you on your travels?', *Guillaume d'Orange: chansons de geste*, ed. M. W. J. A. Jonckbloet, 2 vols. (The Hague: Nijhoff, 1854), i. 286–7.

4. There has been some debate as to which language borrowed from the other in this lexical change. See T. E. Hope, *Lexical Borrowing in the Romance Languages*, 2 vols. (Oxford: Blackwell, 1971), i. 184–5, who suggests that the French 'courtiser' derived directly from the Italian 'corteggiare'.

5. 'People are saying I've got a girl, but I really don't want one yet: I wouldn't know how to go courting. I'd rather have a drop myself than kiss', 'Le Vin l'Emporte sur l'Amour', lines 1–4; 'I'd give up love and courting ladies. It's enough for me to drink my fill and take it easy', 'Les Gales Bon-Temps', lines 1–4, in *Vaux-de-vire d'Olivier Basselin et de Jean le Houx*, ed. P. L. Jacob (Paris: Delahays, 1858), 11–12, 92. See also E. Littré, *Dictionnaire de la langue française*, s.v. 'courtiser'.

6. 'I love you, lady, so faithfully that Love can no longer grant me another mistress. But He permits me to pay court to others, and by this means I imagine that I am distancing my great sorrow', Guillem de Cabestanh, 'Lo jorn qu'je·us vi, dompna, primeiramen', lines 15–18, in *Anthology of the Provençal Troubadours*, ed. Raymond Thompson Hill and Thomas Goddard Bergin (New Haven, Conn.: Yale University Press, 1941), 113.

7. 'There were some who must needs complain that the ladies would neither entertain nor hold their court at once, but they had ridden a long way, and this, with the heat of the day, had made them tired',

anon., *Le Roman de Flamenca*, ed. Ulrich Gschwind, 2 vols. (Berne: Francke, 1976), i. 34–5.

8. 'My friend is full of himself and pleased with his appearance; he's hale, boastful and full of charms; doffing his cap, he courts and flatters, and sometimes steps beyond the call of duty'; 'Let him have that spur which goads us all on, of wanting to be great; let him court and flatter, let him carp at those who have some social grace: if he pleases you thus, he doesn't displease me', Olivier de Magny, sonnet 94, followed by du Bellay's reply, in *Les Souspirs d'Olivier de Magny*, ed. E. Courbet (Paris: Lemerre, 1874), 67–8.

9. 'Happy the man who can court her; and happier still he who can kiss her; but a hundred times happier is he who finds himself loved by her', sonnet 104, ibid. 75.

10. 'One has to court great lords and seek them out, attending their lever and their coucher', *La Promesse ... de la Royne* (1564), in *Pierre de Ronsard: Œuvres Complètes*, ed. Paul Laumonier, 20 vols. (Paris: Droz, 1914–67), xiii. 12.

11. 'One has to lie, to flatter, and to court, to laugh without laughter, to hide one's face behind another's mask', 'La Salade', *Le Sixième Livre des poèmes* (1569), ibid. xv. 78.

12. 'He wouldn't want to kiss your hands, embrace your knees, to make love, or to adore you', *Discours au Roy, après son retour de Pologne* (1575), ibid. xvii. 31.

13. 'Courting and seeking out flirtatious ladies, being always seated in the midst of the most handsome men, yet feeling neither Love's darts nor his flames – Believe me, my lady, these are monstrous things', 'Les Amours diverses', sonnet 28, *Les Œuvres* (1578), ibid. xvii. 310.

14. 'Now that, in Padua, young Nerino had cultivated the friendship of many students in whose company he was every day, it happened that among them there was a doctor who called himself Maestro Raimondo Brunello', Giovan Francesco Straparola, *Le piacevoli notti* (1550–3), Notte quarta, favola 4, in *Le piacevoli notti*, ed. Giuseppe Rua, 2 vols. (Bari: Laterza, 1927), i. 189.

15. 'Whoever fails to court him [the despot], or to present himself at his house or in the street, is labelled as an enemy', Girolamo Savonarola, *Trattato Secondo* (1494), ch. 2, in *Trattato circa il reggimento e governo della città di Firenze*, ed. Audin de Rians, 6th edn (Florence: Barachi, 1847), 29.

16. 'When I spoke of arms and emblems and of the beauty of our language and our poets, or even of courtesy and matters pertaining to courts and to courtiership, what I had to say was sometimes well received', Torquato Tasso, *Il Minturno* (c. 1593), in *Tasso's Dialogues: A Selection*, ed. and trans. Carnes Lord and Dain A. Trafton (Berkeley: University of California Press, 1982), 198–9.

17. 'For your fellows will show great wisdom if they will court this Prince in the future in the same way that they courted their ladies in the past', Pietro Bembo, *Gli Asolani* (1505), book III, in *Gli Asolani et Le Rime*, ed. Carlo Dionisotti-Casalone (Turin: Unione Tipografico–Editrice Torinese, 1932), 156–7.

18. 'But have you heard of any house, where graceful ladies live, that is not frequented by young men wanting to court them, whether or not their husbands are at home?', Ludovico Ariosto, *Il Negromante* (1509–20), I. iv. 504–8, in *Opere minori*, ed. Cesare Segre (Milan: Ricciardi, 1954), 437.

19. 'I tell you, boss, he has a sister who is classier than he is, and who has more than a few knights courting her', Ludovico Dolce, *Il Ragazzo* (1541), I. i. 5–6, in *Commedie del Cinquencento*, ed. Ireneo Sanesi, 2 vols. (Bari: Laterza, 1912), ii. 209.

20. 'There'd been others who – not fully understanding the kind of girl she was – set about to court her, and even to make love to her; but after she had played them along with sweet looks, she had dismissed them with one trick or another, so that these foolhardy lovers were left miserably mocked', Matteo Bandello, *La Prima Parte de le Novelle* (1554), in *Tutte le opere di Matteo Bandello*, ed. Francesco Flora, 2 vols. (Verona: Mondadori, 1942), i. 45.

21. Alexander Barclay, *The Eclogues of Alexander Barclay*, ed. Beatrice White (Early English Text Society, 1928), 93.

22. *Memoirs of the Life and Times of Sir Christopher Hatton*, ed. Harris Nicolas (London: Bentley, 1847), 357.

23. *The Letters of John Chamberlain*, ed. Norman E. McClure, 2 vols. (Philadelphia: American Philosophical Society, 1939), i. 130.

24. Henry Chettle, *Englands Mourning Garment* (1603), sig. E2.

25. Thomas Wilson, *The Arte of Rhetorique* (1553), ed. Robert Hood Bowers (Gainesville, Fla.: Scholars' Facsimiles, 1962), 196.

26. Christopher Marlowe, *Edward II* (1594), II. i. 31–43, in *The Complete Works of Christopher Marlowe*, ed. Fredson Bowers, 2 vols. (Cambridge: Cambridge University Press, 1973), ii. 37.

27. George Peele, *Polyhymnia* (1590), in *The Life and Works of George Peele*, ed. C. T. Prouty, 3 vols. (New Haven, Conn.: Yale University Press, 1952–70), i. 238.

28. Christopher Marlowe, *Tamburlaine*, part 2 (1591), IV. ii. 93–4, in *The Complete Works of Christopher Marlowe*, ed. Bowers, i. 200.

29. John Donne, 'The Will', in *John Donne: The Elegies and The Songs and Sonnets*, ed. Helen Gardner (Oxford: Clarendon Press, 1965), 54.

30. *Richard II* (c.1595), I. iv. 24–8. All references to Shakespeare are to the *Riverside Shakespeare*, ed. G. Blakemore Evans (Boston: Houghton Mifflin, 1974).

31. Ben Jonson, *Cynthia's Revels* (1601), V. iii. 93; *Sejanus* (1603), III. i. 668,

in *Ben Jonson*, ed. C. H. Herford and Percy Simpson, 11 vols. (Oxford: Clarendon Press, 1925–52), iv. 138, 415.

32. Thomas Nashe, *Pierce Pennilesse Supplication to the Devil* (1592), and *The Unfortunate Traveller* (1594), in *The Works of Thomas Nashe*, ed. R. B. McKerrow, 5 vols. (Oxford: Blackwell, 1904–10), i. 177, ii. 298.

33. Thomas Nashe, *Have with yow to Saffron Walden* (1596), ibid. iii. 92.

34. Edmund Spenser, *The Ruines of Time* (1591), lines 200–3.

35. *The Faerie Queene*, vi. v. 38; i. x. 7.

36. Giovanni della Casa, *Galateo*, trans. Robert Peterson (1576), in *A Renaissance Courtesy Book: Galateo of Manners and Behaviours by Giovanni della Casa*, ed. J. E. Spingarn (London: Grant Richards, 1914), 58–9.

37. Sir Philip Sidney, *The Countess of Pembroke's Arcadia (The New Arcadia)* (1590), ed. Victor Skretkowicz (Oxford: Clarendon Press, 1987), 318.

38. John Donne, *Satire I*, in *John Donne: The Satires, Epigrams and Verse Letters*, ed. W. Milgate (Oxford: Clarendon Press, 1967), 3; Holy Sonnet 3, in *John Donne, The Divine Poems*, ed. Helen Gardner (Oxford: Clarendon Press, 1978), 16.

39. *As You Like It* (1599), iii. ii. 343–6.

40. John Florio, *Queen Anna's New World of Words* (1611), ed. R. C. Alston (Menston: Scolar Press, 1968), s.v. 'corteggiare' and 'corteseggiare'.

41. Sir Geoffrey Fenton, *Certaine Tragicall Discourses* (1567), fols. 123ᵛ, 161, 207. François de Belleforest, *Histoires tragiques*, ii (Paris, 1565) 196, 50, 262ᵛ. Four of Belleforest's *Histoires* (13ᵉ, 18ᵉ in vol. i, and 20ᵉ, 21ᵉ in vol. ii) have been edited separately by Frank S. Hook in *The French Bandello* (Columbia: University of Missouri Press, 1948). These correspond to Fenton's 11th, 13th, 7th, and 1st tales respectively. References to Belleforest's 13ᵉ, 18ᵉ, 20ᵉ, and 21ᵉ *Histoires* will therefore be to Hook's edition; all others to the first editions of vol. i (1564) and vol. ii (1565).

42. *Certaine Tragicall Discourses*, fols. 68ᵛ, 95ᵛ, 113, 126. See also fols. 46, 63ᵛ, 139ᵛ, for similar examples.

43. See: 'courted by a crew of veneryan & carpet knights', *Certaine Tragicall Discourses*, fol. 39ᵛ, from the French, 'amouraischées par une bonne troupe de Gentils-hommes', 22ᵉ *Histoire*, ii. 88; 'such as cold make best court to Ladies', fol. 141ᵛ, from, 'cherie & amourachée de plusieurs', 20ᵉ *Histoire*, 132; 'he forgat not to court & embrase her', fol. 139ᵛ, from, '[il] la caressoit', 20ᵉ *Histoire*, 131.

44. See: 'when he made court to her', *Certaine Tragicall Discourses*, fol. 246, from the French, 'il luy faisoit l'amour', 13ᵉ *Histoire*, 77; 'suche as vse to court vs simple Ladyes', fol. 162ᵛ, from 'qu'ils offrent leur service seigneurial aux dames', 20ᵉ *Histoire*, 151.

45. See: 'courtlike wooing', *Certaine Tragicall Discourses*, fol. 153ᵛ, from the French, 'langage', 20ᵉ *Histoire*, 142; 'seruices of court', fol. 304, from

'services', 13^e *Histoire*, 126; 'proffers of court', fol. 31, from, 'estant recueilly', 21^e *Histoire*, 181.

46. *Certaine Tragicall Discourses*, 123^v, 131^v, 63^v.

47. William Painter, *The Palace of Pleasure* (1566–7), ed. Joseph Jacobs, 3 vols. (London: Nutt, 1890), ii. 155, iii. 197, ii. 110.

48. George Gascoigne, *A Hundreth Sundrie Flowers* (1573), ed. C. T. Prouty (Columbia: University of Missouri Press, 1942), 116.

49. In *The Steele Glass* (1579), Gascoigne uses 'to court' in the first, generalized sense: the poet catches his reflection in the mirror of Satire, 'Wherein I see, a corps of comely shape / (And such as might beseeme the courte full wel) / Is cast at heele, by courting al to soone', *The Complete Works of George Gascoigne*, ed. J. W. Cunliffe, 2 vols. (Cambridge: Cambridge University Press, 1907–10), ii. 149.

50. Painter, *The Palace of Pleasure*, iii. 57.

51. *Love's Labour's Lost* (*c.*1595), v. ii. 780; George Chapman, *Chapman's Homer* (1614–16), ed. Allardyce Nicoll, 2 vols. (London: Routledge and Kegan Paul, 1957), ii. 320.

52. John Webster, *The Duchess of Malfi* (1614), I. i. 379–81, in *The Complete Works of John Webster*, ed. F. L. Lucas, 4 vols. (London: Chatto and Windus, 1927), ii. 46.

53. Barnaby Rich, *Rich's Farewell to Military Profession* (1581), ed. Thomas M. Cranfill (Austin: University of Texas Press, 1959), 130.

54. Thomas Nashe, *Pierce Pennilesse* (1592), in *The Works of Thomas Nashe*, ed. McKerrow, i. 210.

55. *The Autobiography of Thomas Whythorne: Modern Spelling Edition* (*c.*1576), ed. J. M. Osborn (Oxford: Clarendon Press, 1962), 24, 80–1.

56. George Puttenham, *The Arte of English Poesie* (1589), ed. G. D. Willcock and Alice Walker (Cambridge: Cambridge University Press, 1936), 186.

57. Stefano Guazzo, *La civile conversatione*, trans. George Pettie and Bartholomew Young, *The Civile Conversation of M. Steeven Guazzo* (1581–6), ed. Charles Whibley, 2 vols. (London: Constable, 1925), i. 233.

58. Thomas Lodge, *A Margarite of America* (1595), ed. G. B. Harrison (Oxford: Blackwell, 1927), 140.

59. Robert Greene, *Mamillia*, part 1 (1583), in *The Life and Complete Works in Prose and Verse of Robert Greene*, ed. A. B. Grosart, 15 vols. (London: private publication, 1881–6), ii. 20–1.

60. Edmund Spenser, *The Faerie Queene*, I. ii. 14; vi. 4; III. x. 6; IV. ii. 8; II. iv. 25. Sansfoy and Sansloy are also found 'Feasting and courting both in bowre and hall', I. iv. 43; while Perissa and Elissa, the extreme sisters of Medina, are found 'Accourting each her friend with lauish fest', II. ii. 16.

61. Thomas Heywood, *Troia Britanica, or Great Britaines Troy* (1609), 194; George Peele, *The Tale of Troy* (1589), in *The Life and Works of George Peele*, ed. Prouty, i. 189.

62. George Gascoigne, *The Complaint of Philomène* (1576), in *The Complete Works of George Gascoigne*, ed. Cunliffe, ii. 205.
63. Christopher Marlowe, *Hero and Leander* (?1593), in *The Complete Works of Christopher Marlowe*, ed. Bowers, ii. 442.
64. Sidney, *The New Arcadia*, ed. Skretkowicz, 91.
65. John Lyly, *Euphues and his England* (1580), in *The Complete Works of John Lyly*, ed. R. W. Bond, 3 vols. (Oxford: Clarendon Press, 1902), ii. 121; Giles Fletcher the elder, *Licia* (1593), in *The English Works of Giles Fletcher the Elder*, ed. Lloyd E. Berry (Madison: University of Wisconsin Press, 1964), 111.
66. Thomas North, *The Diall of Princes* (1568), fol. 159ᵛ.
67. Thomas Kyd, *The Spanish Tragedy* (?1585–7), IV. i. 53–5, in *The Works of Thomas Kyd*, ed. F. S. Boas, rev. edn (Oxford: Clarendon Press, 1955), 83.
68. Thomas Lodge, *Wits Miserie, and the Worlds Madnesse* (1596), sig. G3ᵛ.
69. George Whetstone, *An Heptameron of Ciuil Discourses* (1582), sig. K3.
70. George Pettie, *A Petite Pallace of Pettie his Pleasure* (1576), ed. Herbert Hartman (New York: Oxford University Press, 1938), 219–20.
71. Lyly, *Euphues and his England* (1580), in *The Complete Works of John Lyly*, ed. Bond, ii. 105, 119.
72. Brian Melbancke, *Philotimus: The Warre betwixt Nature and Fortune* (1583), sig. C1ᵛ.
73. Lyly, *Euphues* (1578), in *The Complete Works of John Lyly*, ed. Bond, i. 181.
74. Philip Massinger, *The Parliament of Love* (c.1624), III. iii. 38–9, in *The Plays and Poems of Philip Massinger*, ed. Philip Edwards and Colin Gibson, 5 vols. (Oxford: Clarendon Press, 1976), ii. 139; Florio, *Queen Anna's New World of Words*, s.v. 'amoreggiare'.
75. *The Poems of Sir John Davies*, ed. R. Kreuger (Oxford: Clarendon Press, 1975), 180.
76. Michael Drayton, *Endimion and Phoebe* (1595), in *The Works of Michael Drayton*, ed. J. Hebel *et al.*, 5 vols. (Oxford: Blackwell, 1931–41), i. 131.
77. Barnaby Rich, *The Straunge and Wonderfull Aduentures of Don Simonides* (1581), sig. Q2ᵛ; George Wilkins, *The Miseries of Inforst Mariage* (1607), ed. Glenn H. Blayney (Oxford: Malone Society, 1963), sig. G3ᵛ.
78. 'Gad not abroad at ev'ry quest and call / Of an untrained hope or passion. / To court each place or fortune that doth fall, / Is wantonnesse in contemplation', from 'Content', in *The English Poems of George Herbert*, ed. C. A. Patrides (London: Dent, 1974), 85.
79. Ludovico Ariosto, *Orlando Furioso*, trans. Sir John Harington (1591), ed. Robert McNulty (Oxford: Clarendon Press, 1972), 78.
80. From a poem published in *The Phoenix Nest* (1593), printed in *The Life and Works of George Peele*, ed. Prouty, i. 263.
81. *The Faerie Queene*, I. vii. 7, 38; II. ix. 2.

82. Ibid. II. ii. 15; ix. 20. The severe Elissa, on the other hand, 'did deeme / Such entertainment base . . . No solace could her Paramour intreat / Her once to show, ne court, nor dalliance', II. ii. 35.

83. Ibid. II. ix. 34, 36, 44.

84. Puttenham, *The Arte of English Poesie*, ed. Willcock and Walker, 158–9.

85. Whetstone, *An Heptameron of Ciuil Discourses*, title page and sig. B4ᵛ.

86. Robert Greene, *Ciceronis Amor* (1589), in *The Life and Complete Works of Robert Greene*, ed. Grosart, vii. 170.

87. From *Entertainments for Elizabeth I*, ed. Jean Wilson (Woodbridge: Boydell and Brewer, 1980), 94.

88. Henry Wotton, *A Courtlie Controuersie of Cupids Cautels* (1578), sig. E4.

89. Nicholas Breton, *The Arbor of Amorous Deuises* (1597), ed. H. E. Rollins (Cambridge, Mass.: Harvard University Press, 1936), 2.

90. Robert Greene, *A Quip for an Vpstart Courtier* (1592), in *The Life and Complete Works of Robert Greene*, ed. Grosart, xi. 235.

91. Ben Jonson, *The Alchemist* (1610), I. ii. 57–8, in *Ben Jonson*, ed. Herford and Simpson, v. 304; Rich, *Rich's Farewell to Military Profession*, ed. Cranfill, 186.

92. George Pettie, trans., *The Civile Conversation*, ed. Whibley, ii. 32.

93. Barnaby Rich, *The Second Tome of the Trauailes and Aduentures of Don Simonides* (1584), sig. H2.

94. Thomas Kyd, *Soliman and Perseda* (?1592), IV. i. 147–8, in *The Works of Thomas Kyd*, ed. Boas, 209.

95. George North, *The Philosopher of the Court* (1575), 32.

96. John Grange, *The Golden Aphroditis* (1577), sig. M3.

97. Robert Greene, *Mamillia*, part 2 (1583), in *The Life and Complete Works of Robert Greene*, ed. Grosart, ii. 219.

98. Thomas Campion, *The Lords' Masque* (1613), from *A Book of Masques*, ed. T. J. B. Spencer and Stanley Wells (Cambridge: Cambridge University Press, 1967), 113.

99. Michael Drayton, *England's Heroicall Epistles* (1599), in *The Works of Michael Drayton*, ed. Hebel *et al.*, ii. 202, 204.

100. Robert Greene, *Menaphon* (1589), ed. G. B. Harrison (Oxford: Blackwell, 1927), 45, 42, 83.

101. George Wither, *Epithalamion* (1613), in *The English Spenserians*, ed. William B. Hunter (Salt Lake City: University of Utah Press, 1977), 132.

102. Puttenham, *The Arte of English Poesie*, ed. Willcock and Walker, 293.

103. See Frank Whigham, *Ambition and Privilege: The Social Tropes of Elizabethan Courtesy Theory* (Berkeley: University of California Press, 1984); and Lauro Martines, *Society and History in English Renaissance Verse* (Oxford: Blackwell, 1985).

104. Whythorne, *The Autobiography of Thomas Whythorne*, ed. Osborn, 24.

3 COURTSHIP AT COURT

1. Francis Bacon, *In Felicem Memoriam* (1608), Bacon's translation, in *The Works of Francis Bacon*, ed. J. Spedding *et al.*, 14 vols., repr. (New York: Longman, 1968), vi. 317.

2. For some historical accounts of Elizabeth's own courtships, see Martin Hume, *The Courtships of Queen Elizabeth: A History of the Various Negotiations for her Marriage* (London: Nash, 1906); Elizabeth Jenkins, *Elizabeth and Leicester* (London: Gollancz, 1961); and Alison Plowden, *Marriage with my Kingdom: The Courtships of Elizabeth I* (London: Macmillan, 1977).

3. Anon., *The Quenes Maiesties Passage through the Citie of London to Westminster the Day before her Coronacion* (1559), ed. James M. Osborn (New Haven, Conn.: Yale University Press, 1960), 28.

4. First quotation taken from Neville Williams, *All the Queen's Men: Elizabeth I and her Courtiers* (London: Weidenfeld and Nicolson, 1972), 138; second quotation from T[homas] R[ogers], *Leicester's Ghost* (?1602–4), ed. Franklin B. Williams (Chicago: University of Chicago Press, 1972), 45.

5. Sir Robert Naunton, *Fragmenta Regalia, or Observations on Queen Elizabeth, her Times and Favorites* (1641), ed. John S. Cerovski (Washington DC: Folger Shakespeare Library, 1985), 84.

6. David Norbrook, *Poetry and Politics in the English Renaissance* (London: Routledge and Kegan Paul, 1984), 117.

7. Jonathan Goldberg, *Endlesse Worke: Spenser and the Structures of Discourse* (Baltimore: Johns Hopkins University Press, 1981), 152; Wallace T. MacCaffrey, 'Place and Patronage in Elizabethan Politics', in S. T. Bindoff *et al.*, eds., *Elizabethan Government and Society: Essays presented to Sir John Neale* (London: Athlone Press, 1961), 97.

8. See e.g. G. R. Elton, *The Tudor Revolution in Government: Administrative Changes in the Reign of Henry VIII* (Cambridge: Cambridge University Press, 1953); Conyers Read, *Mr Secretary Walsingham and Queen Elizabeth*, 3 vols. (Oxford: Clarendon Press, 1925), *Mr Secretary Cecil and Queen Elizabeth* (London: Cape, 1955), and *Lord Burghley and Queen Elizabeth* (London: Cape, 1960).

9. See also Penry Williams, *The Tudor Regime* (Oxford: Clarendon Press, 1979), 421–56; G. W. Bernard, *The Power of the Early Tudor Nobility: A Study of the Fourth and Fifth Earls of Shrewsbury* (Brighton: Harvester, 1985); Simon Adams, 'Eliza Enthroned? The Court and its Politics', in Christopher Haigh, ed., *The Reign of Elizabeth I* (London: Macmillan, 1984), 55–77; and David Starkey, 'Intimacy and Innovation: The Rise of the Privy Chamber, 1485–1547', in David Starkey, ed., *The English Court from the Wars of the Roses to the Civil War* (London: Longman, 1987).

10. Louis Adrian Montrose, 'Celebration and Insinuation: Sir Philip

Sidney and the Motives of Elizabethan Courtship', *Renaissance Drama* 8 (1977), 3–35 (4).

11. Philippa Berry, *Of Chastity and Power: Elizabethan Literature and the Unmarried Queen* (London: Routledge and Kegan Paul, 1989), 85.

12. 'This is all against me,' Elizabeth is reported to have said, *Calendar of State Papers: Spanish 1558–67*, 404.

13. Gerard Legh, *The Accedens of Armory* (1562), fols. 202ᵛ–225. All references are to this edition.

14. Francis Bacon, 'Of Counsel', in *The Works of Francis Bacon*, ed. Spedding *et al.*, vi. 424.

15. See, Marie Axton: 'Robert Dudley and the Inner Temple Revels', *Historical Journal* 13 (1970), 365–78; 'The Tudor Mask and Elizabethan Court Drama', in M. Axton and R. Williams, eds., *English Drama: Forms and Development: Essays in Honour of Muriel Clara Bradbrook* (Cambridge: Cambridge University Press, 1977), 24–47; and *The Queen's Two Bodies: Drama and the Elizabethan Succession* (London: Royal Historical Society, 1977), 39–48.

16. For summaries and accounts of this pageant, see Glynne Wickham, *Early English Stages 1300–1660*, 3 vols., 2nd edn (London: Routledge and Kegan Paul, 1980–1), this quotation from i. 209; Sydney Anglo, *Spectacle, Pageantry, and Early Tudor Policy* (Oxford: Clarendon Press, 1969), 102–3; and Gordon Kipling, *The Triumph of Honour: Burgundian Origins of the Elizabethan Renaissance* (The Hague: Leiden University Press, 1977), 102–5.

17. See Sydney Anglo, ed., *The Great Tournament Roll of Westminster* (Oxford: Clarendon Press, 1968), 56.

18. Anglo, *Spectacle, Pageantry, and Early Tudor Policy*, 112–13, 120–2. For an account of the 1522 show, see also Edward Hall, *The Vnion of the Two Noble and Illustre Famelies of Lancastre and Yorke* (1548–50), ed. Henry Ellis (London: Johnson, 1809), 631.

19. In a pageant presented before the Queen on a royal progress through Norwich in 1578, for example, the figure of Apollo is advised by his 'vertuous desire'; see Bernard Garter, *The Ioyfull Receyuing of the Queenes Maiestie into Norwich* (1578), sig. E2ᵛ. In *The Four Foster Children of Desire* (1581), Desire is legitimized as 'vertuous' and 'honourable', and again as 'chast desires' in a show performed at Cowdray in 1591; see *Entertainments for Elizabeth I*, ed. Jean Wilson (Woodbridge: Boydell and Brewer, 1980), 67, 89. The use of oxymoron served to strip desire of sexual attributes and to transform a sexual vocabulary into a language of loyalty, honour and reverence.

20. The text of this masque has been preserved in one of the Lansdowne manuscripts, and is reproduced in *Malone Society Collections*, part 1, vol. ii (Oxford: Malone Society, 1904), ed. E. K. Chambers and W. W. Greg, 144–8.

21. Ibid. 146.

22. Bruce R. Smith, 'Landscape with Figures: The Three Realms of Queen Elizabeth's Country-House Revels', *Renaissance Drama* 8 (1977), 57–115 (58). For other studies of Renaissance country-house literature, see Don E. Wayne, *Penshurst: The Semiotics of Place and the Poetics of History* (London: Methuen, 1984); G. R. Hibbard, 'The Country House Poem of the Seventeenth Century', *Journal of the Warburg and Courtauld Institutes* 19 (1956), 159–74; and William A. McClung, *The Country House in English Renaissance Poetry* (Berkeley: University of California Press, 1977).

23. There are two main accounts of the Kenilworth show: George Gascoigne, 'The Princely Pleasures at Kenilworth Castle', in *The Complete Works of George Gascoigne*, ed. J. W. Cunliffe, 2 vols. (Cambridge: Cambridge University Press, 1907–10), ii. 91–131; and Richard Lanham, *A Letter whearin Part of the Entertainment vntoo the Queenz Maiesty at Killingwoorth Castl iz Signified* (1575).

24. I take the phrase 'functional ambiguity' primarily from Annabel Patterson's discussion in *Censorship and Interpretation: The Conditions of Writing and Reading in Early Modern England* (Madison: University of Wisconsin Press, 1984), 18. For Bourdieu's use of the term, see Pierre Bourdieu, *Outline of a Theory of Practice*, trans. Richard Nice (Cambridge: Cambridge University Press, 1977), 49.

25. Sir William Dugdale, *The Antiquities of Warwickshire*, ed. William Thomas, 2 vols. (1730), i. 249[a].

26. Ibid. 247[b].

27. John Stow, *Annales of England* (1592), 299; Michael Drayton, *Mortimeriados*, lines 78–83, *The Barons' Wars*, i. 177–84, and *England's Heroicall Epistles*, 'Mortimer to Queen Isabel', lines 53–8, in *The Works of Michael Drayton*, ed. J. Hebel *et al.*, 5 vols. (Oxford: Blackwell, 1931–41), i. 311, ii. 15, 169.

28. Dugdale, *The Antiquities of Warwickshire*, 247[b].

29. Lanham, *A Letter*, 18.

30. See e.g. some of the 'greenwood' songs reproduced by John Stevens, *Music and Poetry in the Early Tudor Court* (London: Methuen, 1961), 338, 400, 408, 410. For an account of the salvage-man motif, see Richard Bernheimer, *Wild Men in the Middle Ages: A Study in Art, Sentiment, and Demonology* (Cambridge, Mass.: Harvard University Press, 1952).

31. *The Complete Works of George Gascoigne*, ed. Cunliffe, ii. 99–101.

32. Ibid. 123–4.

33. Ibid. 124–6. The device of arborified lovers was to be repeated in a show performed by Leicester's protégé, Sir Henry Lee, at Woodstock later that summer. As she was departing from Woodstock, Elizabeth confronted the figure of Despair, who was concealed 'closelie in an Oke'. See J. W. Cunliffe, 'The Queenes Majesties Entertainment at Woodstock', *PMLA* 26 (1911), 92–141 (101).

34. *The Complete Works of George Gascoigne*, ed. Cunliffe, ii. 126.
35. John Lyly, *The Honorable Entertainment gieuen to the Queenes Maiestie in Progresse, at Eluetham* (1591), in *The Complete Works of John Lyly*, ed. R. Warwick Bond, 3 vols. (Oxford: Clarendon Press, 1902), i. 445.
36. *The Complete Works of George Gascoigne*, ed. Cunliffe, ii. 130, 126–7.
37. See Muriel Bradbrook, *The Rise of the Common Player: A Study of Actor and Society in Shakespeare's England* (London: Chatto and Windus, 1964), 250; Bruce R. Smith, 'Landscape with Figures', 58; and Axton, *The Queen's Two Bodies*, 63.
38. *The Complete Works of John Lyly*, ed. Bond, i. 480.
39. From the song 'Grene Growith the Holy', reproduced by Stevens, *Music and Poetry in the Early Tudor Court*, 399.
40. See *Entertainments for Elizabeth I*, ed. Wilson, 127.
41. *The Complete Works of George Gascoigne*, ed. Cunliffe, ii. 126, 125.
42. Ibid. 126.
43. Montrose, 'Celebration and Insinuation', 10.
44. For a recent study of Sidney's relation to a 'culture of institutionalized obliquity', see Dennis Kay, ' "She Was a Queen and therefore Beautiful": Sidney, his Mother, and Queen Elizabeth', *Review of English Studies* (Feb. 1992).
45. Puttenham, *The Arte of English Poesie*, ed. Willcock and Walker, 38.
46. See *The Victoria History of The Counties of England*, 8 vols. (London: Oxford University Press, 1903–83), vi: *Essex*, 323–4.
47. See *Documents Relating to the Office of the Revels in the Time of Queen Elizabeth*, ed. Albert Feuillerat (Louvain: Materialen, 1908), 227. In January 1579, the Earl of Leicester's Men performed a 'pastorell or historie of A Greeke maide' at court, another early example of the form. Ibid. 286.
48. Sidney, *The New Arcadia* (1590), ed. Victor Skretkowicz (Oxford: Clarendon Press, 1987), 255. There is also evidence of another entertainment (associated with the Accession Day Tilts) in which Sidney may have entered the lists as 'Philisides, the shepherd good and true' with a group of ploughmen and to the accompaniment of 'rusticall musick'. See Bernard M. Wagner, 'New Poems by Sir Philip Sidney', *PMLA* 53 (1938), 118–24; Peter Beal, 'Poems by Sir Philip Sidney: The Ottley Manuscript', *The Library*, 5th series, 33 (1978), 284–95; and Alan Young, *Tudor and Jacobean Tournaments* (London: George Philip, 1987), 127–8.
49. George Peele, *Polyhymnia* (1590), in *The Life and Works of George Peele*, ed. C. T. Prouty, 3 vols. (New Haven, Conn.: Yale University Press, 1952–70), i. 236. See also Spenser's *Astrofell* (1595).
50. On the similarities, both thematic and textual, between Sidney's writings and *As You Like It*, see D. C. Kay, 'Sidney: A Critical Heritage', in D. C. Kay, ed., *Sir Philip Sidney: An Anthology of Modern Criticism* (Oxford: Clarendon Press 1987), 19–21.

51. Sidney, *The Old Arcadia*, ed. Jean Robertson (Oxford: Clarendon Press, 1973), 166.
52. See George Peele, *The Arraygnement of Paris* (1584), in which Paris, having first kept the golden apple for himself, is obliged to surrender it to the incomparable Eliza. During an entertainment at Ditchley in 1592, Elizabeth's superlative presence miraculously resolves the argument between Constancy and Inconstancy; and, in a show performed at Mitcham in 1598, a contention between a poet, painter, and musician is resolved when they agree that not one of them is capable of depicting her satisfactorily. See *The Life and Works of George Peele*, ed. Prouty, iii. 61–114; *Entertainments for Elizabeth I*, ed. Wilson; and anon., *Queen Elizabeth's Entertainment at Mitcham*, ed. Leslie Hotson (New Haven, Conn.: Yale University Press, 1953), 16–30.
53. John Hoskins, *Directions for Speech and Style*, in *The Life, Letters, and Writings of John Hoskyns 1566–1638*, ed. Louise Brown Osborn (New Haven, Conn.: Yale University Press, 1937), 135.
54. *Rhetorica ad Herennium*, ed. and trans. Harry Caplan, Loeb edition (Cambridge, Mass.: Harvard University Press, 1954), 157.
55. Thomas Wilson, *The Arte of Rhetorique* (1553), ed. Robert Hood Bowers (Gainesville, Fla.: Scholars' Facsimiles, 1962), 105, 43.
56. Boccaccio, *Filocolo*, trans. H[enry] G[rantham], *Thirtene most Plesant and Delectable Questions* (1566, 2nd edn 1571).
57. Ibid. sig. B8.
58. Puttenham, *The Arte of English Poesie*, ed. Willcock and Walker, 159; John Lyly, *Euphues and his England* (1580), in *The Complete Works of John Lyly*, ed. Bond, ii. 375.
59. See Thomas Wilson, *The Rule of Reason* (1567), fols. 3ᵛ, 14ᵛ–15: 'When we go about to expounde any matter, first we must beginne with the definicion ... As a definition therefore doeth declare, what a thing is, so the diuision sheweth, how many things are contained in the same.' Contrast Astrophil's inversion of normal rhetorical procedure when he puts *elocutio* before *inventio* in the first sonnet of *Astrophil and Stella*: discussed by W. A. Ringler, *The Poems of Sir Philip Sidney*, ed. Ringler (Oxford: Clarendon Press, 1962), 458–9; and Thomas Roche, '*Astrophil and Stella*: A Radical Reading', *Spenser Studies* 3 (1982), 139–91.
60. Wilson, *The Rule of Reason*, fol. 4ᵛ.
61. See Thomas Wilson, *The Arte of Rhetorique*, ed. Bowers, 19–20.
62. From a letter to Sidney dated 30 Jan. 1580, in *The Correspondence of Sir Philip Sidney and Hubert Languet*, ed. and trans. Steuart A. Pears (London: William Pickering, 1845), 170.
63. Thomas Churchyard, *A Discourse of the Queenes Maiesties Entertainement in Suffolk and Norffolk* (1578), sig. F1.
64. Sidney, *The Old Arcadia*, 135. Stephen Orgel, *The Jonsonian Masque* (Cambridge, Mass.: Harvard University Press, 1965), 53, and David

Kalstone, *Sidney's Poetry: Contexts and Interpretations* (Cambridge, Mass.: Harvard University Press, 1965), 46, both interpret the final song as a débâcle. For Ringler, on the other hand (*The Poems of Sir Philip Sidney*, ed. Ringler, 363), the song 'was ingeniously devised to be appropriate to whichever suitor was adjudged victor by the Queen'. Ringler is followed by Katherine Duncan-Jones and Jan van Dorsten, *The Miscellaneous Prose of Sir Philip Sidney*, ed. Duncan-Jones and van Dorsten (Oxford: Clarendon Press, 1973), 14–15; Robert Kimbrough and Philip Murphy, 'The Helmingham Hall Manuscript of *The Lady of May*: A Commentary and Transcription', *Renaissance Drama* NS 1 (1968), 103–19 (106); and by Montrose, 'Celebration and Insinuation', 20.

65. Henry Goldwell, *A Briefe Declaration of the Shews, Devices, Speeches, and Inventions, Done & Performed before the Queene's Maiestie, & the French Ambassadors* (1581), in *Entertainments for Elizabeth I*, ed. Wilson, 63–85. All page references are to this edition.

66. Robert Carey, *Memoirs*, ed. F. H. Mares (Oxford: Clarendon Press, 1972), 4.

67. The month-long delay between the issue of the challenge and the tournament (unexplained by Goldwell) may have been owing to the French Commissioners' late arrival in London. See Burghley's memoranda and revised schedule of events, *Calendar of State Papers: Foreign 1581–2*, 144–5.

68. A blank score-cheque for this tilt survives in Bodleian MS Ashmole 845, fol. 166, entitled 'The Tournay holden at Westminster on Monday the 15. of May. 1581. when as the prince dolphine of Auuergne and the frenche commissioners were heer'.

69. *Calendar of State Papers: Spanish 1580–6*, 110.

70. See Ivan L. Schulze, 'The Final Protest against the Elizabeth–Alençon Marriage Proposal', *Modern Language Notes* 58 (1943), 54–7; Conyers Read, *Lord Burghley and Queen Elizabeth* (London: Cape, 1960), 258–60; Ronald A. Rebholz, *The Life of Fulke Greville, First Lord Brooke* (Oxford: Clarendon Press, 1971), 36–8; David Bergeron, *English Civic Pageantry 1558–1642* (London: Edward Arnold, 1971), 44–6; Norman Council, 'O Dea Certe: The Allegory of The Fortress of Perfect Beauty', *Huntington Library Quarterly* 39 (1975–6), 329–42.

71. Rebholz, *The Life of Fulke Greville*, 38. See also Read, *Lord Burghley and Queen Elizabeth*, 260: 'The symbolism is obvious.'

72. See Montrose, 'Celebration and Insinuation', 20–31.

73. Most notably by John Stubbs, in his *Discoverie of a Gaping Gulf whereinto England is like to be Swallowed by an other French Mariage* (1579).

74. See Henry Woudhuysen, 'Leicester's Literary Patronage: A Study of the English Court 1578–1582', D.Phil. thesis, Oxford, 1981, 340–5.

75. *Astrophil and Stella*, 41.

76. William Segar, *The Booke of Honor and Armes* (1589), 98.

77. *Astrophil and Stella*, 1, 46.
78. Montrose, 'Celebration and Insinuation', 26.
79. Quoted by Wickham, *Early English Stages 1300–1660*, i. 208–9.
80. Hall, *The Vnion of the Two Noble and Illustre Famelies of Lancastre and Yorke*, 631.
81. See R. S. Loomis, 'The Allegorical Siege in the Art of the Middle Ages', *American Journal of Archaeology* NS 23 (1919), 255–69; Kipling, *The Triumph of Honour*; Anglo, *Spectacle, Pageantry, and Early Tudor Policy*.
82. Sir Thomas Elyot, *The Book Named the Governor*, ed. Henry Croft, 2 vols. (London: Kegan Paul, 1880), i. 233.
83. Luigi Gonzaga, Duke of Nevers, *Mémoires*, 2 vols. (Paris, 1665), i. 556: 'on a chariot made like a rock. Love and Fate led him – tied with great chains of gold – toward her Majesty.'
84. Ibid.: 'not to suffer the pride of your cruelty, but that – in his loving your chaste beauty – you will finally transform his imprisonment into honourable liberty'.
85. Ibid. 557: 'by means of the most excellent and magnanimous Prince, the most constant lover of all time; and of the most chaste, virtuous, and heroic princess in the world'.
86. Sir Henry Wotton, *Reliquiae Wottonianae* (1651), 21.
87. George Peele, *Anglorum Feriae* (1595), in *The Life and Works of George Peele*, ed. Prouty, i. 270. Contrast a poem attributed to the Earl of Oxford: 'I went abroad to take the Ayre, and in the meedes I mette a knyght, / Clad in Carnation Colour fayre, I did salute this gentle wyght, / Of him I did his name enquyre, / He syghed and sayd he was desyre', quoted by Steven May, 'The Poems of Edward de Vere, Seventeenth Earl of Oxford and of Robert Devereux, Second Earl of Essex', *Studies in Philology* 77 (1980), 1–132 (31).
88. Some of the speeches survive in Bacon's hand, and some in that of another secretary, Edward Reynolds. The show seems to have consisted of the following parts: (1) a speech by Philautia (*Calendar of State Papers: Domestic 1595–7*, 133–4); (2) a speech or letter from Philautia addressed to the Queen (*The Works of Francis Bacon*, ed. Spedding *et al.*, viii. 376–7); (3) the squire's speech (ibid., viii. 378); (4) speeches by a Hermit, Soldier, and Secretary, and an answer by the squire (anon., *An Elizabethan Manuscript at Alnwick Castle, Northumberland*, ed. F. J. Burgoyne (London: Longman, 1904), 57–63). George Peele commemorates the tilting in *Anglorum Feriae* (1595), and there is an account of the device in a letter from Rowland Whyte to Robert Sidney, dated 22 Nov. 1595, repr. in *The Life and Works of George Peele*, i. 179–81.
89. *Calendar of State Papers: Domestic 1595–7*, 133.
90. Ibid. 134.
91. Anon., *An Elizabethan Manuscript at Alnwick Castle*, 62.

92. Ibid. 63.
93. Ibid.
94. G. B. Harrison, *The Life and Death of Robert Devereux, Earl of Essex* (London: Cassell, 1937), 90–1. See also E. K. Chambers, *The Elizabethan Stage*, 4 vols. (Oxford: Clarendon Press, 1923), iii. 212; Roy Strong, *The Cult of Elizabeth: Elizabethan Portraiture and Pageantry* (London: Thames and Hudson, 1977), 141; and Young, *Tudor and Jacobean Tournaments*, 173–6.
95. *The Works of Francis Bacon*, viii. 376.
96. Anon., *An Elizabethan Manuscript at Alnwick Castle*, 60.
97. *The Works of Francis Bacon*, viii. 377.
98. *The Life and Works of George Peele*, i. 181.
99. Ibid. 270–1.
100. Cf. Ray Heffner, 'Essex, the Ideal Courtier', *Journal of English Literary History* 1 (1934), 7–36; and May, 'The Poems of Edward de Vere and Robert Devereux', both of whom associate Essex with the Hermit figure.
101. The speech is printed in *The Works of Francis Bacon*, viii. 388–90. Bacon's editors associate the Indian Prince with Sir Walter Ralegh, recently returned from his Guiana voyage.
102. Ibid. 388.
103. *The Life and Works of George Peele*, i. 273.
104. *The Works of Francis Bacon*, viii. 389. Cf. the transcription of the speech by Walter Bourchier Devereux, *Lives and Letters of the Devereux, Earls of Essex*, 2 vols. (London: Murray, 1853), ii. 501–5: Devereux transcribes 'seemly Love' rather than 'Seeing Love', although, as we shall see, internal evidence suggests that the latter is the correct reading.
105. *The Works of Francis Bacon*, viii. 388.
106. Ibid. 390.
107. Ibid.
108. *The Complete Works of John Lyly*, ed. Bond, iii. 16–80. All references are to this edition.
109. See N. J. Halpin, *Oberon's Vision in the Midsummer Night's Dream* (London: Shakespeare Society, 1843); Josephine W. Bennett, 'Oxford and *Endimion*', *PMLA* 57 (1942), 354–69; and F. S. Boas, *Queen Elizabeth in Drama and Related Studies* (London: Allen and Unwin, 1950).
110. Many critics have commented on the play's enigmatic nature: see Peter Saccio, 'The Oddity of Lyly's *Endimion*', *Elizabethan Theatre* 5 (1975), 92–111, and *The Court Comedies of John Lyly* (Princeton, NJ.: Princeton University Press, 1969), 169–86, where he writes of the play's 'perplexity' and its 'mysterious' nature (169); Percy W. Long, 'The Purport of Lyly's *Endimion*', *PMLA* 24 (1909), 164–84, calls the play 'enigmatic' (175); Robert S. Knapp, 'The Monarchy of Love in Lyly's *Endimion*', *Modern Philology* 73 (1975–6), 353–67, an 'enigma'

(353); the play remains a 'puzzle' for Susan D. Thomas, '*Endimion* and its Sources', *Comparative Literature* 30 (1978), 35–52 (35).

111. Entertaining the Queen at Ditchley in 1592, Sir Henry Lee allegorized his exclusion from Elizabeth's favour as an enchanted sleep.

112. Baldassare Castiglione, *The Book of the Courtier*, trans. Sir Thomas Hoby, ed. W. H. D. Rouse (London: Dent, 1928), 315.

4 COURTLY COURTESIES

1. Baldassare Castiglione, *The Book of the Courtier*, trans. Sir Thomas Hoby, ed. W. H. D. Rouse (London: Dent, 1928), 315; Thomas Whythorne, *The Autobiography of Thomas Whythorne: Modern Spelling Edition* (*c.*1576), ed. J. M. Osborn (Oxford: Clarendon Press, 1962), 24.

2. Shakespeare, *A Lover's Complaint*, line 125.

3. Roger Ascham, *The Schoolmaster* (1570), ed. Lawrence V. Ryan (Ithaca, NY: Cornell University Press, 1967), 73–4.

4. Ibid. 74.

5. *Euphues* (1578), 186 (two examples), 242; *Euphues and his England* (1580), 24, 49, 68, 88, 93, 105, 107, 119, 121, 138, 156, 181, 184, 221, 227, in *The Complete Works of John Lyly*, ed. R. Warwick Bond, 3 vols. (Oxford: Clarendon Press, 1902). All references are to this edition, *E* referring to *Euphues*, *EE* to *Euphues and his England*.

6. All quotations from *Rosalynde* are taken from the Variorum edition of *As You Like It*, ed. Richard Knowles and Evelyn Joseph Mattern (New York: Modern Language Association, 1977), 383–475 (385). I am grateful to the editors of the *Review of English Studies* for permission to reproduce here a version of my article ' "A Large Occasion of Discourse": John Lyly and the Art of Civil Conversation', 42 (1991), 1–18.

7. Lodge's error is all the more culpable because, being inserted into the second (and subsequent) editions of *Rosalynde*, it stands as a correction to his original text.

8. Annibale Romei, *Discorsi*, trans. John Keepers, *The Courtiers Academie* (1598), sig. E1; see also *EE* 72.

9. There is an obvious model for the distinction between courtly and pedagogic utterance in Sir Thomas Hoby's prefatory epistle to *The Book of the Courtier*: 'Both Cicero and Castilio professe, they folow not any certaine appointed order of precepts or rules, as is used in the instruction of youth, but call to rehearsall, matters debated in their times too and fro in the disputation of most eloquent men and excellent wittes', in Castiglione, *The Book of the Courtier*, 3.

10. Edmund Tilney, *A Briefe and Pleasaunt Discourse of Duties in Mariage, Called the Flower of Friendshippe* (1568), sig. A5: 'But M. *Pedro* nothing

at all lyking of such deuises, wherein the Ladies should be left out, said, y^t he wel remembred how *Boccace* & Countie *Baltizar* with others recounted many proper deuises for exercise, both pleasant, & profitable, which, quoth he, were vsed in ye courts of Italie, and some much like to them, are practised at this day in the English court, wherein is not onely delectable, but pleasure ioyned with profite, and *exercise of the wyt*', my italics.

11. Barnaby Rich, *The Second Tome of the Trauailes and Aduentures of Don Simonides* (1584), sig. I3. See also Thomas Lodge, *Euphues Shadow, the Battaile of the Sences* (1592), in *The Complete Works of Thomas Lodge*, ed. E. Gosse, 4 vols. repr. (New York: Russell and Russell, 1963), ii. 104: 'if [Euphues'] courting hath wrought you any content, I doubte not but his contemplations shall yeeld forth good conceit'.

12. John Hoskins, *Directions for Speech and Style*, in *The Life, Letters, and Writings of John Hoskyns 1566–1638*, ed. Louise Brown Osborn (New Haven, Conn.: Yale University Press, 1937), 130.

13. Sir Philip Sidney, *Apology for Poetry*, ed. Geoffrey Shepherd (Manchester: Manchester University Press, 1973), 139, my italics.

14. Castiglione, *The Book of the Courtier*, 154.

15. For other examples of quandary in *Euphues*, see *E* 194, 204, 224, 240.

16. George Gascoigne, *The Aduentures of Master F.J.*, in *A Hundreth Sundrie Flowers* (1573), ed. C. T. Prouty (Columbia: University of Missouri Press, 1942), 87. See also Henry Wotton, *A Courtlie Controuersie of Cupids Cautels* (1578), sig. M2^v: 'It is a great matter, replied *Sir bel Aceueil*, how these Maidens continually desire quarels and contention'; and Boccaccio, *Filocolo*, trans. H[enry] G[rantham], *Thirtene most Plesant and Delectable Questions* (1566), sig. L7: 'we haue according to our small knowledge, made answere, following rather pleasant reasoning, than matter of contention'.

17. Boccaccio, *Filocolo*, trans. G[rantham], *Thirtene Most Plesant and Delectable Questions*, sig. F4; Romei, *Discorsi*, trans. Keepers, *The Courtiers Academie*, sigs. E3–E3^v.

18. Thomas Nashe, *Anatomie of Absurditie* (1589), in *The Works of Thomas Nashe*, ed. R. B. McKerrow, 5 vols. (Oxford: Clarendon Press, 1904–10, repr. 1966), i. 7.

19. Wotton, *A Courtlie Controuersie of Cupids Cautels*, sig. 2H4.

20. Stefano Guazzo, *La civile conversatione*, trans. George Pettie and Bartholomew Young, *The Civile Conversation of M. Steeven Guazzo* (1581–6), ed. Charles Whibley, 2 vols. (London: Constable, 1925), i. 41.

21. Pietro Bembo, *Gli Asolani* (1505), trans. Rudolf B. Gottfried (Bloomington: Indiana University Press, 1954), 147. In *The Baynes of Aquisgrane* (pub. 1617, but written, according to the printer's note, 'in the tyme of the late Queene Elizabeth'), Roger Baynes defends the dialogue form – which he models on Castiglione, Boethius, and

Plato – as follows: 'in Dialogues it is not to be expected, that all which is written, is to be continuate doctrine, but that some Interlocutions are to enter betwixt; the which being passed ouer, then the matter of doctrine returneth againe ... The which Interlocutions though perhaps they may not fall out still to be so pleasing as the doctrine it selfe; yet so long as they be not vnproportionable to the matter which they concerne, they may be permitted to passe: because when all is done, he who will haue good store of corne, must be content withall to take some chaffe', sigs. *3–*3ᵛ.

22. For accounts of Lyly's debt to this tradition, see Violet M. Jeffery, *John Lyly and the Italian Renaissance* (Paris: Champion, 1929); Joel B. Altman, *The Tudor Play of Mind* (Berkeley: University of California Press, 1978), ch. 7; and Arthur F. Kinney, *Humanist Poetics: Thought, Rhetoric, and Fiction in Sixteenth-Century England* (Amherst: University of Massachusetts Press, 1986), ch. 4.

23. Robert Y. Turner, 'Some Dialogues of Love in Lyly's Comedies', *Journal of English Literary History*, 29 (1962), 276–88 (284). See also Jocelyn Powell: 'Most of Lyly's plays revolve around some sort of debate. Debate was in its own right an important entertainment form in the courts of the sixteenth century', 'John Lyly and the Language of Play', *Stratford-upon-Avon Studies*, 9 (1966), 146–67 (159).

24. The qualities of Lyly's 'courtliness' have frequently been misrepresented by their contradistinction with humanist values. The comparison is a commonplace one: see G. K. Hunter, *John Lyly: The Humanist as Courtier* (London: Routledge and Kegan Paul, 1962), 34; Albert Feuillerat, *John Lyly: Contribution à l'histoire de la Renaissance en Angleterre* (Cambridge: Cambridge University Press, 1910); and Kinney, *Humanist Poetics*, ch. 4. The two forces are present throughout Lyly's work, and their intimate relation is one of the chief characteristics of his fiction. But in an attempt to redress some of the imbalances of Lyly criticism, with its constant stress on humanist values, I shall – at the risk of some distortion and over-emphasis – concentrate primarily on the *courtliness* of Lyly's narratives.

25. The tradition behind the Italian *questioni d'amore* is discussed by Thomas F. Crane, *Italian Social Customs of the Sixteenth Century* (New Haven, Conn.: Yale University Press, 1920); Wayne A. Rebhorn, *Courtly Performances: Masking and Festivity in Castiglione's* Book of the Courtier (Detroit: Wayne State University Press, 1978), ch. 5; David Marsh, *The Quattrocento Dialogue: Classical Tradition and Humanist Innovation* (Cambridge, Mass.: Harvard University Press, 1980); and Peter Burke, 'The Renaissance Dialogue', *Renaissance Studies*, 3 (1989), 1–12. On the dialogue form in the English Renaissance, see K. J. Wilson, *Incomplete Fictions: The Formation of English Renaissance Dialogue* (Washington, DC: Catholic University of America Press, 1985).

26. The convention is so common in *questione d'amore* texts as to be

virtually universal. On Castiglione's use of this formula, see Rebhorn, *Courtly Performances*, 134–5.

27. George Whetstone, *An Heptameron of Ciuill Discourses* (1582), sigs. H3–H3ᵛ; Bembo, *Gli Asolani*, trans. Gottfried, 172.

28. Tilney, *A Brief and Pleasaunt Discourse ... Called the Flower of Friendshippe*, sig. B7. Robert Greene, *Morando: The Tritameron of Love* (1587), in *The Life and Complete Works in Prose and Verse of Robert Greene*, ed. A. B. Grosart, 15 vols. (London: private publication, 1881–6), iii. 84. See also Bembo, *Gli Asolani*, trans. Gottfried, 17: Gismondo says that his companions should criticize love because 'even though they believed the very opposite, [they] ought at least to decry that quality by way of jest, in order that we might debate so excellent a theme among us here today'. In book III of *The Book of the Courtier*, Gasparo Pallavicino and the Magnifico take up opposing positions as misogynist and *defensor feminae*. In the course of their debate Gasparo admits that the two positions are necessarily complementary in giving women their due praise: 'But they are so wise above other, that they love truth better (although it make not so much with them) than false prayses', Castiglione, *The Book of the Courtier*, 196. See Ruth Kelso, *Doctrine for the Lady of the Renaissance* (Urbana: University of Illinois Press, 1956), on the traditional two-sidedness of the *querelle des femmes*.

29. This explains, perhaps, the ambiguous mixture of praise and blame that Theodore Steinberg confusingly calls an 'odd stance for a reputed courtesy-book', 'The Anatomy of *Euphues*', *Studies in English Literature*, 17 (1977), 27–38 (31).

30. Sir Philip Sidney, *An Apology for Poetry*, ed. Shepherd, 104.

31. Kinney, *Humanist Poetics*, 141. The passage is full of erotic overtones. Lucilla, we are told, hankers for Euphues' conclusion 'as women are wont for things that like them', she is 'inflamed' by his presence, and she craves his 'naked' proof (*E* 215–16).

32. 'She was striken sodaynely beeinge troubled with no sickenesse: It may be, for it is commonly seene, that a sinfull lyfe is rewarded with a soddayne deathe, and a sweete beginning with a sowre ende' (*E* 312).

33. In Castiglione, *The Book of the Courtier*, 3. Steinberg, on the other hand, does not see the ambivalence of the ending as characteristically courtly: 'the narrator refuses to tell how or why she died, a reluctance which is indeed strange in a courtesy book', 'The Anatomy of *Euphues*', 33.

34. *Love's Labour's Lost*, v. ii. 874.

35. Lodge, *Rosalynde*, 475.

36. *Love's Labour's Lost*, v. ii. 901–2.

37. Sidney, *The New Arcadia* (1590), ed. Victor Skretkowicz (Oxford:

Clarendon Press, 1987), 506; Gascoigne, *A Hundreth Sundrie Flowers*, ed. Prouty, 105.

38. Wotton, *A Courtlie Controuersie of Cupids Cautels*, sigs. A2–A2ᵛ, A4.
39. Guazzo, *La civile conversatione*, trans. Pettie, *The Civil Conversation*, i. 8.
40. *Pericles*, i. Cho. 8. On the traditionally restorative nature of story-telling, see Peter Burke, *Popular Culture in Early Modern Europe* (London: Temple Hill, 1978), ch. 5; Margaret Spufford, *Small Books and Pleasant Histories: Popular Fiction and its Readership in Seventeenth-Century England* (London: Methuen, 1981); and Dennis Kay, ' "To Hear the Rest Untold": Shakespeare's Postponed Endings', *Renaissance Quarterly*, 37 (1984), 207–27.
41. Gascoigne, *A Hundreth Sundrie Flowers*, ed. Prouty, 101.
42. Etienne Pasquier, *Le Monophile*, trans. Sir Geoffrey Fenton, *Monophylo* (1572), sig. B1.
43. Sidney, *The New Arcadia*, ed. Skretkowicz, 13.
44. Guazzo, *La civile conversatione*, trans. Pettie, *The Civil Conversation*, i. 238.
45. 'Thus oftentimes had we conference, but no conclusion, many meetinges, but few pastimes, vntill at the last *Surius* one that could quickly perceiue, on which side my bread was buttered, beganne to breake with me touching *Frauncis*, not as though he had heard any thing, but as one that would vnderstand some-thing. I durst not seeme straunge when I founde him so curteous, knowing that in this matter he might almoste worke all to my lyking' (*EE* 221).
46. The texts I will be using in the following discussion are: *The Old Arcadia*, ed. Jean Robertson (Oxford: Clarendon Press, 1973) (hereafter *OA*); *The New Arcadia*, ed. Victor Skretkowicz (Oxford: Clarendon Press, 1987) (hereafter *90*); and *The Countess of Pembroke's Arcadia* (being the 1593 composite version), ed. Maurice Evans (Harmondsworth: Penguin, 1977) (hereafter *93*). This quotation, *90* 88.
47. John Carey, 'Structure and Rhetoric in Sidney's *Arcadia*', repr. in Dennis Kay, ed., *Sir Philip Sidney: An Anthology of Modern Criticism* (Oxford: Oxford University Press, 1987), 245–64 (261).
48. Gabriel Harvey, *Pierce's Supererogation* (1593), in *Elizabethan Critical Essays*, ed. G. Gregory Smith, 2 vols. (Oxford: Clarendon Press, 1904), ii. 263.
49. See William Painter, *The Palace of Pleasure* (1566–7), and George Pettie, *A Petite Pallace of Pettie his Pleasure* (1576). In his *Certaine Tragicall Discourses* (1567), Sir Geoffrey Fenton offers to present 'the meruellous effects of loue', which are even more remarkable than 'the curious construction and frame of any Pallais for necessitie or pleasure, theatrie or place of solace buylded by art or industrie of man, or other stately Court' (fol. 1).
50. Thomas Lodge, *Rosalynde* (1590), 454; *The Faerie Queene*, vi. ix. 34.

51. Walter R. Davis goes so far as to suggest that Nico's song is an 'anti-epithalamion, since its plot is the collapse of marriage', *A Map of Arcadia: Sidney's Romance in its Tradition* (New Haven, Conn.: Yale University Press, 1965), 108.

52. For two recent studies of the *Old Arcadia* as a Calvinistic tract, see F. Marenco, *Arcadia Puritana* (Bari: Adriatica Editrice, 1968); and A. D. Weiner, *Sir Philip Sidney and the Poetics of Protestantism: A Study of Contexts* (Minneapolis: University of Minnesota Press, 1978).

53. In the *Old Arcadia*, Musidorus muses that 'such was as then the state of the duke as it was no time by direct means to seek her [Pamela], and such was the state of his captived will as he could delay no time of seeking her' (*OA* 105). Compare Amphialus in the *New Arcadia*: '[Basilius] had set his daughters (in whom the whole estate, as next heirs thereunto, had no less interest than himself) in so unfit and ill-guarded a place as it was not only dangerous for their persons but (if they should be conveyed to any foreign country) to the whole commonwealth pernicious' (*90* 325–6).

54. *As You Like It*, v. iv. 102–3.

55. Davis, *A Map of Arcadia*, 68–9.

56. See e.g. Desdemona's 'liberal hand', *Othello*, III. iv. 46; and Hermione and Polixenes, in *The Winter's Tale*, whom Leontes accuses of provocatively 'paddling palms and pinching fingers', I. ii. 115.

57. Ronald Levao, *Renaissance Minds and their Fictions: Cusanus, Sidney, Shakespeare* (Berkeley: University of California Press, 1985), 196.

58. This point has been made by Dorothy Connell, *Sir Philip Sidney: The Maker's Mind* (Oxford: Clarendon Press, 1977), 28–9.

59. See Richard C. McCoy, *Sir Philip Sidney: Rebellion in Arcadia* (New Brunswick, NJ: Rutgers University Press, 1979), x, who suggests that the *Arcadia* reflects the 'social and personal predicament of an Elizabethan aristocrat, caught up in a tangle of diminishing feudal power . . . courtly dependence and intrigue, and a cult of devotion to a formidable, emasculating queen'.

60. Quoted in *New Arcadia*, ed. Skretkowicz, lxi.

61. R. W. Zandvoort, *Sidney's Arcadia: A Comparison between the Two Versions* (Amsterdam: Swets and Zeitlinger, 1929). See also A. G. D. Wiles, 'Parallel Analyses of the Two Versions of Sidney's *Arcadia*', *Studies in Philology* 39 (1942), 167–206.

62. See *The Poems of Sir Philip Sidney*, ed. W. A. Ringler (Oxford: Clarendon Press, 1962), 375–9; *The Old Arcadia*, ed. Robertson, lviii–lxiii; William Leigh Godshalk, 'Sidney's Revision of the *Arcadia*, Books III—V', *Philological Quarterly* 43 (1964), 171–84; and Michael McCanles, *The Text of Sidney's Arcadian World* (Durham, NC: Duke University Press, 1989), 134–43.

63. In *The Poems of Sir Philip Sidney*, Ringler, suggests that this interpolation could only have been made by someone who had studied

Mercator's edition of Ptolemy's *Geographiae Libri Octo* (Cologne, 1584), and concludes that the episode 'could not have been written by any editor, but only by Sidney himself' (377–8).

64. Nancy R. Lindheim suggests that 'the alterations in vision between the *Old* and the *New Arcadia* are significant enough to make us wonder whether the reason for Sidney's failure to complete the *New Arcadia* was not that his original plan was no longer workable', 'Vision, Revision, and the 1593 Text of the *Arcadia*', repr. in Arthur F. Kinney, ed., *Sidney in Retrospect: Selections from English Literary Renaissance* (Amherst: University of Massachusetts Press, 1988), 180.

65. Jon S. Lawry, *Sidney's Two Arcadias: Pattern and Proceeding* (Ithaca, NY: Cornell University Press, 1972), 167.

66. See Christopher Martin, 'Misdoubting his Estate: Dynastic Anxiety in Sidney's *Arcadia*', *English Literary Renaissance*, 18 (1988) 369–88 (386 n). For a general study of marriage in relation to the *Arcadia*, see Mark Rose, *Heroic Love: Studies in Sidney and Spenser* (Cambridge, Mass.: Harvard University Press, 1968).

67. See McCoy, *Rebellion in Arcadia*; Arthur Marotti, ' "Love Is Not Love": Elizabethan Sonnet Sequences and the Social Order', *Journal of English Literary History* 49 (1982), 396–428; Daniel Javitch, 'The Impure Motives of Elizabethan Poetry', *Genre* 15 (1982), 225–38; and Peter Stallybrass and Ann Jones, 'The Politics of *Astrophil and Stella*', *Studies in English Literature* 24 (1984), 53–68.

68. In *Argalus and Parthenia* (1629), a 'puritan' version of the tale, Francis Quarles attempts to 'legitimize' Parthenia's last-minute change of heart by inserting a long debate (not in Sidney) on the binding nature of the vows that are passed between her and Argalus – 'plighted faith and *sacro-sanctius* vowe'. See Francis Quarles, *Argalus and Parthenia*, ed. David Freeman (Washington DC: Folger Books, 1986), 106.

69. Robert Burton, *The Anatomy of Melancholy*, ed. Floyd Dell and Paul Jordan-Smith (New York: Tudor Publishing Company, 1948), 651.

70. For Davis, for example, Argalus and Parthenia 'exemplify the ideal heroic marriage', *A Map of Arcadia*, 130.

71. Torquato Tasso, *Discourses on the Heroic Poem* (1594), trans. Mariella Cavalchini and Irene Samuel (Oxford: Clarendon Press, 1973), 48.

72. For a summary of the chief textual differences between the *Old* and *New* versions of this tale, see Zandvoort, 96–102.

73. From a letter to the Earl of Leicester, dated 2 Aug. 1580, in *The Prose Works of Sir Philip Sidney*, ed. A. Feuillerat, 4 vols. (Cambridge: Cambridge University Press, 1962), iii. 129.

74. Castiglione, *The Book of the Courtier*, 315.

75. 'The opaque surface and the body's "valleys" acquire an essential meaning as the border of a closed individuality that does not merge with other bodies and with the world', Mikhail Bakhtin, *Rabelais and his World*, trans. Helene Iswolsky (Cambridge, Mass.: MIT Press,

1968), 320; see also Francis Barker, *The Tremulous Private Body: Essays on Subjection* (London: Methuen, 1984); and Peter Stallybrass, 'Patriarchal Territories: The Body Enclosed', in Margaret Ferguson *et al.*, eds., *Rewriting the Renaissance: The Discourses of Sexual Difference in Early Modern Europe* (Chicago: University of Chicago Press, 1986), 123–42.

76. George Puttenham, *The Arte of English Poesie* (1589), ed. G. D. Willcock and Alice Walker (Cambridge: Cambridge University Press, 1936), 244.

77. In *The Faerie Queene*, II. ix. 25–6, Spenser includes an almost identical image of the locked mouth in his castle of Alma. As the home of 'a virgin Queene most bright' (*FQ* II. xi. 2), Alma's castle suggests an immediate and obvious link with Elizabeth. See Robin Headlam Wells, *Spenser's Faerie Queene and the Cult of Elizabeth* (London: Croom Helm, 1983), 58–61.

78. R. E. Stillman, *Sidney's Poetic Justice: The Old Arcadia, its Eclogues, and Renaissance Pastoral Traditions* (Lewisburg, Pa.: Bucknell University Press, 1986), 136. For a detailed commentary on the poem, see Dorothy Jones, 'Sidney's Eroticism: An Interpretation of One of the *Arcadia* Poems', *Journal of English and Germanic Philology*, 73 (1974), 32–47.

79. See Levao, *Renaissance Minds and their Fictions*, 220–1.

80. Mrs Stanley, *Sir Philip Sidney's Arcadia Moderniz'd* (London, 1725), sig. b2.

5 'OF COURT IT SEEMES, MEN COURTESIE DOE CALL'

1. For a transcript of the document which details this award, see F. I. Carpenter, *A Reference Guide to Edmund Spenser* (Chicago: University of Chicago Press, 1923), 70.

2. *Amoretti* 74; *The Teares of the Muses*, line 573. All references to Spenser's poetry are taken from *The Works of Edmund Spenser*, ed. Edwin Greenlaw *et al.*, Variorum edition, 8 vols. (Baltimore: Johns Hopkins University Press, 1932–8).

3. George Peele, *The Honour of the Garter* (1593), lines 66–8, in *The Life and Works of George Peele*, ed. C. T. Prouty, 3 vols. (New Haven, Conn.: Yale University Press, 1952–70), i. 247.

4. *Diary of John Manningham of the Middle Temple, 1602–1603*, ed. Robert Parker Sorlien (Hanover, NH: University Press of New England, 1976), 78. For another version of these lines, again attributed to Spenser, see Thomas Fuller, *Fuller's Worthies of England*, ed. J. Freeman (London: Allen and Unwin, 1952), 366.

5. Roger A. Geimer notes that the verse quoted here in Manningham's diary was attributed elsewhere to Thomas Churchyard, and uses the evidence to suggest that the payment of Churchyard's first royal

pension was delayed by several years, 'Spenser's Rhyme and Church-yard's Reason: Evidence of Churchyard's First Pension', *Review of English Studies* NS 20 (1969), 306–9. Contrast M. H. Goldwyn, who finds that Churchyard's first pension (of 18*d.* per diem) *was* paid, 'Notes on the Biography of Thomas Churchyard', *Review of English Studies* NS 17 (1966), 1–15. The inference is that contemporaries clearly felt both Churchyard and Spenser to have good reason for rebuking their supposed patrons, even if, in the event, they had no real cause for doing so.

6. Ben Jonson, *Conversations with William Drummond*, quoted in *Ben Jonson*, ed. C. H. Herford and Percy Simpson, 11 vols. (Oxford: Clarendon Press, 1925–52), i. 137.

7. See anon., *The None-Such Charles his Character* (1651), 170: 'Now men may see, how much reason *Ben. Jonson* had, when as, lying sicke in his bed, very poore, and that after much importunity of Courtiers, ten pounds were sent to him by the King, after the receit of which, *Ben.* threw them through the glasse windowes, saying, *this mans soule was not fit to live in an alley*', quoted in *Ben Jonson*, ed. Herford and Simpson, i. 183.

8. *Mother Hubberds Tale*, lines 896–902. On the tendency of biographers to read into Spenser's words evidence for Burghley's failure to pay the pension, see the Variorum edition, vi. 271–2.

9. I am grateful to the editors of *Criticism* for permission to reproduce here a version of my article 'The Politics of Spenser's *Amoretti*', 33 (1991), 73–89.

10. William C. Johnson, *Spenser's* Amoretti: *Analogies of Love* (Lewisburg, Pa.: Bucknell University Press, 1990), 29. For a similar interpretation of the *Amoretti* and *Epithalamion*, see John N. Wall, *Transformations of the Word: Spenser, Herbert, Vaughan* (Athens: University of Georgia Press, 1988), 129–65.

11. Peter Stallybrass and Ann Jones, 'The Politics of *Astrophil and Stella*', *Studies in English Literature* 24 (1984), 53–68 (54).

12. The publication history of the *Amoretti and Epithalamion* (1595) is somewhat problematic. William Ponsonby entered 'Amoretti and Epithalamion written not longe since by Edmund Spenser' in the Stationers' Register on 19 Nov. 1594, having received a packet containing the two poems from Sir Robert Needham, the dedicatee of the 1595 volume. As there was no precedent for the publication of a marriage-poem at the end of a sonnet-sequence, it has been suggested (by the Variorum editors) that Ponsonby's joint volume was merely the result of an accident by which both manuscripts came into his hands at the same time. Critics have commented on the apparently careless production of the 1595 volume, noting in particular the notorious repetition of sonnet 35 as 83.

13. Sonnet-sequences have traditionally been interpreted as a site for

numerological structures and patterns, a practice initially authorized by Petrarch's *I Trionfi*. See Alastair Fowler, *Triumphal Forms: Structural Forms in Elizabethan Poetry* (Cambridge: Cambridge University Press, 1970), 174–97, for a discussion of the sonnet-sequences by Sidney, Spenser, and Shakespeare; and A. Kent Hieatt, *Short Time's Endless Monument* (New York: Columbia University Press, 1960), for a seminal study of the numerological structures of the *Amoretti* and *Epithalamion*. Other Elizabethan sonnet-sequences which portray a static, irresolvable courtship include: Thomas Watson, *The Hekatompathia* (1582); John Soowthern, *Pandora, the Musyque of the Beautie of his Mistress Diana* (1584); Henry Constable, *Diana* (1592); Samuel Daniel, *Delia* (1592); Barnabe Barnes, *Parthenophil and Parthenope* (1593); Giles Fletcher the elder, *Licia* (1593); Thomas Lodge, *Phillis* (1593); Thomas Watson, *The Tears of Fancie* (1593); anon., *Zepheria* (1594); Michael Drayton, *Idea's Mirrour* (1594); William Percy, *Coelia* (1594); Richard Barnfield, *The Affectionate Shepherd* (1594), and *Cynthia* (1595); E.C., *Emaricdulfe* (1595); Bartholomew Griffin, *Fidessa* (1596); R[ichard] L[inche], *Diella* (1596); William Smith, *Chloris* (1596); R[obert] T[ofte], *Laura* (1597); and Sir William Alexander, *Aurora* (1604).

14. See also Giles Fletcher's sequence, *Licia* (1593), which concludes with a lament-poem – 'The Rising to the Crowne of Richard III' – modelled on the style of the *Mirror for Magistrates*. Likewise, R[ichard] L[inche] follows his sonnet-sequence *Diella* (1596) with an 'amorous poem of Dom Diego and Gineura', a narrative which traces a history of feminine wilfulness and inconstancy, before the two lovers are finally allowed to marry at the close.

15. George Puttenham, *The Arte of English Poesie*, ed. G. D. Willcock and Alice Walker (Cambridge: Cambridge University Press, 1936), 50.

16. Quoted by A. L. Rowse, *Simon Forman: Sex and Society in Shakespeare's Age* (London: Weidenfeld and Nicolson, 1974), 20. See Louis A. Montrose, ' "Shaping Fantasies": Figurations of Gender and Power in Elizabethan Culture', in Stephen Greenblatt, ed., *Representing the Renaissance* (Berkeley: University of California Press, 1988), 31–64.

17. So J. W. Lever argues, in *The Elizabethan Love Sonnet* (London: Methuen, 1956), 97–102.

18. This is one of the interpretations of the Actaeon story given by Abraham Fraunce, in *The Third Part of the Countesse of Pembrokes Iuychurch* (1592), sig. M: 'a wiseman ought to refraine his eyes, from beholding sensible and coporall bewty, figured by *Diana*: least, as *Actaeon* was deuoured of his owne doggs, so he be distracted and torne in peeces with his owne affections, and perturbations'. For a recent discussion of Spenser's other allusion to the Actaeon myth, in the *Mutabilitie Cantos*, see David Quint, *Origin and Originality in Renaissance*

Literature: Versions of the Source (New Haven, Conn.: Yale University Press, 1983), 163–6.

19. In ' "Love Doth Hold My Hand": Writing and Wooing in the Sonnets of Sidney and Spenser', *Journal of English Literary History* 46 (1979), 541–58, Jacqueline T. Miller traces the tense relation between the mistress's ascendancy and the poet's apparent subordination in the *Amoretti*. Contrast A. Leigh DeNeef, *Spenser and the Motives of Metaphor* (Durham, NC: Duke University Press, 1982), 69–73, who interprets the captivity of both the lady and the lover within a Christian context, as sustaining, educating, and nourishing. For a similar interpretation, see J. C. Gray, 'Bondage and Deliverance in *The Faerie Queene*', *Modern Language Review* 70 (1975), 1–12.

20. Sir Philip Sidney, *The Old Arcadia*, ed. Jean Robertson (Oxford: Clarendon Press, 1973), 260. Geron's epithalamion immediately follows the seduction scene between Pyrocles and Philoclea, providing an ironic commentary on the difference between the shepherds' courtship (which concludes in legitimate marriage) and the indulgence of the prince and princess, who find themselves 'otherwise occupied' at the time, ibid. 245.

21. *The Shorter Poems of Edmund Spenser*, ed. William A. Oram *et al.*, Yale edition (New Haven, Conn.: Yale University Press, 1989), 590–1.

22. Puttenham, *The Arte of English Poesie*, ed. Willcock and Walker, 51.

23. Ibid. 51–2.

24. Louis A. Montrose, 'The Elizabethan Subject and the Spenserian Text', in Patricia Parker and David Quint, eds., *Literary Theory/Renaissance Texts* (Baltimore: Johns Hopkins University Press, 1986), 303–40 (320).

25. *The Prose Works of Fulke Greville, Lord Brooke*, ed. John Gouws (Oxford: Clarendon Press, 1986), 37.

26. For detailed discussions of Spenser's anacreontic poems, see James Hatton, 'Cupid and the Bee', *PMLA* 56 (1941), 1036–57; Peter M. Cummings, 'Spenser's *Amoretti* as an Allegory of Love', *Texas Studies in Language and Literature* 12 (1970), 163–79; Carol Kaske, 'Spenser's *Amoretti and Epithalamion* of 1595: Structure, Genre, and Numerology', *English Literary Renaissance* 8 (1978), 271–95; and Robert S. Miola, 'Spenser's Anacreontics: A Mythological Metaphor', *Studies in Philology* 77 (1980), 50–66.

27. Soowthern, *Pandora* (1584), sigs. D2^v, D3.

28. Louis L. Martz, 'The *Amoretti*: "Most Goodly Temperature" ', in William Nelson, ed., *Form and Convention in the Poetry of Edmund Spenser* (New York: Columbia University Press, 1961), 152. See also G. K. Hunter, 'Spenser's *Amoretti* and the English Sonnet Tradition', in Judith M. Kennedy and James A. Reither, eds., *A Theatre for Spenserians* (Toronto: University of Toronto Press, 1973), 124–44.

29. It will be clear that I am indebted to the challenging study of Spenser's 1596 revisions to the Amoret story in Jonathan Goldberg's *Endlesse Worke: Spenser and the Structures of Discourse* (Baltimore: Johns Hopkins University Press, 1981). See also Thomas P. Roche, *The Kindly Flame: A Study of the Third and Fourth Books of Spenser's Faerie Queene* (Princeton, NJ: Princeton University Press, 1964).

30. Sidney couterbalances Geron's epithalamion in the *Old Arcadia*, for example, with Nico's fabliau of married discord and feminine inconstancy ('A neighbour mine not long ago there was'), and with Histor's 'detestation of marriage', *Old Arcadia*, 249, 260. Spenser's *Epithalamion* seems, in particular, to have lent itself to an ambivalent response among its contemporary readers, for critics remain divided about the most famous imitation of Spenser's poem, Donne's *Epithalamion Made at Lincolnes Inne*. Donne's startling and disturbing image of the bride's ritual disembowelment on her wedding night has been interpreted both as a horrible parody of Spenser's hymn, and as a serious attempt to imitate its tone. For the first interpretation, see David Novarr, *The Disinterred Muse: Donne's Texts and Contexts* (Ithaca, NY: Cornell University Press, 1980), 65–84, and Celeste Marguerite Schenk, *Mourning and Panegyric: The Poetics of Pastoral Ceremony* (University Park: Pennsylvania State University Press, 1988), 73–90; for the second, see Heather [Ousby] Dubrow, 'Donne's "Epithalamion Made at Lincolnes Inne": An Alternative Interpretation', *Studies in English Literature* 16 (1976), 131–43, and *A Happier Eden: The Politics of Marriage in the Stuart Epithalamium* (Ithaca, NY: Cornell University Press, 1990), 156–70. I suggest that Donne's poem picks up on the ambivalence that was internal to Spenser's poem and that was a recognized characteristic of the epithalamic genre.

31. See e.g. Thomas M. Greene, 'Spenser and the Epithalamic Convention', *Comparative Literature* 9 (1957), 215–28; and Douglas Anderson, ' "Vnto My Selfe Alone": Spenser's Plenary Epithalamion', *Spenser Studies* 5 (1984–5), 149–66.

32. Samuel Daniel, *Delia* (1592), in *Samuel Daniel: Poems and* A Defence of Ryme, ed. Arthur Colby Sprague (Chicago: University of Chicago Press, 1930), 36.

33. For a recent discussion of the echo motif in the *Epithalamion*, see Joseph Lowenstein, 'Echoes Ring: Orpheus and Spenser's Career', *English Literary Renaissance* 16 (1986), 287–302. For more general studies of the device, see John Hollander, *The Figure of Echo: A Mode of Allusion in Milton and After* (Berkeley: University of California Press, 1981); Joseph Lowenstein, *Responsive Readings: Versions of Echo in Epic, Pastoral, and the Jonsonian Masque* (New Haven, Conn.: Yale University Press, 1984); and Jonathan Goldberg, *Voice Terminal Echo: Postmodernism and English Renaissance Texts* (London: Methuen, 1986).

34. George Peele, *The Honour of the Garter* (1593), lines 35–40, in *The Life and Works of George Peele*, ed. Prouty, i. 247.
35. See e.g. Thomas H. Cain, *Praise in* The Faerie Queene (Lincoln: University of Nebraska Press, 1978), 14–24; David Norbrook, *Poetry and Politics in the English Renaissance* (London: Routledge and Kegan Paul, 1984), 84–9; and Annabel Patterson, *Pastoral and Ideology: Virgil to Valéry* (Oxford: Clarendon Press, 1988), 121–32.
36. The Variorum editors adopt the 1611 reading 'froward' here, and are followed by J. C. Smith, Ernest de Selincourt, and A. C. Hamilton in their editions of the poem. For a defence of which reading, see DeWitt T. Starnes and Ernest W. Talbert, *Classical Myth and Legend in Renaissance Dictionaries* (Chapel Hill: University of North Carolina Press, 1955), 50–5; Humphrey Tonkin, *Spenser's Courteous Pastoral* (Oxford: Clarendon Press, 1972), 248–59, and *The Faerie Queene* (London: Unwin Hyman, 1989), 184–89; Lila Geller, 'The Acidalian Vision: Spenser's Graces in Book VI of *The Faerie Queene*', *Review of English Studies* NS 23 (1972), 267–77; and Robin Headlam Wells, 'Spenser and the Courtesy Tradition: Form and Meaning in the Sixth Book of *The Faerie Queene*', *English Studies* 58 (1977), 221–9.
37. E.K. glosses the Graces in the April eclogue as follows: 'the one having her backe towarde us, and her face fromwarde, as proceeding from us; the other two toward us'. In his *Thesaurus linguae Romanae et Britannicae* (1565), Thomas Cooper similarly describes how 'the ones backe should be towarde vs, and hir face fromwarde, as proceeding from vs, the other twoo towarde vs'; see also Fraunce, *The Third Part of the Countesse of Pembrokes Iuychurch* (1592), 46: 'Two of them looke towards vs, and one fromwards vs: we must yeeld double thanks, and double requitall for good turnes.' While most editors assume 'froward' to be the correct reading at VI. x. 24 on the basis of such contemporary usage, they use the evidence, of course, to support the fact that Spenser there *reverses* the traditional positioning of the Graces found in E.K., Cooper, and Fraunce.
38. This, alternative, reading is supported by Edgar Wind, *Pagan Mysteries in the Renaissance*, 2nd edn (Oxford: Oxford University Press, 1980), 28–30; A. Kent Hieatt, in *Spenser: Selected Poetry*, ed. Hieatt (New York: 1970); and Thomas Roche Jr., in *The Faerie Queene*, ed. Roche (Harmondsworth: Penguin, 1978).
39. A position persuasively argued by Seth Weiner, 'Minims and Grace Notes: Spenser's Acidalian Vision and Sixteenth-Century Music', *Spenser Studies* 5 (1984), 91–112.
40. James Nohrnberg, *The Analogy of* The Faerie Queene (Princeton, NJ: Princeton University Press, 1976), 709.
41. C. S. Lewis, *The Allegory of Love: A Study of Medieval Tradition* (Oxford: Clarendon Press, 1936), 350; see also A. C. Hamilton, *The Structure*

of Allegory in The Faerie Queene (Oxford: Clarendon Press, 1961), 200.

42. See Michael Baybak *et al.*, 'Placement "in the Middest"', in *The Faerie Queene*', in Alastair Fowler, ed., *Silent Poetry: Essays in Numerological Analysis* (London: Routledge and Kegan Paul, 1970), 141–52; Alastair Fowler, *Spenser and the Numbers of Time* (London: Routledge and Kegan Paul, 1964); See also Gerald Snare, 'Spenser's Fourth Grace', *Journal of the Warburg and Courtauld Institutes* 34 (1971), 350–5, on the fourth grace as an 'encyclopaedic symbol'.

43. On the growing reflexiveness of *The Faerie Queene*, and its portrayal of the relation between the poet and a corrupt and unpredictable world, see Nohrnberg, *Analogy of* The Faerie Queene; Harry Berger, 'A Secret Discipline: *The Faerie Queene* Book VI', in *Revisionary Play: Studies in the Spenserian Dynamics* (Berkeley: University of California Press, 1988); William V. Nestrick, 'The Virtuous and Gentle Discipline of Gentlemen and Poets', *Journal of English Literary History* 29 (1962), 357–71; and Kathleen Williams, *Spenser's World of Glass: A Reading of* The Faerie Queene (Berkeley: University of California Press, 1966).

44. An earlier use of the river–ocean image suggests that the act of return enacts a double tribute – for the tide returns to the ocean 'with double gaine / And tribute eke withall, as to his Soueraine' (*FQ* IV. iii. 27) – anticipating, perhaps, the 'double thanke' Spenser feels is his due in the second half of *The Faerie Queene*.

45. *Pace* Kathleeen Williams, who suggests that the Graces figure the 'benevolent life of the universe ... [and the] reciprocal goodwill ... [of a] divinely ordered universe', *Spenser's World of Glass*, 223.

46. Humphrey Tonkin describes book VI as a 'poetry of reconciliation', *Spenser's Courteous Pastoral*, *passim*; I am also most grateful to Michael Schoenfeldt for allowing me to see the transcript of a conference paper on a similar theme: 'The Poetry of Conduct: Accommodation and Transgression in *The Faerie Queene*, Book 6', Politics, Patronage and Literature in England, 1558–1658, University of Reading, 1989.

47. On the ambivalence surrounding Calidore's truancy, see J. C. Maxwell, 'The Truancy of Calidore', *Journal of English Literary History* 19 (1952), 143–9 (147); Harry Rusche, 'The Lesson of Calidore's Truancy', *Studies in Philology* 76 (1979), 149–61 (159); and A. Leigh DeNeef, 'Ploughing Virgilian Furrows: The Genres of *Faerie Queene* VI', *John Donne Journal* 1 (1982), 151–66 (160).

48. At V. x. 10, and V. xi. 23, Echidna and Typhaeon are the parents of Orthrus. In legend, Echidna is the mother of Cerberus.

49. Dante, *Convivio*, II. xi. 64, in *Dante's Convivio*, trans. W. W. Jackson (Oxford: Clarendon Press, 1909), 101.

50. S[imon] R[obson], *A Newe Yeeres Gift: The Courte of Ciuill Courtesie* (1577), sig. A3ᵛ; George Herbert, *The Church Porch* (1633), line 292.

51. See A. J. Denomy, 'Courtly Love and Courtliness', *Speculum* 28

(1953), 44–63; Moshé Lazar, 'Les Eléménts constitutifs de la "corte-zia" dans la lyrique des troubadours', *Studi Mediolatini et Volgari* 6 (1959), 67–96, and *Amour courtois et 'fin'amors' dans la littérature du XIIe* siècle* (Paris: Klinckseick, 1964); and Jean Frappier, 'Vues sur les conceptions courtoises dans les littératures d'oc et d'oïl au XIIe siècle', *Cahiers de Civilisation Médiévale* 2 (1959), 135–56.

52. Marcabru, song 15, 'Cortesamen vuoill comenssar', line 20, in *Poésies complètes du troubadour Marcabru*, ed. J. M. L. Dejeanne (Toulouse: private publication, 1909), 62 ('to have courtesy is to love'); Cerca-mon, song 1, 'Quant l'aura doussa s'amarzis', lines 57–8, in *Les Poésies de Cercamon*, ed. Alfred Jeanroy (Paris: Champion, 1922), 4 ('hardly will that man be courteous who gives up all hope of love'); Peire d'Auvergne, in a debate with Bernart de Ventadorn, song 2, 'Amics Bernartz de Ventadorn', lines 15–16, in *Bernart von Ventadorn: Seine Lieder*, ed. Carl Appel (Halle: Niemeyer, 1915), 11 ('hardly will that man be worthy or courteous who cannot abide in love').

53. Guillaume IX, song 9, 'Mout jauzens me prenc en amar', lines 25–30, in *Les Chansons de Guillaume IX, Duc d'Aquitaine (1071–1127)*, ed. Alfred Jeanroy (Paris: Champion, 1913), 23 ('Through joy the sick man can grow well, through sadness the healthy man can die, and the wise man become a fool, the handsome man alter his good looks, the most courtly become vile, and the completely base become courtly').

54. Richard Lanham, *A Letter whearin Part of the Entertainment vntoo the Queenz Maiesty at Killingwoorth Castl iz Signified* (1575), sig. C5.

55. Thomas Churchyard, *A Discourse of the Queenes Maiesties Entertainement in Suffolk and Norffolk* (1578), sig. B1.

56. John Webster, *The White Devil*, I. ii. 318–19, in *The Complete Works of John Webster*, ed. F. L. Lucas, 4 vols. (London: Chatto and Windus, 1927), i. 121.

57. Robert Greene, *Menaphon* (1589), ed. G. B. Harrison (Oxford: Black-well, 1927), 45.

58. Parts of Guazzo's treatise are included in Ludovick Bryskett's *Dis-course of Civill Life* (1606), which purports to describe a conversation with Spenser on moral philosophy and on the plan of *The Faerie Queene*. Spenser alludes explicitly to Guazzo's treatise when he refers to courtesy as the 'roote of ciuill conuersation' (*FQ* VI. i. 1).

59. J. W. Nicholls, *The Matter of Courtesy: Medieval Courtesy Books and the Gawain-Poet* (Cambridge: Brewer, 1985), 7. On the polysemy of 'courtesy' in French and English, see Henri Dupin, *La Courtoisie au Moyen Age* (Paris: Picard, 1931); Constance West, *'Courtoisie' in Anglo-Norman Literature* (Oxford: Medium Aevum Monographs, 1938); D. S. Brewer, 'Courtesy and the *Gawain*-Poet', in *Patterns of Love and Courtesy: Essays in Memory of C. S. Lewis*, ed. J. Lawlor (London: Edward Arnold, 1966); and W. O. Evans, ' "Cortaysye" in Middle English', *Medieval Studies* 29 (1967), 143–57.

60. For some studies of the semantic development of 'courtoisie' in French, see Glyn S. Burgess, *Contribution à l'étude du vocabulaire pré-courtois* (Geneva: Droz, 1970); K. J. Hollyman, *Le Développement du vocabulaire féodale* (Geneva: Droz, 1957); Georges Matoré, *Le Vocabulaire et la société médiévale* (Paris: Presses Universitaires de France, 1985); Stanley L. Galpin, *Cortois and Vilain: A Study of the Distinctions Made between them by the French and Provençal Poets of the 12th, 13th and 14th Centuries* (New Haven, Conn.: Ryder, 1905); and Frappier, 'Vues sur les conceptions courtoises'.

61. 'And here is kydde cortaysye, as I haf herd carp, / And þat hatz wayned me hider, iwyis, at þis tyme', *Sir Gawain and the Green Knight*, lines 263–4, ed. Norman Davis, 2nd edn (Oxford: Clarendon Press, 1967), 8.

62. Chaucer, *The Parson's Tale*, line 245, in *The Works of Geoffrey Chaucer*, ed. F. N. Robinson (Oxford: Oxford University Press, 1957), 234.

63. Anon., *Dan Michel's Ayenbite of Inwyt*, ed. R. Morris (Early English Text Society, 1886), 97; *Cursor Mundi* (Cotton MS), line 13355, ed. R. Morris (Early English Text Society, 1876), 766; and ibid., line 2256.

64. *Purity*, line 1097, ed. R. J. Menner (New Haven, Conn.: Yale University Press, 1920), 42. *Pearl*, line 432, ed. E. V. Gordon (Oxford: Clarendon Press, 1953), 16. Spenser's use of 'courtesy' in this sense is discussed by Peter Bayley, 'Order, Grace, and Courtesy in Spenser's World', in John Lawlor, ed., *Patterns of Love and Courtesy: Essays in Memory of C. S. Lewis* (London: Edward Arnold, 1966), 197–8; and by Tonkin, *Spenser's Courteous Pastoral*, ch. 9, esp. 239.

65. Evans, ' "Cortaysye" in Middle English', 145; *Sir Degaré*, lines 819–22, in *Middle English Metrical Romances*, ed. W. H. French and C. B. Hale, 2 vols. (New York: Russell and Russell, 1930), i. 312; Chaucer, *General Prologue*, lines 99–100, in *The Works of Geoffrey Chaucer*, ed. Robinson, 18.

66. *Havelok the Dane*, lines 192–5, in *Middle English Metrical Romances*, ed. French and Hale, i. 82.

67. *The Bird with Four Feathers*, lines 93–6, in *Religious Lyrics of the XIVth Century*, ed. Carleton Brown (Oxford: Clarendon Press, 1924), 211.

68. *Sapho and Phao*, I. iv. 15–16, in *The Complete Works of John Lyly*, ed. R. Warwick Bond, 3 vols. (Oxford: Clarendon Press, 1902), ii. 379.

69. Richard Neuse, 'Book VI as Conclusion to *The Faerie Queene*', *Journal of English Literary History* 35 (1968), 329–53 (341).

70. On the apparently cyclical structure of *The Faerie Queene*, see Northrop Frye, 'The Structure of Imagery in *The Faerie Queene*', *University of Toronto Quarterly* 30 (1960–1), 109–27; Neuse, 'Book VI as Conclusion to *The Faerie Queene*'; Williams, *Spenser's World of Glass, passim*; Nohrnberg, *Analogy of* The Faerie Queene, ch. 5; Tonkin, *Spenser's Courteous Pastoral, passim*; and Susanne Woods, 'Closure in *The Faerie Queene*', *Journal of English and Germanic Philology* 76 (1977), 195–216.

Contrast Stanley Stewart, for whom the 'primary feature of organization [in book VI] ... is disjunction', 'Sir Calidore and "Closure" ', *Studies in English Literature* 24 (1984), 69–86 (85).

71. Nohrnberg, *Analogy of* The Faerie Queene, 664.
72. DeNeef, 'Ploughing Virgilian Furrows', 152.
73. 'But now my teme begins to faint and fayle, / All woxen weary of their iournall toyle' (*FQ* III. xii. 47, 1590 edn); 'But here my wearie teeme nigh ouer spent / Shall breath it selfe awhile, after so long a went' (IV. v. 46); 'And turne we here to this faire furrowes end / Our wearie yokes, to gather fresher sprights' (v. iii. 40). The image, together with the image of weariness, derives from Chaucer's *Knight's Tale*, lines 886–8: 'I have, God woot, a large feeld to ere, / And wayke been the oxen in my plough. / The remenant of the tale is long ynough', in *The Works of Geoffrey Chaucer*, ed. Robinson, 26.
74. From Giraldi Cinthio, *Discorsi de M. Giovambattista Giraldi Cinthio* (Vinegia, 1554), 25 ('the poet ought to be careful to treat ... digressions so that one depends on another and so that they are well linked with the parts of the material which with a continuous thread and with a continuous chain he has set out to tell', trans. Henry L. Snuggs, *Giraldi Cinthio on Romances* (Lexington: University of Kentucky Press, 1968), 23.

EPILOGUE

1. 'Of Truth', from *Essays or Counsels Civil and Moral* (1625), in *The Works of Francis Bacon*, ed. J. Spedding *et al.*, 14 vols., repr. (New York: Longman, 1968), vi. 377–8.
2. Annabel Patterson, *Censorship and Interpretation: The Conditions of Writing and Reading in Early Modern England* (Madison: University of Wisconsin Press, 1984), 71.
3. *The Works of Francis Bacon*, ed. Spedding *et al.*, vi. 378, 377.

Bibliography

PRIMARY SOURCES

COLLECTIONS AND ANTHOLOGIES

Anthology of the Provençal Troubadours, ed. Raymond Thompson Hill and Thomas Goddard Bergin (New Haven, Conn.: Yale University Press, 1941).

A Book of Masques, ed. T. J. B. Spencer and Stanley Wells (Cambridge: Cambridge University Press, 1967).

Calendar of State Papers: Domestic.

Calendar of State Papers: Foreign.

Calendar of State Papers: Spanish.

Documents Relating to the Office of the Revels in the Time of Queen Elizabeth, ed. Albert Feuillerat (Louvain: Materialen, 1908).

Elizabethan Critical Essays, ed. G. Gregory Smith, 2 vols. (Oxford: Clarendon Press, 1904).

The English Spenserians, ed. William B. Hunter (Salt Lake City: University of Utah Press, 1977).

Entertainments for Elizabeth I, ed. Jean Wilson (Woodbridge: Boydell and Brewer, 1980).

Middle English Metrical Romances, ed. W. H. French and C. B. Hale, 2 vols. (New York: Russell and Russell, 1930).

Religious Lyrics of the XIVth Century, ed. Carleton Brown (Oxford: Clarendon Press, 1924).

ANONYMOUS WORKS

Anon., *La Chanson des Quatre Fils Aymon d'après le manuscrit de Vallière*, ed. Ferdinand Castets (Montpellier: Coulet, 1909).

Anon., *Cursor Mundi*, ed. R. Morris (Early English Text Society, 1874–6).

Anon., *Dan Michel's Ayenbite of Inwyt*, ed. R. Morris (Early English Text Society, 1886).

Anon., *An Elizabethan Manuscript at Alnwick Castle, Northumberland*, ed. F. J. Burgoyne (London: Longman, 1904).

Anon., *The None-Such Charles his Character* (1651).

Anon., *Pearl*, ed. E. V. Gordon (Oxford: Clarendon Press, 1953).

Purity, ed. R. J. Menner (New Haven, Conn.: Yale University Press, 1920).

Sir Gawain and the Green Knight, ed. Norman Davis, 2nd edn (Oxford: Clarendon Press, 1967).

Anon., *Queen Elizabeth's Entertainment at Mitcham*, ed. Leslie Hotson (New Haven, Conn.: Yale University Press, 1953).

Anon., *The Quenes Maiesties Passage through the Citie of London to Westminster the Day before her Coronacion* (1559), ed. James M. Osborn (New Haven, Conn.: Yale University Press, 1960).

Anon., *Rhetorica ad Herennium*, ed. and trans. Harry Caplan, Loeb edition, (Cambridge, Mass: Harvard University Press, 1954).

Anon., *Le Roman de Flamenca*, ed. Ulrich Gschwind, 2 vols. (Berne: Francke, 1976).

Anon., *Zepheria* (1594).

WORKS BY INDIVIDUAL AUTHORS

Alexander, Sir William, *Aurora* (1604).

Ariosto, Ludovico, *Opere minori*, ed. Cesare Segre (Milan: Ricciardi, 1954).

Orlando Furioso, trans. Sir John Harington (1591), ed. Robert McNulty (Oxford: Clarendon Press, 1972).

Ascham, Roger, *The Schoolmaster* (1570), ed. Lawrence V. Ryan (Ithaca, NY: Cornell University Press, 1967).

Bacon, Francis, *The Works of Francis Bacon*, ed. J. Spedding, R. L. Ellis, and D. D. Heath, 14 vols., repr. (New York: Longman, 1968).

Bandello, Matteo, *Tutte le opere di Matteo Bandello*, ed. Francesco Flora, 2 vols. (Verona: Mondadori, 1942).

Barclay, Alexander, *The Eclogues of Alexander Barclay*, ed. Beatrice White (Early English Text Society, 1928).

Barnes, Barnabe, *Parthenophil and Parthenope* (1593).

Barnfield, Richard, *The Affectionate Shepherd* (1594).

Cynthia (1595).

Basselin, Olivier, *Vaux-de-vire d'Olivier Basselin et de Jean le Houx*, ed. P. L. Jacob (Paris: Delahays, 1858).

Baynes, Roger, *The Baynes of Aquisgrane* (1617).

Belleforest, François de, *Histoires tragiques*, 2 vols. (Paris, 1564–5), ed. and trans. Frank S. Hook, in *The French Bandello* (Columbia: University of Missouri Press, 1948).

Bembo, Pietro, *Gli Asolani et Le Rime*, ed. Carlo Dionisotti-Casalone (Turin: Unione Tipografico–Editrice Torinese, 1932); *Gli Asolani*, trans. Rudolf B. Gottfried (Bloomington: Indiana University Press, 1954).

Bernart de Ventadorn, *Bernart von Ventadorn: Seine Lieder*, ed. Carl Appel (Halle: Niemeyer, 1915).

Boccaccio, Giovanni, *Filocolo*, trans. H[enry] G[rantham], *Thirtene Most Plesant and Delectable Questions* (1566, 2nd edn 1571).

Breton, Nicholas, *The Arbor of Amorous Deuises* (1597), ed. H. E. Rollins (Cambridge, Mass.: Harvard University Press, 1936).

Burton, Robert, *The Anatomy of Melancholy*, ed. Floyd Dell and Paul Jordan-Smith (New York: Tudor Publishing Company, 1948).

E.C., *Emaricdulfe* (1595).

Carey, Robert, *Memoirs*, ed. F. H. Mares (Oxford: Clarendon Press, 1972).

Castiglione, Baldassare, *The Book of the Courtier*, trans. Sir Thomas Hoby (1561), ed. W. H. D. Rouse (London: Dent, 1928).

Cercamon, *Les Poésies de Cercamon*, ed. Alfred Jeanroy (Paris: Champion, 1922).

Chamberlain, John, *The Letters of John Chamberlain*, ed. Norman E. McClure, 2 vols. (Philadelphia: American Philosophical Society, 1939).

Chapman, George, *Chapman's Homer* (1614–16), ed. Allardyce Nicoll, 2 vols. (London: Routledge and Kegan Paul, 1957).

Chaucer, Geoffrey, *The Works of Geoffrey Chaucer*, ed. F. N. Robinson (Oxford: Oxford University Press, 1957).

Chettle, Henry, *Englands Mourning Garment* (1603).

Churchyard, Thomas, *A Discourse of the Queenes Maiesties Entertainement in Suffolk and Norffolk* (1578).

Cinthio, Giraldi, *Discorsi de M. Giovambattista Giraldi Cinthio* (Vinegia, 1554), trans. Henry L. Snuggs, *Giraldi Cinthio on Romances* (Lexington: University of Kentucky Press, 1968).

Congreve, William, *The Complete Plays of William Congreve*, ed. Herbert Davis (Chicago: University of Chicago Pres, 1967).

Constable, Henry, *Diana* (1592).

Cooper, Thomas, *Thesaurus linguae Romanae et Britannicae* (1565).

Daniel, Samuel, *Samuel Daniel: Poems and* A Defence of Ryme, ed. Arthur Colby Sprague (Chicago: University of Chicago Press, 1930).

Dante Alighieri, *Dante's Convivio*, trans. W. W. Jackson (Oxford: Clarendon Press, 1909).

   La Divina Commedia, ed. Natalino Sapegno (Milan: Ricciardi, 1957).

Davies, Sir John, *The Poems of Sir John Davies*, ed. R. Kreuger (Oxford: Clarendon Press, 1975).

della Casa, Giovanni, *Galateo* (1576), trans. Robert Peterson, in *A Renaissance Courtesy Book: Galateo of Manners and Behaviours by Giovanni della Casa*, ed. J. E. Spingarn (London: Grant Richards, 1914).

Devereux, Robert, 'The Poems of Edward de Vere, Seventeenth Earl of Oxford, and of Robert Devereux, Second Earl of Essex', ed. Steven May, *Studies in Philology* 77 (1980), 1–132.

Devereux, Walter Bourchier, *Lives and Letters of the Devereux, Earls of Essex*, 2 vols. (London: Murray, 1853).

Dolce, Ludovico, *Commedie del Cinquecento*, ed. Ireneo Sanesi, 2 vols. (Bari: Laterza, 1912).

Donne, John, *The Elegies and The Songs and Sonnets*, ed. Helen Gardner (Oxford: Clarendon Press, 1965).

John Donne: The Satires, Epigrams and Verse Letters, ed. W. Milgate (Oxford: Clarendon Press, 1967).

John Donne: The Divine Poems, ed. Helen Gardner (Oxford: Clarendon Press, 1978).

Drayton, Michael, *The Works of Michael Drayton*, ed. J. Hebel, K. Tillotson, and B. Newdigate, 5 vols. (Oxford: Blackwell, 1931–41).

Dugdale, Sir William, *The Antiquities of Warwickshire*, ed. William Thomas, 2 vols. (London, 1730).

Elyot, Sir Thomas, *The Book Named the Governor*, ed. Henry Croft, 2 vols. (London: Kegan Paul, 1880).

Fenton, Sir Geoffrey, *Certaine Tragicall Discourses* (1567).

Fletcher, Giles, *The English Works of Giles Fletcher the Elder*, ed. Lloyd E. Berry (Madison: University of Wisconsin Press, 1964).

Florio, John, *Queen Anna's New World of Words* (1611), ed. R. C. Alston (Menston: Scolar Press, 1968).

Fraunce, Abraham, *The Third Part of the Countesse of Pembrokes Iuychurch* (1592).

Fuller, Thomas, *Fuller's Worthies of England*, ed. J. Freeman (London: Allen and Unwin, 1952).

Garter, Bernard, *The Ioyfull Receyuing of the Queenes Maiestie into Norwich* (1578).

Gascoigne, George, *A Hundreth Sundrie Flowers* (1573), ed. C. T. Prouty (Columbia: University of Missouri Press, 1942).

The Complete Works of George Gascoigne, ed. J. W. Cunliffe, 2 vols. (Cambridge: Cambridge University Press, 1907–10).

Gonzaga, Luigi, Duke of Nevers, *Mémoires*, 2 vols. (Paris, 1665).

Grange, John, *The Golden Aphroditis* (1577).

Greene, Robert, *The Life and Complete Works in Prose and Verse of Robert Greene*, ed. A. B. Grosart, 15 vols. (London: private publication, 1881–6).

Menaphon (1589), ed. G. B. Harrison (Oxford: Blackwell, 1927).

Greville, Fulke, *The Prose Works of Fulke Greville, Lord Brooke*, ed. John Gouws (Oxford: Clarendon Press, 1986).

Griffin, Bartholomew, *Fidessa* (1596).

Guazzo, Stefano, *La civile conversatione*, trans. George Pettie and Bartholomew Young, *The Civile Conversation of M. Steeven Guazzo* (1580–6), ed. Charles Whibley, 2 vols. (London: Constable, 1925).

Guevara, Antonio de, *Aviso de Privados* (Valladolid, 1539), trans. F.B., 'The Larum of the Court', Houghton Library MS Eng. 517.

Guillaume IX, *Les Chansons de Guillaume IX, Duc d'Aquitaine (1071–1127)*, ed. Alfred Jeanroy (Paris: Champion, 1913).

Guillaume d'Orange, *Guillaume d'Orange: chansons de geste*, ed. M. W. J. A. Jonckbloet, 2 vols. (The Hague: Nijhoff, 1854).

Hall, Edward, *The Vnion of the Two Noble and Illustre Famelies of Lancastre and Yorke* (1548–50), ed. Henry Ellis (London: Johnson, 1809).

Hatton, Sir Christopher, *Memoirs of the Life and Times of Sir Christopher Hatton*, ed. Harris Nicolas (London: Bentley, 1847).

Herbert, George, *The English Poems of George Herbert*, ed. C. A. Patrides (London: Dent, 1974).

Heywood, Thomas, *Troia Britanica, or Great Britaines Troy* (1609).

Hoskins, John, *Directions for Speech and Style* (1599), in *The Life, Letters, and Writings of John Hoskyns 1566–1638*, ed. Louise Brown Osborn (New Haven, Conn.: Yale University Press, 1937).

Jonson, Ben, *Ben Jonson*, ed. C. H. Herford and Percy Simpson, 11 vols. (Oxford: Clarendon Press, 1925–52).

Kyd, Thomas, *The Works of Thomas Kyd*, ed. F. S. Boas, rev. edn (Oxford: Clarendon Press, 1955).

Lanham, Richard, *A Letter whearin Part of the Entertainment vntoo the Queenz Maiesty at Killingwoorth Castl iz Signified* (1575).

Legh, Gerard, *The Accedens of Armory* (1562).

L[inche], R[ichard], *Diella* (1596).

Lodge, Thomas, *Wits Miserie, and the Worlds Madnesse* (1596).

   A Margarite of America (1595), ed. G. B. Harrison (Oxford: Blackwell, 1927).

   The Complete Works of Thomas Lodge, ed. E. Gosse, 4 vols., repr. (New York: Russell and Russell, 1963).

Lorris, Guillaume de, and Jean de Meun, *The Romaunt of the Rose*, ed. Ronald Sutherland (Oxford: Blackwell, 1968).

Lyly, John, *The Complete Works of John Lyly*, ed. R. Warwick Bond, 3 vols. (Oxford: Clarendon Press, 1902).

Magny, Olivier de, *Les Souspirs d'Olivier de Magny*, ed. E. Courbet (Paris: Lemerre, 1874).

Manningham, John, *Diary of John Manningham of the Middle Temple, 1602–1603*, ed. Robert Parker Sorlien (Hanover, NH: University Press of New England, 1976).

Marcabru, *Poésies complètes du troubadour Marcabru*, ed. J. M. L. Dejeanne (Toulouse: private publication, 1909).

Marlowe, Christopher, *The Complete Works of Christopher Marlowe*, ed. Fredson Bowers, 2 vols. (Cambridge: Cambridge University Press, 1973).

Massinger, Philip, *The Plays and Poems of Philip Massinger*, ed. Philip Edwards and Colin Gibson, 5 vols. (Oxford: Clarendon Press, 1976).

Melbancke, Brian, *Philotimus: The Warre betwixt Nature and Fortune* (1583).

Montaigne, Michel de, *The Complete Works of Montaigne*, ed. Donald M. Frame (London: Hamish Hamilton, 1957).

Nashe, Thomas, *The Works of Thomas Nashe*, ed. R. B. McKerrow, 5 vols. (Oxford: Blackwell, 1904–10, repr. 1966).

Naunton, Sir Robert, *Fragmenta Regalia, or Observations on Queen Elizabeth, her*

Times and Favorites (1641), ed. John S. Cerovski (Washington DC: Folger Shakespeare Library, 1985).

North, George, *The Philosopher of the Court* (1575).

North, Thomas, *The Diall of Princes* (1568).

Painter, William, *The Palace of Pleasure* (1566–7), ed. Joseph Jacobs, 3 vols. (London: Nutt, 1890).

Pasquier, Etienne, *Le Monophile*, trans. Sir Geoffrey Fenton, *Monophylo* (1572).

Peele, George, *The Life and Works of George Peele*, ed. C. T. Prouty, 3 vols. (New Haven, Conn.: Yale University Press, 1952–70).

Percy, William, *Coelia* (1594).

Pettie, George, *A Petite Pallace of Pettie his Pleasure* (1576), ed. Herbert Hartman (New York: Oxford University Press, 1938).

Puttenham, George, *The Arte of English Poesie* (1589), ed. G. D. Willcock and Alice Walker (Cambridge: Cambridge University Press, 1936).

Quarles, Francis, *Argalus and Parthenia*, ed. David Freeman (Washington DC: Folger Books, 1986).

Rich, Barnaby, *Rich's Farewell to Military Profession* (1581), ed. Thomas M. Cranfill (Austin: University of Texas Press, 1959).

The Straunge and Wonderfull Aduentures of Don Simonides (1581).

The Second Tome of the Trauailes and Aduentures of Don Simonides (1584).

Richardson, Samuel, *Clarissa*, ed. Angus Ross (Harmondsworth: Penguin, 1985).

R[obson], S[imon], *A Newe Yeeres Gift: The Courte of Ciuill Courtesie* (1577).

R[ogers], T[homas], *Leicester's Ghost* (?1602–4), ed. Franklin B. Williams (Chicago: University of Chicago Press, 1972).

Romei, Annibale, *Discorsi*, trans. John Keepers, *The Courtiers Academie* (1598).

Ronsard, Pierre de, *Pierre de Ronsard: Œuvres Complètes*, ed. Paul Laumonier, 20 vols. (Paris: Droz, 1914–67).

Savonarola, Girolamo, *Trattato circa il reggimento e governo della città di Firenze*, ed. Audin de Rians, 6th edn (Florence: Barachi, 1847).

Segar, William, *The Booke of Honor and Armes* (1589).

Shakespeare, William, *The Riverside Shakespeare*, ed. G. Blakemore Evans (Boston: Houghton Mifflin, 1974).

As You Like It, ed. Richard Knowles and Evelyn Joseph Mattern, Variorum edition (New York: Modern Language Association, 1977).

Sidney, Sir Philip, *The Correspondence of Sir Philip Sidney and Hubert Languet*, ed. and trans. Steuart A. Pears (London: William Pickering, 1845).

The Poems of Sir Philip Sidney, ed. W. A. Ringler (Oxford: Clarendon Press, 1962).

The Prose Works of Sir Philip Sidney, ed. A. Feuillerat, 4 vols. (Cambridge: Cambridge University Press, 1962).

An Apology for Poetry, ed. Geoffrey Shepherd (Manchester: Manchester University Press, 1973).

The Countess of Pembroke's Arcadia (The Old Arcadia), ed. Jean Robertson (Oxford: Clarendon Press, 1973).

The Miscellaneous Prose of Sir Philip Sidney, ed. Katherine Duncan-Jones and Jan van Dorsten (Oxford: Clarendon Press, 1973).

The Countess of Pembroke's Arcadia (being the 1593 composite version), ed. Maurice Evans (Harmondsworth: Penguin, 1977).

The Countess of Pembroke's Arcadia (The New Arcadia) (1590), ed. Victor Skretkowicz (Oxford: Clarendon Press, 1987).

Smith, William, *Chloris* (1596).

Soowthern, John, *Pandora, the Musyque of the Beautie of his Mistresse Diana* (1584).

Spenser, Edmund, *The Works of Edmund Spenser*, ed. Edwin Greenlaw, Charles G. Osgood, Frederick M. Padelford, *et al.*, 8 vols., Variorum edition (Baltimore: Johns Hopkins University Press, 1932–8).

Spenser: Selected Poetry, ed. A. Kent Hieatt (New York: 1970).

The Faerie Queene, ed. Thomas Roche Jr. (Harmondsworth: Penguin, 1978).

The Shorter Poems of Edmund Spenser, ed. William A. Oram *et al.*, Yale edition (New Haven: Yale University Press, 1989).

Stanley, Mrs, *Sir Philip Sidney's Arcadia Moderniz'd* (London, 1725).

Stow, John, *Annales of England* (1592).

Straparola, Giovan Francesco, *Le piacevoli notti* (1550–3), ed. Giuseppe Rua, 2 vols. (Bari: Laterza, 1927).

Stubbs, John, *The Discoverie of a Gaping Gulf whereinto England is like to be Swallowed by an other French Mariage* (1579).

Tasso, Torquato, *Discourses on the Heroic Poem* (1594), trans. Mariella Cavalchini and Irene Samuel (Oxford: Clarendon Press, 1973).

Tasso's Dialogues: A Selection, ed. and trans. Carnes Lord and Dain A. Trafton (Berkeley: University of California Press, 1982).

Tilney, Edmund, *A Briefe and Pleasaunt Discourse of Duties in Mariage, Called the Flower of Friendshippe* (1568).

T[ofte], R[obert], *Laura* (1597).

Vere, Edward de, 'The Poems of Edward de Vere, Seventeenth Earl of Oxford, and of Robert Devereux, Second Earl of Essex', ed. Steven May, *Studies in Philology* 77 (1980), 1–132.

Watson, Thomas, *The Hekatompathia* (1582).

The Tears of Fancie (1593).

Webster, John, *The Complete Works of John Webster*, ed. F. L. Lucas, 4 vols. (London: Chatto and Windus, 1927).

Whetstone, George, *An Heptameron of Ciuil Discourses* (1582).

Whythorne, Thomas, *The Autobiography of Thomas Whythorne: Modern Spelling Edition (c.*1576), ed. J. M. Osborn (Oxford: Clarendon Press, 1962).

Wilkins, George, *The Miseries of Inforst Mariage* (1607), ed. Glenn H. Blayney (Oxford: Malone Society, 1963).

Wilson, Thomas, *The Arte of Rhetorique* (1553), ed. Robert Hood Bowers (Gainesville, Fla.: Scholars' Facsimiles, 1962).

The Rule of Reason (1567).

Wotton, Henry, *A Courtlie Controuersie of Cupids Cautels* (1578).

Wotton, Sir Henry, *Reliquiae Wottonianae* (1651).

SECONDARY SOURCES

Adams, Simon, 'Eliza Enthroned?' The Court and its Politics', in Christopher Haigh, ed., *The Reign of Elizabeth I* (London: Macmillan, 1984).

Altman, Joel B., *The Tudor Play of Mind* (Berkeley: University of California Press, 1978).

Anderson, Douglas, ' "Vnto My Selfe Alone": Spenser's Plenary Epithalamion', *Spenser Studies* 5 (1984–5), 149–66.

Anglo, Sydney, *Spectacle, Pageantry, and Early Tudor Policy* (Oxford: Clarendon Press, 1969).

ed., *The Great Tournament Roll of Westminster* (Oxford: Clarendon Press, 1968).

Ariès, Philippe, and André Béjin, *Western Sexuality: Practice and Precept in Past and Present Times* (Oxford: Blackwell, 1985).

Axton, Marie, 'Robert Dudley and the Inner Temple Revels', *Historical Journal* 13 (1970), 365–78.

The Queen's Two Bodies: Drama and the Elizabethan Succession (London: Royal Historical Society, 1977).

'The Tudor Mask and Elizabethan Court Drama', in M. Axton and R. Williams, eds., *English Drama: Forms and Development: Essays in Honour of Muriel Clara Bradbrook* (Cambridge University Press, 1977).

Bakhtin, Mikhail, *Rabelais and his World*, trans. Helen Iswolsky (Cambridge, Mass.: MIT Press, 1968).

Barker, Francis, *The Tremulous Private Body: Essays on Subjection* (London: Methuen, 1984).

Barthes, Roland, *Criticism and Truth*, trans. Katrine Pilcher Keuneman (London: Athlone Press, 1987).

Baybak, Michael, Paul Delany, and A. Kent Hieatt, 'Placement "in the Middest", in *The Faerie Queene*', in Alastair Fowler, ed., *Silent Poetry: Essays in Numerological Analysis* (London: Routledge and Kegan Paul, 1970).

Bayley, Peter, 'Order, Grace, and Courtesy in Spenser's World', in John Lawlor, ed., *Patterns of Love and Courtesy: Essays in Memory of C. S. Lewis* (London: Edward Arnold, 1966).

Beal, Peter, 'Poems by Sir Philip Sidney: The Ottley Manuscript', *The Library*, 5th series, 33 (1978), 284–95.

Bennett, Josephine W., 'Oxford and *Endimion*', *PMLA* 57 (1942), 354–69.

Berger, Harry, 'A Secret Discipline: *The Faerie Queene* Book VI', in *Revisionary Play: Studies in the Spenserian Dynamics* (Berkeley: University of California Press, 1988).

Bergeron, David, *English Civic Pageantry 1558–1642* (London: Edward Arnold, 1971).

Bernard, G. W., *The Power of the Early Tudor Nobility: A Study of the Fourth and Fifth Earls of Shrewsbury* (Brighton: Harvester, 1985).

Bernheimer, Richard, *Wild Men in the Middle Ages: A Study in Art, Sentiment, and Demonology* (Cambridge, Mass.: Harvard University Press, 1952).

Berry, Philippa, *Of Chastity and Power: Elizabethan Literature and the Unmarried Queen* (London: Routledge and Kegan Paul, 1989).

Bloch, Marc, *Feudal Society*, trans. L. A. Manyon (London: Routledge and Kegan Paul, 1961).

Bloch, R. Howard, *Medieval French Literature and Law* (Berkeley and Los Angeles: University of California Press, 1977).

Etymologies and Genealogies: A Literary Anthropology of the French Middle Ages (Chicago: University of Chicago Press, 1983).

Boas, F. S., *Queen Elizabeth in Drama and Related Studies* (London: Allen and Unwin, 1950).

Boase, Roger, *The Origin and Meaning of Courtly Love: A Critical Study of European Scholarship* (Manchester: Manchester University Press, 1977).

Bourdieu, Pierre, *Outline of a Theory of Practice*, trans. Richard Nice (Cambridge: Cambridge University Press, 1977).

Bradbrook, Muriel, *The Rise of the Common Player: A Study of Actor and Society in Shakespeare's England* (London: Chatto and Windus, 1964).

Brewer, D. S., 'Courtesy and the *Gawain*-Poet', in J. Lawlor, ed., *Patterns of Love and Courtesy: Essays in Memory of C. S. Lewis* (London: Edward Arnold, 1966).

Burgess, Glyn S., *Contribution à l'étude du vocabulaire pré-courtois* (Geneva: Droz, 1970).

ed., *Court and Poet* (Liverpool: Cairns, 1981).

Burke, Peter, *The Renaissance Sense of the Past* (London: Edward Arnold, 1969).

Popular Culture in Early Modern Europe (London: Temple Hill, 1978).

'The Renaissance Dialogue', *Renaissance Studies* 3 (1989), 1–12.

Cain, Thomas H., *Praise in* The Faerie Queene (Lincoln: University of Nebraska Press, 1978).

Carey, John, 'Structure and Rhetoric in Sidney's *Arcadia*', in Dennis Kay, ed., *Sir Philip Sidney: An Anthology of Modern Criticism* (Oxford: Oxford University Press, 1987).

Carpenter, F. I., *A Reference Guide to Edmund Spenser* (Chicago: University of Chicago Press, 1923).

Cave, Terence, *The Cornucopian Text: Problems of Writing in the French Renaissance* (Oxford: Oxford University Press, 1979).

Chambers, E. K., *The Elizabethan Stage*, 4 vols. (Oxford: Clarendon Press, 1923).

Connell, Dorothy, *Sir Philip Sidney: The Maker's Mind* (Oxford: Clarendon Press, 1977).

Council, Norman, 'O Dea Certe: The Allegory of The Fortress of Perfect Beauty', *Huntington Library Quarterly* 39 (1975–6), 329–42.

Crane, Thomas F., *Italian Social Customs of the Sixteenth Century* (New Haven, Conn.: Yale University Press, 1920).

Cummings, Peter M., 'Spenser's *Amoretti* as an Allegory of Love', *Texas Studies in Language and Literature* 12 (1970), 163–79.

Cunliffe, J. W., 'The Queenes Majesties Entertainment at Woodstock', *PMLA* 26 (1911), 92–141.

Davis, Natalie Zemon, *Society and Culture in Early Modern France* (London: Duckworth, 1975).

Davis, Walter R., *A Map of Arcadia: Sidney's Romance in its Tradition* (New Haven, Conn.: Yale University Press, 1965).

DeNeef, A. Leigh, 'Ploughing Virgilian Furrows: The Genres of *Faerie Queene* VI', *John Donne Journal* 1 (1982), 151–66.

Spenser and the Motives of Metaphor (Durham, NC: Duke University Press, 1982).

Denomy, A. J., 'Courtly Love and Courtliness', *Speculum* 28 (1953), 44–63.

Derrida, Jacques, *Of Grammatology* (Baltimore: Johns Hopkins University Press, 1976).

Donaldson, E. T., 'The Myth of Courtly Love', in *Speaking of Chaucer* (London: Athlone Press, 1970).

Dronke, Peter, *Medieval Latin and the Rise of European Love-Lyric*, 2 vols. (Oxford: Clarendon Press, 1965–6).

Dubrow, Heather [Ousby], 'Donne's "Epithalamion made at Lincolnes Inne": An Alternative Interpretation', *Studies in English Literature* 16 (1976), 131–43.

A Happier Eden: The Politics of Marriage in the Stuart Epithalamium (Ithaca, NY: Cornell University Press, 1990).

Duby, Georges, *The Knight, the Lady, and the Priest: The Making of Modern Marriage in Medieval France*, trans. Barbara Bray (Harmondsworth: Penguin, 1983).

Mâle Moyen Age (Paris: Flammarion, 1988).

ed., *A History of Private Life*, ii: *Revelations of the Medieval World* (Cambridge, Mass.: Harvard University Press, 1988).

Dupin, Henri, *La Courtoisie au Moyen Age* (Paris: Picard, 1931).

Durkheim, Emile, *The Rules of Sociological Method* (New York: Free Press, 1965).

Elias, Norbert, *The Civilizing Process*, trans. Edmund Jephcott, 2 vols. (Oxford: Blackwell, 1982).

The Court Society, trans. Edmund Jephcott (Oxford: Blackwell, 1983).

Elton, G. R., *The Tudor Revolution in Government: Administrative Changes in the Reign of Henry VIII* (Cambridge: Cambridge University Press, 1953).

Evans, W. O., ' "Cortaysye" in Middle English', *Medieval Studies* 29 (1967), 143–57.

Feuillerat, Albert, *John Lyly: Contribution à l'histoire de la Renaissance en Angleterre* (Cambridge: Cambridge University Press, 1910).

Flandrin, Jean-Louis, *Le Sexe et l'Occident* (Paris: Editions de Seuil, 1981).

Foucault, Michel, *The History of Sexuality*, trans. Robert Hurley, 4 vols. (Harmondsworth: Penguin, 1981–).

Fowler, Alastair, *Spenser and the Numbers of Time* (London: Routledge and Kegan Paul, 1964).

   Triumphal Forms: Structural Forms in Elizabethan Poetry (Cambridge: Cambridge University Press, 1970).

   ed., *Silent Poetry: Essays in Numerological Analysis* (London: Routledge and Kegan Paul, 1970).

Frappier, Jean, 'Vues sur les conceptions courtoises dans les littératures d'oc et d'oïl au XIIe siècle', *Cahiers de Civilisation Médiévale* 2 (1959), 135–56.

Frye, Northrop, 'The Structure of Imagery in *The Faerie Queene*', *University of Toronto Quarterly* 30 (1960–1), 109–27.

Galpin, Stanley L., *Cortois and Vilain: A Study of the Distinctions Made between them by the French and Provençal Poets of the 12th, 13th and 14th Centuries* (New Haven, Conn.: Ryder, 1905).

Garin, Eugenio, *Italian Humanism: Philosophy and Civic Life in the Renaissance*, trans. Peter Munz (Oxford: Blackwell, 1965).

Geertz, Clifford, *The Interpretation of Culture* (London: Hutchinson, 1975).

Geimer, Roger A., 'Spenser's Rhyme and Churchyard's Reason: Evidence of Churchyard's First Pension', *Review of English Studies* NS 20 (1969), 306–9.

Geller, Lila, 'The Acidalian Vision: Spenser's Graces in Book VI of *The Faerie Queene*', *Review of English Studies* NS 23 (1972), 267–77.

Godshalk, William Leigh, 'Sidney's Revision of the *Arcadia*, Books III–V', *Philological Quarterly* 43 (1964), 171–84.

Goldberg, Jonathan, *Endlesse Worke: Spenser and the Structures of Discourse* (Baltimore: Johns Hopkins University Press, 1981).

   Voice Terminal Echo: Postmodernism and English Renaissance Texts (London: Methuen, 1986).

Goldwyn, M. H., 'Notes on the Biography of Thomas Churchyard', *Review of English Studies* NS 17 (1966), 1–15.

Gray, J. C., 'Bondage and Deliverance in *The Faerie Queene*', *Modern Language Review* 70 (1975), 1–12.

Greene, Thomas, *The Light in Troy: Imitation and Discovery in Renaissance Poetry* (New Haven, Conn.: Yale University Press, 1982).

   'Spenser and the Epithalamic Convention', *Comparative Literature* 9 (1957), 215–28.

Halpin, N. J., *Oberon's Vision in the Midsummer Night's Dream* (London: Shakespeare Society, 1843).

Hamilton, A. C., *The Structure of Allegory in* The Faerie Queene (Oxford: Clarendon Press, 1961).

Harrison, G. B., *The Life and Death of Robert Devereux, Earl of Essex* (London: Cassell, 1937).

Hatton, James, 'Cupid and the Bee', *PMLA* 56 (1941), 1036–57.

Heer, Friedrich, *The Medieval World: Europe 1100–1350*, trans. Janet Sond-
heimer (London: Weidenfeld and Nicolson, 1962).
Heffner, Ray, 'Essex, the Ideal Courtier', *Journal of English Literary History* 1
(1934), 7–36.
Hibbard, G. R., 'The Country House Poem of the Seventeenth Century',
Journal of the Warburg and Courtauld Institutes 19 (1956), 159–74.
Hieatt, A. Kent, *Short Time's Endless Monument* (New York: Columbia
University Press, 1960).
Hollyman, K. J., *Le Développement du vocabulaire féodale* (Geneva: Droz,
1957).
Hope, T. E., *Lexical Borrowing in the Romance Languages*, 2 vols. (Oxford:
Blackwell, 1971).
Huizinga, Johan, *Homo Ludens: A Study of the Play Element in Culture*, trans. R.
F. C. Hull (London: Routledge and Kegan Paul, 1949).
Hume, Martin, *The Courtships of Queen Elizabeth: A History of the Various
Negotiations for her Marriage* (London: Nash, 1906).
Hunter, G. K., *John Lyly: The Humanist as Courtier* (London: Routledge and
Kegan Paul, 1962).
  'Spenser's *Amoretti* and the English Sonnet Tradition', in *A Theatre for
Spenserians*, ed. Judith M. Kennedy and James A. Reither (Toronto:
University of Toronto Press, 1973).
Huppert, George, *The Idea of Perfect History: Historical Erudition and Historical
Philosophy in Renaissance France* (Urbana: University of Illinois Press,
1970).
Jackson, W. T. H., *The Literature of the Middle Ages* (New York: Columbia
University Press, 1960).
Javitch, Daniel, *Poetry and Courtliness in Renaissance England* (Princeton, NJ:
Princeton University Press, 1978).
  'The Impure Motives of Elizabethan Poetry', *Genre* 15 (1982), 225–
38.
Jeffery, Violet M., *John Lyly and the Italian Renaissance* (Paris: Champion,
1929).
Jenkins, Elizabeth, *Elizabeth and Leicester* (London: Gollancz, 1961).
Johnson, William C., *Spenser's* Amoretti: *Analogies of Love* (Lewisburg, Pa.:
Bucknell University Press, 1990).
Jones, Dorothy, 'Sidney's Eroticism: An Interpretation of One of the
Arcadia Poems', *Journal of English and Germanic Philology*, 73 (1974),
32–47.
Kalstone, David, *Sidney's Poetry: Contexts and Interpretations* (Cambridge,
Mass.: Harvard University Press, 1965).
Kaske, Carol, 'Spenser's *Amoretti and Epithalamion* of 1595: Structure, Genre,
and Numerology', *English Literary Renaissance* 8 (1978), 271–95.
Kay, D. C., ' "To Hear the Rest Untold": Shakespeare's Postponed
Endings', *Renaissance Quarterly*, 37 (1984), 207–27.
  'Sidney: A Critical Heritage', in D. C. Kay, ed., *Sir Philip Sidney: An
Anthology of Modern Criticism* (Oxford: Clarendon Press 1987).

' "She Was a Queen and therefore Beautiful": Sidney, his Mother, and Queen Elizabeth', *Review of English Studies* (Feb. 1992).

Kelley, Donald, *Foundations of Modern Historical Scholarship: Language, Law, and History in the French Renaissance* (New York: Columbia University Press, 1970).

Kelso, Ruth, *Doctrine for the Lady of the Renaissance* (Urbana: University of Illinois Press, 1956).

Kimbrough, Robert, and Philip Murphy, 'The Helmingham Hall Manuscript of *The Lady of May*: A Commentary and Transcription', *Renaissance Drama* NS 1 (1968), 103–19.

Kinney, Arthur F., *Humanist Poetics: Thought, Rhetoric, and Fiction in Sixteenth-Century England* (Amherst: University of Massachusetts Press, 1986).

Kipling, Gordon, *The Triumph of Honour: Burgundian Origins of the Elizabethan Renaissance* (The Hague: Leiden University Press, 1977).

Knapp, Robert S., 'The Monarchy of Love in Lyly's *Endimion*', *Modern Philology* 73 (1975–6), 353–67.

Köhler, Eric, *Ideal und Wirklichkeit in der höfischen Epik* (Tübingen: Niemeyer, 1956).

Trobadorlyrik und höfischen Roman (Berlin: Rütten and Loening, 1962).

'Observations historiques et sociologiques sur la poésie des troubadours', *Cahiers de Civilisation Médiévale* 7 (1964), 27–51.

Lawry, Jon S., *Sidney's Two Arcadias: Pattern and Proceeding* (Ithaca, NY: Cornell University Press, 1972).

Lazar, Moshé, 'Les Eléments constitutifs de la "cortezia" dans la lyrique des troubadours', *Studi Mediolatini et Volgari* 7 (1959), 67–96.

Amour courtois et 'fin' amors' dans la littérature du XIIe siècle (Paris: Klincksieck, 1964).

Levao, Ronald, *Renaissance Minds and their Fictions: Cusanus, Sidney, Shakespeare* (Berkeley: University of California Press, 1985).

Lever, J. W., *The Elizabethan Love Sonnet* (London: Methuen, 1956).

Lewis, C. S., *The Allegory of Love: A Study in Medieval Tradition* (Oxford: Clarendon Press, 1936).

Lindheim, Nancy R., 'Vision, Revision, and the 1593 Text of the *Arcadia*', repr. in Arthur F. Kinney, ed., *Sidney in Retrospect: Selections from English Literary Renaissance* (Amherst: University of Massachusetts Press, 1988).

Long, Percy W., 'The Purport of Lyly's *Endimion*', *PMLA* 24 (1909), 164–84.

Loomis, R. S., 'The Allegorical Siege in the Art of the Middle Ages', *American Journal of Archaeology* NS 23 (1919), 255–69.

Lowenstein, Joseph, *Responsive Readings: Versions of Echo in Epic, Pastoral, and the Jonsonian Masque* (New Haven, Conn.: Yale University Press, 1984).

'Echoes Ring: Orpheus and Spenser's Career', *English Literary Renaissance* 16 (1986), 287–302.

Lukes, Steven, *Emile Durkheim: His Life and Work* (London: Allen Lane, 1973).

MacCaffrey, Wallace T., 'Place and Patronage in Elizabethan Politics', in S. T. Bindoff, J. Hurstfield, and C. H. Williams, eds., *Elizabethan Government and Society: Essays presented to Sir John Neale* (London: Athlone Press, 1961).

McCanles, Michael, *The Text of Sidney's Arcadian World* (Durham, NC: Duke University Press, 1989).

McClung, William A., *The Country House in English Renaissance Poetry* (Berkeley: University of California Press, 1977).

McCoy, Richard C., *Sir Philip Sidney: Rebellion in Arcadia* (New Brunswick, NJ: Rutgers University Press, 1979).

Marcus, Leah, *The Politics of Mirth: Jonson, Herrick, Milton, Marvell, and the Defense of Old Holiday Pastimes* (Chicago: University of Chicago Press, 1986).

Marenco, F., *Arcadia Puritana* (Bari: Adriatica Editrice, 1968).

Marotti, Arthur, ' "Love Is Not Love": Elizabethan Sonnet Sequences and the Social Order', *Journal of English Literary History* 49 (1982), 396–428.

Marsh, David, *The Quattrocento Dialogue: Classical Tradition and Humanist Innovation* (Cambridge, Mass.: Harvard University Press, 1980).

Martin, Christopher, 'Misdoubting his Estate: Dynastic Anxiety in Sidney's *Arcadia*', *English Literary Renaissance*, 18 (1988), 369–88.

Martines, Lauro, *Society and History in English Renaissance Verse* (Oxford: Blackwell, 1985).

Martz, Louis L., 'The *Amoretti*: "Most Goodly Temperature" ', in *Form and Convention in the Poetry of Edmund Spenser*, ed. William Nelson (New York: Columbia University Press, 1961).

Matoré, Georges, *Le Vocabulaire et la société médiévale* (Paris: Presses Universitaires de France, 1985).

Maxwell, J. C., 'The Truancy of Calidore', *Journal of English Literary History* 19 (1952), 143–9.

Miller, D. L., *The Poem's Two Bodies: The Poetics of the 1590 Faerie Queene* (Princeton, NJ: Princeton University Press, 1988).

Miller, Jacqueline T., ' "Love Doth Hold My Hand": Writing and Wooing in the Sonnets of Sidney and Spenser', *Journal of English Literary History* 46 (1979), 541–58.

Miola, Robert S., 'Spenser's Anacreontics: A Mythological Metaphor', *Studies in Philology* 77 (1980), 50–66.

Moller, Herbert, 'The Social Causation of the Courtly Love Complex', *Comparative Studies in Society and History* 1 (1958–9), 137–63.

'The Meaning of Courtly Love', *Journal of American Fiction* 73 (1960), 39–52.

Montrose, Louis Adrian, 'Celebration and Insinuation: Sir Philip Sidney and the Motives of Elizabethan Courtship', *Renaissance Drama* 8 (1977), 3–35.

'The Elizabethan Subject and the Spenserian Text', in Patricia Parker and David Quint, eds., *Literary Theory/Renaissance Texts* (Baltimore: Johns Hopkins University Press, 1986).

' "Shaping Fantasies": Figurations of Gender and Power in Elizabethan Culture', in Stephen Greenblatt, ed., *Representing the Renaissance* (Berkeley: University of California Press, 1988).

Morgan, D. A. L., 'The House of Policy: The Political Role of the Late Plantagenet Household, 1422–1485', in David Starkey, ed., *The English Court from the Wars of the Roses to the Civil War* (London: Longman, 1987).

Nestrick, William V., 'The Virtuous and Gentle Discipline of Gentlemen and Poets', *Journal of English Literary History* 29 (1962), 357–71.

Neuse, Richard, 'Book VI as Conclusion to *The Faerie Queene*', *Journal of English Literary History* 35 (1968), 329–53.

Newman, F. X., ed., *The Meaning of Courtly Love* (Albany: State University of New York Press, 1968).

Nicholls, J. W., *The Matter of Courtesy: Medieval Courtesy Books and the Gawain-Poet* (Cambridge: Brewer, 1985).

Nohrnberg, James, *The Analogy of* The Faerie Queene (Princeton, NJ: Princeton University Press, 1976).

Norbrook, David, *Poetry and Politics in the English Renaissance* (London: Routledge and Kegan Paul, 1984).

Novarr, David, *The Disinterred Muse: Donne's Texts and Contexts* (Ithaca, NY: Cornell University Press, 1980).

Orgel, Stephen, *The Jonsonian Masque* (Cambridge, Mass.: Harvard University Press, 1965).

Paget, Violet (Vernon Lee), *Euphorion: Being Studies of the Antique and the Mediaeval in the Renaissance*, 2 vols. (London: Unwin, 1884).

Paris, Gaston, 'Lancelot de Lac: II. Le Conte de la charrette', *Romania* 12 (1883), 459–534.

Parkin, David, 'Exchanging Words', in Bruce Kapferer, ed., *Transaction and Meaning: Directions in the Anthropology of Exchange and Symbolic Behaviour* (Philadelphia: Institute for the Study of Human Issues, 1976).

Patterson, Annabel, *Censorship and Interpretation: The Conditions of Writing and Reading in Early Modern England* (Madison: University of Wisconsin Press, 1984).

Pastoral and Ideology: Virgil to Valéry (Oxford: Clarendon Press, 1988).

Plowden, Alison, *Marriage with my Kingdom: The Courtships of Elizabeth I* (London: Macmillan, 1977).

Powell, Jocelyn, 'John Lyly and the Language of Play', *Stratford-upon-Avon Studies* 9 (1966), 146–67.

Quilligan, Maureen, 'Sidney and his Queen', in Heather Dubrow and Richard Strier, eds., *The Historical Renaissance: New Essays on Tudor and Stuart Culture and Literature* (Chicago: University of Chicago Press, 1988).

Quint, David, *Origin and Originality in Renaissance Literature: Versions of the Source* (New Haven, Conn.: Yale University Press, 1983).

Read, Conyers, *Mr Secretary Walsingham and Queen Elizabeth*, 3 vols. (Oxford: Clarendon Press, 1925).

Mr Secretary Cecil and Queen Elizabeth (London: Cape, 1955).

Lord Burghley and Queen Elizabeth (London: Cape, 1960).

Rebholz, Ronald A., *The Life of Fulke Greville, First Lord Brooke* (Oxford: Clarendon Press, 1971).

Rebhorn, Wayne A., *Courtly Performances: Masking and Festivity in Castiglione's* Book of the Courtier (Detroit: Wayne State University Press, 1978).

Robertson, D. W., 'The Concept of Courtly Love as an Impediment to the Understanding of Medieval Texts', in Newman, ed., *The Meaning of Courtly Love*.

Roche, Thomas, *The Kindly Flame: A Study of the Third and Fourth Books of Spenser's Faerie Queene* (Princeton: Princeton University Press, 1964).

'*Astrophil and Stella*: A Radical Reading', *Spenser Studies* 3 (1982), 139–91.

Rose, Mark, *Heroic Love: Studies in Sidney and Spenser* (Cambridge, Mass.: Harvard University Press, 1968).

Rougemont, Denis de, *Love in the Western World*, trans. Montgomery Belgion (Princeton, NJ: Princeton University Press, 1983).

Rowse, A. L., *Simon Forman: Sex and Society in Shakespeare's Age* (London: Weidenfeld and Nicolson, 1974).

Rusche, Harry, 'The Lesson of Calidore's Truancy', *Studies in Philology* 76 (1979), 149–61.

Saccio, Peter, *The Court Comedies of John Lyly* (Princeton, NJ: Princeton University Press, 1969).

'The Oddity of Lyly's *Endimion*', *Elizabethan Theatre* 5 (1975), 92–111.

Salter, Elizabeth, 'Courts and Courtly Love', in David Daiches and Anthony Thorlby, eds., *Literature and Western Civilization: The Medieval World* (London: Aldus, 1973).

Saussure, Ferdinand de, *Course in General Linguistics*, ed. Charles Bally and Albert Sechehaye, trans. Roy Harris (London: Duckworth, 1983).

Schenk, Celeste Marguerite, *Mourning and Panegyric: The Poetics of Pastoral Ceremony* (University Park: Pennsylvania State University Press, 1988).

Schulze, Ivan L., 'The Final Protest against the Elizabeth–Alençon Marriage Proposal', *Modern Language Notes* 58 (1943), 54–7.

Sharpe, Kevin, *Criticism and Compliment: The Politics of Literature in the England of Charles I* (Cambridge: Cambridge University Press, 1987).

Silverstein, T., 'Guenevere, or the Uses of Courtly Love', in Newman, ed., *The Meaning of Courtly Love*.

Smith, Bruce R., 'Landscape with Figures: The Three Realms of Queen Elizabeth's Country-House Revels', *Renaissance Drama* NS 8 (1977), 57–115.

Smith, Nathaniel B., and Joseph T. Snow, eds., *The Expansion and Trans-*

formations of Courtly Literature (Athens: University of Georgia Press, 1980).

Snare, Gerald, 'Spenser's Fourth Grace', *Journal of the Warburg and Courtauld Institutes* 34 (1971), 350–5.

Spitzer, Leo, *Linguistics and Literary Theory: Essays in Stylistics* (Princeton, NJ: Princeton University Press, 1948).

Spufford, Margaret, *Small Books and Pleasant Histories: Popular Fiction and its Readership in Seventeenth-Century England* (London: Methuen, 1981).

Stallybrass, Peter, and Ann Rosalind Jones, 'The Politics of *Astrophil and Stella*', *Studies in English Literature* 24 (1984), 53–68.

'Patriarchal Territories: The Body Enclosed', in Margaret Ferguson, Maureen Quilligan, and Nancy Vickers, eds., *Rewriting the Renaissance: The Discourses of Sexual Difference in Early Modern Europe* (Chicago: University of Chicago Press, 1986).

Starkey, David, 'Intimacy and Innovation: The Rise of the Privy Chamber, 1485–1547', in Starkey, ed., *The English Court from the Wars of the Roses to the Civil War*.

ed., *The English Court from the Wars of the Roses to the Civil War* (London: Longman, 1987).

and Christopher Coleman, eds., *Revolution Reassessed: Revisions in the History of Tudor Government and Administration* (Oxford: Clarendon Press, 1986).

Starnes, DeWitt T., and Ernest W. Talbert, *Classical Myth and Legend in Renaissance Dictionaries* (Chapel Hill: University of North Carolina Press, 1955).

Steinberg, Theodore, 'The Anatomy of *Euphues*', *Studies in English Literature*, 17 (1977), 27–38.

Stevens, John, *Music and Poetry in the Early Tudor Court* (London: Methuen, 1961).

Stewart, Stanley, 'Sir Calidore and "Closure" ', *Studies in English Literature* 24 (1984), 69–86.

Stillman, R. E., *Sidney's Poetic Justice:* The Old Arcadia, *its Eclogues, and Renaissance Pastoral Traditions* (Lewisburg, Pa.: Bucknell University Press, 1986).

Stone, Lawrence, *An Open Elite? England 1540–1880* (Oxford: Clarendon Press, 1984).

Streuver, Nancy, *The Language of History in the Renaissance* (Princeton, NJ: Princeton University Press, 1970).

Strong, Roy, *The Cult of Elizabeth: Elizabethan Portraiture and Pageantry* (London: Thames and Hudson, 1977).

Tennenhouse, Leonard, 'Sir Walter Ralegh and the Literature of Clientage', in Guy Fitch Lytle and Stephen Orgel, eds., *Patronage in the Renaissance* (Princeton, NJ: Princeton University Press, 1981).

Thomas, Susan D., '*Endimion* and its Sources', *Comparative Literature* 30 (1978), 35–52.

Tonkin, Humphrey, *Spenser's Courteous Pastoral* (Oxford: Clarendon Press, 1972).

The Faerie Queene (London: Unwin Hyman, 1989).

Turner, Robert Y., 'Some Dialogues of Love in Lyly's Comedies', *Journal of English Literary History* 29 (1962), 276–88.

Ullmann, Stephen, *The Principles of Semantics*, 2nd edn (Oxford: Blackwell, 1957).

Utley, F. L., 'Must we Abandon the Concept of Courtly Love?', *Medievalia et Humanistica* NS 3 (1972), 299–324.

Valency, Maurice, *In Praise of Love: An Introduction to the Love-Poetry of the Renaissance* (New York: Macmillan, 1958).

The Victoria History of the Counties of England, 8 vols. (London: Oxford University Press, 1903–83), vi: *Essex*.

Wagner, Bernard M., 'New Poems by Sir Philip Sidney', *PMLA* 53 (1938), 118–24.

Wall, John N., *Transformations of the Word: Spenser, Herbert, Vaughan* (Athens: University of Georgia Press, 1988).

Waswo, Richard, *Language and Meaning in the Renaissance* (Princeton, NJ: Princeton University Press, 1987).

Wayne, Don E., *Penshurst: The Semiotics of Place and the Poetics of History* (London: Methuen, 1984).

Weiner, A. D., *Sir Philip Sidney and the Poetics of Protestantism: A Study of Contexts* (Minneapolis: University of Minnesota Press, 1978).

Weiner, Seth, 'Minims and Grace Notes: Spenser's Acidalian Vision and Sixteenth-Century Music', *Spenser Studies* 5 (1984), 91–112.

Wells, Robin Headlam, 'Spenser and the Courtesy Tradition: Form and Meaning in the Sixth Book of *The Faerie Queene*', *English Studies* 58 (1977), 221–9.

Spenser's Faerie Queene and the Cult of Elizabeth (London: Croom Helm, 1983).

West, Constance, *'Courtoisie' in Anglo-Norman Literature* (Oxford: Medium Aevum Monographs, 1938).

Whigham, Frank, *Ambition and Privilege: The Social Tropes of Elizabethan Courtesy Theory* (Berkeley: University of California Press, 1984).

Wickham, Glynne, *Early English Stages 1300–1660*, 3 vols., 2nd edn (London: Routledge, and Kegan Paul, 1980–1).

Wiles, A. G. D., 'Parallel Analyses of the Two Versions of Sidney's *Arcadia*', *Studies in Philology* 39 (1942), 167–206.

Williams, Kathleen, *Spenser's World of Glass: A Reading of* The Faerie Queene (Berkeley: University of California Press, 1966).

Williams, Neville, *All the Queen's Men: Elizabeth I and her Courtiers* (London: Weidenfeld and Nicolson, 1972).

Williams, Penry, *The Tudor Regime* (Oxford: Clarendon Press, 1979).

Wilson, K. J., *Incomplete Fictions: The Formation of English Renaissance Dialogue* (Washington DC: Catholic University of America Press, 1985).

Wind, Edgar, *Pagan Mysteries in the Renaissance*, 2nd edn (Oxford: Oxford University Press, 1980).

Woods, Susanne, 'Closure in *The Faerie Queene*', *Journal of English and Germanic Philology* 76 (1977), 195–216.

Woudhuysen, Henry, 'Leicester's Literary Patronage: A Study of the English Court 1578–1582' D. Phil. thesis, Oxford, 1981.

Young, Alan, *Tudor and Jacobean Tournaments* (London: George Philip, 1987).

Zandvoort, R. W., *Sidney's Arcadia: A Comparison between the Two Versions* (Amsterdam: Swets and Zeitlinger, 1929).

Index